Patriotic Professionalism in Urban China

IN THE SERIES *Urban Life, Landscape, and Policy,*

EDITED BY ZANE L. MILLER, DAVID STRADLING, AND LARRY BENNETT

Also in this series:

William Issel, *For Both Cross and Flag: Catholic Action, Anti-Catholicism, and National Security Politics in World War II San Francisco*

Patriotic Professionalism in Urban China

Fostering Talent

LISA M. HOFFMAN

TEMPLE UNIVERSITY PRESS
Philadelphia

Lisa M. Hoffman is Associate Professor in the Urban Studies Program at the University of Washington Tacoma.

TEMPLE UNIVERSITY PRESS
Philadelphia, Pennsylvania 19122
www.temple.edu/tempress

Library of Congress Cataloging-in-Publication Data

Hoffman, Lisa M. (Lisa Mae)
    Patriotic professionalism in urban China : fostering talent / Lisa M. Hoffman.
        p.   cm. — (Urban life, landscape, and policy)
    Includes bibliographical references and index.
    ISBN 978-1-4399-0034-5 (hardcover : alk. paper)
    ISBN 978-1-4399-0035-2 (pbk. : alk. paper)
    1. Professional employees—China—Dalian (Liaoning Sheng).   2. Neoliberalism—China.   I. Title.

    HD8038.A3H645 2010
    331.7'1095182—dc22   2009038152

⊖ The paper used in this publication meets the requirements of the American National Standard for Information Sciences—Permanence of Paper for Printed Library Materials, ANSI Z39.48-1992

Printed in the United States of America

2 4 6 8 9 7 5 3 1

Contents

Acknowledgments

This book would not have been possible without the continued support and encouragement of many people in China and the United States. Most important are those in Dalian who shared their stories and lives with me. I offer my deepest gratitude for their participation in the research, their immeasurable help and guidance, and the friendships we built together. This project first began in 1993, when I was a graduate student at the University of California at Berkeley, and it continued with a decade of research that ended in 2003, when I was an assistant professor at the University of Washington Tacoma (UWT). Along the way, I have received support from many individuals and institutions, including funding for research or writing from the Committee on Scholarly Communication with China, the Foreign Language and Area Studies Fellowship, the Center for Studies in Higher Education at Berkeley, the Institute of East Asian Studies at Berkeley, Robert H. Lowie Graduate Scholarships, and the University of Washington's Harry Bridges Center for Labor Studies Research Grant; a UWT junior faculty research leave; and a sabbatical from the Urban Studies Program to finish the manuscript.

My debt to individuals is even greater and wider. I thank Aihwa Ong, in particular, for providing intellectual inspiration, for offering invaluable insights as she read and reread chapters, for engaging me as a colleague, and especially for sharing her continued friendship over the years. I also thank Paul Rabinow and Allan Pred for challenging me while at Berkeley and for opening doors to new spaces of critique. I was deeply saddened by Allan's recent passing; it is a great loss in many respects. The influence that Aihwa, Paul, and Allan had on me and my work is not only intellectual but also personal, and I am grateful to them for this. Ann Anagnost, Joe Bosco, Greg Guldin, Stevan Harrell, Xin Liu, Liz Perry, and Lisa Rofel also guided me at important moments in my graduate work, and I thank them for their engagement and support.

My colleagues at the University of Washington (in Tacoma and in Seattle) have provided lively debates and good humor, creating an enjoyable work space. Many have had a direct impact on this book as well, including Dan Abramson, Kam Wing Chan, Brian Coffey, Yonn Dierwechter, Katharyne Mitchell, Mark Pendras, and—again—Ann and Steve, who in many ways originally inspired me to pursue a doctorate in anthropology when I was studying for my master's degree in China regional studies at the University of Washington. My cohorts at the University of Washington and at Berkeley made academia and the study of China interesting and enjoyable, especially Neil Diamant, Sandra Hyde, Ralph Litzinger, Heather Merrill, Tim Oakes, Hai Ren, Louisa Schein, and Athena Wolfe. I have also benefited from collegial and stimulating conversations about China and contemporary issues with Alana Boland, David Bray, Elaine Jeffreys, Ananya Roy, Gary Sigley, Jesook Song, Wing Shing Tang, Luigi Tomba, and Li Zhang. Without a doubt, this book owes a great deal to the conversations we have had together.

A special acknowledgment goes to the members of my writing group, Monica DeHart and Jennifer Hubbert, who went above and beyond the call of duty by reading multiple drafts of papers and chapters and by energizing me over the years. I have enjoyed all our exchanges, personal and intellectual, whether at I-5 road stops or American Anthropological Association meetings. I also thank Stephen Collier and Monica for very productive workshops on neoliberalism and anthropology. Not only has my analysis benefited from those conversations and readings but through these exchanges I learned the true meaning of collective work. Thank you for your friendship and your scholarship.

Students in my courses, and particularly in independent studies, have challenged me to think about ideas in new ways and pushed me to reduce my use of jargon (which I hope is reflected in this text). Shane Muchow, Wang Xiuping, Yan Jiang, and Xia Zhang provided helpful research assistance;

I thank Xiongjiu Liao for producing the maps and Qu Bin and his colleagues for the cover photo. I am grateful as well to Aubyn Eakle for her careful work on the references, editing, and general support, and to Andrew Liu for his last-minute editing help.

Among those who offered support in China is Professor Liu Zhongquan at Dalian University of Technology (DUT), who has been incredibly helpful over the years. I am enormously indebted to him, and I thank him for his constant encouragement, questions, and continuing friendship. I also thank Gao Lin, He Yan, Li Huimin, Qi Yue, Wang Xiuping, and Zhou Liping and her extended family not only for their help with my research but also for their warmth and welcome over the years. Dong Liqun, Ge Cuihua, Professor Li Mingfei, Tang Yongqiang, and Professor Yu Kaicheng also graciously provided helpful research materials and engaged the work in interesting ways. Bai Zhongxiao from DUT's Foreign Affairs Office also always welcomed me to campus. Of course, my sincere gratitude and respect go to the numerous students, employees, company and unit representatives, talent market administrators, and university personnel who remain anonymous and who willingly answered my queries and allowed me to participate in their work and lives.

I also thank Mick Gusinde-Duffy at Temple University Press for his commitment to this project and Zane Miller, David Stradling, and Larry Bennett for embracing a book about China and subject formation for their *Urban Life, Landscape, and Policy* series. I am very grateful for the support and encouragement that they provided along the way and for the fine work by the editorial staff. Comments from the three anonymous reviewers were also helpful, and I am grateful to them for their time and constructive criticism. Any flaws that remain are my own.

Parts of Chapters 1, 2, and 4 were previously published. I thank Taylor and Francis for permission to use portions of "Enterprising Cities and Citizens: The Re-figuring of Urban Spaces and the Making of Post-Mao Professionals," *Provincial China* 8, no. 1 (2003): 5–26, and parts of "Autonomous Choices and Patriotic Professionalism: On Governmentality in Late-Socialist China," *Economy and Society* 35, no. 4 (2006): 550–570.

I thank my mother, Susan Hoffman, for reading and editing the full manuscript several times. I credit her for the lucidity of the writing. My father, Allan Hoffman, has inspired me to do careful research and to understand the wonders of academic life, and my brother, David, has always encouraged me in the marathon of life. Kaitak and Orly deserve special thanks for being such good company, especially when my husband, Bill Driscoll, was gone, and for only once creating chaos by trying to steal the treats on my desk. My deepest gratitude goes to Bill for being there when I need him, while also listening to ideas, helping me talk through arguments, and giving me the space to write when necessary. This book is dedicated to him and to John Saul, who arrived in our lives at the perfect moment.

1

Talent in the Global City

Preparing Dalian for the Twenty-first Century

"In the global knowledge economy, people's skills, learning, talents and attributes—their human capital—have become key to both their ability to earn a living and to wider economic growth" (Keeley 2007). This quote from a recent Organization for Economic Co-operation and Development (OECD) publication reiterates what has become common-sense to many around the world: "Human capital" development is fundamental for economic growth and social progress. Few nations, cities, or development agencies question the link between talented human resources and local prosperity. Even in times of economic crisis, politicians have referred to workers as a fundamental of the economy that remains "strong" and "sound."[1] In the United States, laid-off factory workers have been offered retraining classes to learn skills appropriate for the growing knowledge economy so that they may earn a living and help generate local economic growth in places suffering from global competition and the outsourcing of production. Although the international division of labor sought cheap manual workers for the production of light-industry consumer goods in the 1970s, more recent practices have targeted employees with higher education, language skills, and technological knowledge. Singapore, for instance, recently launched a coordinated effort to attract foreign experts to train the city-state's next generation of high-tech and biotech researchers and employees. In Bangalore, India, a complex network of universities and corporate training centers prepares people to work in multinational call centers and service operations, making the city competitive in the global knowledge economy. In addition to manufacturing facilities, transnational corporations have established computer and airline call centers in India and Ireland, U.S. tax preparation in Asia, communication corridors in Malaysia, and a biotech research web in Singapore. This celebration of talent in the global city is a worldwide phenomenon, and China is no exception.

A clear example of China's investment in talent is the opening of "talent markets" and "talent exchange centers" in cities across the country. These centers are designated sites for people with special skills, talents, and knowledge to meet employers through job fairs, computer databanks, and resume distribution. Although the first talent markets were small and attracted only a few people, they quickly expanded in the mid- to late 1990s, becoming important sites for the constitution of talented and professional employees. I distinctly remember the day in 1996 when I went to the Spring Festival job fair organized by the Personnel Bureau in Dalian, a major port city in northeast China. I had visited many such events (the first in 1993), but never had I seen so many people waiting to get into the fair. The line, about four people wide, snaked through the neighboring used-car market located just outside the large building where the fair was held. College seniors, their parents, friends, and others who wanted to change jobs came to the fair to look for new employment or to support their friends and relatives. Inside the building, representatives from state-run units, private and foreign-owned companies, and cooperative enterprises sat at tables with the list of positions for which they were hiring posted on the walls behind them, ready to engage in the new mechanism of labor allocation termed "mutual choice" (*shuangxiang xuanze*). These markets facilitated the newly prioritized "flow" of talent across and between cities, so it could be used "efficiently."

Although the image of a college graduates' job fair is commonsense to many Westerners, the spread of talent markets across China's cities is emblematic of significant changes in urban life in the past twenty years. After Mao Zedong died and the new leadership ushered in the "reform era" (1979–present) and the Four Modernizations (in agriculture, industry, science and technology, and national defense), China turned away from central planning, adopted a socialist market economy, and actively engaged the global market.[2] State-owned units no longer dominated urban economies, migrants moved to cities in search of work, and college graduates looked for employment on

TABLE 1.1   BREAKDOWN OF WORKFORCE IN CHINA (BY NUMBER OF WORKERS IN EACH SECTOR)

Year	State-owned sector	Collectively owned sector	Other ownership
National workforce			
1980	80,190,000	24,250,000	n.a.[a]
1990	103,460,000	35,490,000	1,640,000
2000	78,780,000	14,470,000	19,350,000[b]
2003	66,212,800	9,510,000	29,200,000[c]
Dalian workforce			
2000	544,017	123,130	316,394[d]

[a] The first statistic available for the "other ownership" category is for 1984.

[b] *China Labor Statistical Yearbook 2001*, p. 21. "Other ownership" units include foreign-funded, private, share holding, limited liability, and joint venture corporations. For details, see *China Labor Statistical Yearbook 2001*, p. 7.

[c] See "Employment Staff and Workers of China for 2003" statistics at China Data Center Online.

[d] This number includes, for example, foreign-funded and private, limited, and joint venture ownership structures. The foreign-funded numbers account for a total of 16 percent of the workforce, with 81 percent of that sector in enterprises that are not Hong Kong, Macau, and Taiwan owned. See *Dalian Statistical Yearbook 2000*, p. 35.

their own instead of receiving state-directed job assignments (Table 1.1). With private wealth accumulation, new social and class identities began to emerge, taking shape in the intersection of new work experiences, leisure pursuits, family histories, and policy shifts. The global competition for highly mobile capital and human resources also led to place-wars between cities and more entrepreneurial city-management policies.[3] Municipalities in China maneuvered to compete in the globalized world by establishing special economic zones, creating new city-marketing campaigns, and investing in the "quality" of its population through higher education and training opportunities. China's investment in human capital development is apparent in the dramatic increase in university enrollments and the number of college graduates in the past several decades; graduates increased, for instance, from 147,000[4] in 1980, to 614,000 in 1990, to 950,000 in 2000—an increase of almost 650 percent in twenty years, and more than 50 percent from 1990 to 2000[5] (Table 1.2). With new investments in human capital and ideas about how best to manage population (and labor) flows, it had become "thinkable" for municipalities to open sites where labor—and specifically *talented* labor—could be marketized. This practice directly contrasted ways of doing things under central planning of the high-socialist era (1949–1978). In other words, a new "regime of practices" and "rationality of governing" (governmentality) emerged in the reform era that aimed to optimize the prosperity, comfort, health, and

TABLE 1.2 INCREASE IN NUMBER OF COLLEGE ENROLLMENTS AND GRADUATES IN CHINA

Year	Newly enrolled students	Total enrolled	Number of graduates
1980	281,000[a]	1,144,000[b]	147,000[c]
1990	609,000	2,063,000	614,000
1993	924,000[d]	2,536,000[e]	571,000[f]
1995	926,000	2,906,000	805,000
2000	2,206,000	5,561,000	950,000
2002	3,205,000	9,034,000	1,337,000
2003	3,822,000	11,086,000	1,877,000[g]
2008	6,077,000	20,210,000	5,120,000[h]

[a] *China Statistical Yearbook 2004*, table 21-6 ("Number of New Students Enrollment by Level and Type of School"). These numbers are for graduates of all regular institutions of higher education.

[b] *China Statistical Yearbook 2004*.

[c] *China Statistical Yearkbook 2004*, table 21-7 ("Number of Graduates by Level and Type of School").

[d] *China Statistical Yearbook 2004*, table 21-6 ("Number of New Students Enrollment by Level and Type of School").

[e] *China Statistical Yearbook 2004*.

[f] *China Statistical Yearbook 2004*, table 21-7 ("Number of Graduates by Level and Type of School"). This number is low, likely because of the crackdown after student protests in 1989; the number of graduates in 1994 was 637,000, and in 1995 it was 805,000.

[g] All data in this table through 2003 are from *China Statistical Yearbook 2004*.

[h] The 2008 data are from China Data Center Online.

happiness of the population in new ways.[6] In the process, an urban professional subject emerged who was distinct from the socialist revolutionary cadre of the Maoist era. In this book, I examine the emergence of this urban professional subject and how it is linked with a new way of doing things (practices, mechanisms, techniques of governing) and a new governmental rationality, specifically the contemporary emphasis on talent and strategies for local urban growth.

Dalian, a port city of approximately six million in the late 2000s and the focus of this study, is an intriguing place to examine these processes (Figure 1.1). Under the leadership of Mayor Bo Xilai (1993–2000), followed by Lin Yongjin (2000–2003) and Xia Deren (2003–present), Dalian began advertising itself to potential investors and visitors as the "Hong Kong of the North," a "Garden City," and the "Pearl of the North." Municipal marketing campaigns boasted of the city's expertise and talent, research universities, the new Software Park, and the abundance of quality human resources. Officials also produced images and representations of Dalian as a hub of finance, trade, and tourism for the global economy, emphasizing the concentration of universities and "high-quality" personnel in the city. In fact, the number of college enrollments and graduates in Dalian increased significantly in the

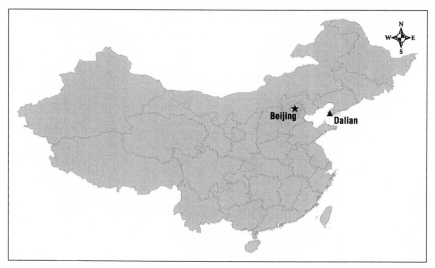

FIGURE 1.1   Dalian, China. (*Created by Xiongjiu Liao.*)

1990s and early 2000s, mirroring the national trend (Table 1.3).[7] Although less familiar to Westerners than Shanghai or Beijing, recently Dalian has drawn international attention for being named "China's Bangalore" because of its concentration of information technology companies (Thompson 2006), for hosting the "Summer Davos" conference of the World Economic Forum Global Growth Companies, for becoming the "fresh air" training location for U.S. track and field athletes prior to the 2008 Beijing Olympic Games, for receiving the accolade of most "livable" city in China (Fu 2006), and for being the subject of a National Public Radio feature on how Dalian University of Technology has used State University of New York as a model for its new automotive school (Abramson 2008a, 2008b). Intel also recently announced a US$2.5-million investment in a chip plant in Dalian. Echoing municipal campaigns, the CEO of Intel noted Dalian's "geographical advantages, sound infrastructure, and abundant human resources" as reasons for choosing the city.[8]

The urban professionals I met in Dalian worked in white-collar jobs in the city as managers and assistants, civil servants and private entrepreneurs, and researchers and translators. They were not the top elite or "princeling" children of high leaders, nor were they the individuals who resisted the "professionalization" of their worlds and lived more alternative urban lives. Rather, they were common urban employees who hoped for social mobility, satisfying careers, and perhaps families. As talented human capital, they focused on

TABLE 1.3 INCREASE IN NUMBER OF COLLEGE ENROLLMENTS AND INSTITUTES
OF HIGHER EDUCATION IN DALIAN AND THREE COMPARABLE PORT CITIES

Year	No. of institutions of higher education	Student enrollment	City population
Dalian			
1996	12[a]	53,100	5,374,000
2000	14	85,800	5,514,700
2003	18	150,000	5,601,600
Tianjin			
1996	20	71,400	8,984,500
2000	21	119,100	9,120,000
2003	37	245,200	9,260,000
Ningbo			
1996	4	10,400	5,300,800
2000	8	25,900	5,409,400
2003	12	80,100	5,490,700
Qingdao			
1996	4	26,100	6,902,700
2000	6	46,100	7,066,500
2003	25	164,840	7,206,800

Source: China Data Center Online.

Note: College enrollments were expanded in 1998.

[a] In 1980, Dalian had ten institutions of higher education (*China Statistical Yearbook 1981,* pp. 81–82).

career development and personal advancement, developed a specialized set of skills or knowledge bases, aimed to be creative and enterprising, and were considered critical to the success of the global city in China. In the following chapters, I examine who this new professional subject is; how he or she made choices; and how he or she negotiated often-conflicting demands and regulatory schemes from state, market, and familial regimes. I argue in particular that the new professional in China remains closely connected with the nation—although not necessarily the Communist Party—leading to a new social form that I call "patriotic professionalism." This professionalism weds career planning and individual professional development with national projects of state-strengthening and urban projects of local growth and prosperity in interesting and unexpected ways.

Many studies of the processes addressed here (urban entrepreneurialism, practices of self-enterprise, valorization of autonomy, and use of the market mechanism) have turned to the concept of "neoliberalism" to explain such shifts in urban life. Although I argue that neoliberal techniques of governing, such as more autonomous decision making and the marketization of labor, have been adopted in China, I also argue that these neoliberal techniques of governing are being combined with *non*liberal ways of governing the self and others—such as Maoist-era politics of socialist modernization and ethics of concern for the well-being of the nation. It thus does not make sense to describe the new urban professionals as "neoliberal subjects," for that assumes too much about the ethics and politics of these young people.[9] My analysis challenges more traditional understandings of neoliberalism as a particular combination of political, technical, and ideological elements that necessarily emerges as a "package" in disparate locations (Hoffman, DeHart, and Collier 2006). I thus aim to contribute to understandings of changing urban life in China, anthropological studies of subject-formation in global city spaces, and analyses of neoliberalism itself.

In the next section, I discuss reforms in China that valued knowledge workers in new ways; my argument is that these reforms included neoliberal ways of doing things, producing what I term "late-socialist neoliberalism" and a subject form I call "patriotic professionalism." In the second half of the chapter, I argue that this emergence of professionalism is similar to human capital development found elsewhere in the world, particularly as a strategy for urban growth.

Reforms in China: The Planned System as a "Problem"

The social, political, and economic transformations that frame the discussion in this book are numerous and have led to unprecedented change in China's cities. This is particularly true of the reform era after Deng Xiaoping's much-cited 1992 tour of southern China and the Special Economic Zones (*nanxun*), when he embraced—and thus accelerated—reforms in the planned system and urged the country to move ahead with "the socialist market economy."[10] These transformations also correspond with a decade of research that I conducted from 1993 to 2003 on professionalism and urban transformation in Dalian. During this time, China welcomed foreign direct investments (FDI), promoted new sectors of the economy and industries as "growth points," and even brought entrepreneurs into the Party and sanctioned the commodification of real estate and labor.[11] Urban economies were diversified, and college graduates were no longer required to work for the state upon graduation.

Instead, they chose jobs on their own and wrote resumes, attended job fairs, scoured newspaper ads, and used connections to find employment. With their families, they made decisions about working for the state or in the private sector, considering the advantages of each.

Since the early 1990s, this new professional middle class has exploded onto the urban scene, increasingly familiar to Western viewers through CNN broadcasts, newspaper articles, and *Business Week* reports, especially with extensive coverage of the 2008 Beijing Olympic Games. Images of young families shopping in shiny new plazas, well-heeled women and men taking taxis and private cars to work, and couples on dates spending leisurely hours together in new malls, restaurants, and tea shops have become commonplace representations of global cities in China, especially those on the eastern seaboard. Additionally, Western observers of China are increasingly aware of the dramatic rural-to-urban migration and low-paid factory production that have been fueling the growth of this urban middle class and the dramatic expansion of the urban population, from just under 18 percent in 1978 to just over 36 percent of the population in 2000 (K. Zhang 2004: 30–31).[12]

What lies behind the new urban landscapes of high-rise offices, export-processing zones, and middle-class social identities is a series of critical reflections on Maoist-era governing of the economy and society. These critical reflections, by government officials and academic elite in China and economic and political observers outside China, identify the Maoist-planned system of high socialism as "a problem" of "excessive government," principally in relation to a market-based, liberal democratic system (Foucault 1997a: 77). For example, in the late 1970s and early 1980s, direct distribution of labor assets by state-planning agencies began to be identified as inefficient, irrational, wasteful, and poor management. In 1982, for instance, Deng said:

> We do have talented people, but *the problem is how to organize them properly,* arouse their enthusiasm and give scope to their talents. On the one hand, there is a great demand for scientists and technicians. On the other hand, there are cases of serious waste, because they are not assigned enough work due to poor organization, or cannot apply what they have learned or put their specialized skills to best use. We should consider the problem of organizing and managing scientists and technicians, because the present method of management doesn't work. *How to use their talents and use them properly is quite a problem.* (Deng 1985: 8; emphasis added)

Economists and foreign investors accused state units of monopolizing educated workers and blamed the units for wasting talent through overstaffing, poorly utilizing their skills, and labor hoarding. Economic reforms that expanded ownership to private, joint venture, and foreign-owned enterprises also highlighted the need for college-educated workers in sectors outside state ownership. The failure of the assignment system to let talent flow to where it was most needed and into positions where the workers would be satisfied were newly identified as serious obstacles to national development. While debates about possible interventions certainly were contentious (see H. Wang 2004), in these discussions the socialist labor-allocation system was identified as a problem. Various actors, in other words, had "problematized" the command economy and raised new questions about "what should be ruled, by whom and through what procedures" (Rose 1993: 285).[13]

With this problematization of socialist planning and acceptance of new truth statements about the command economy, China entered a new campaign of reform and opening up (*gaige kaifang*; 1979–present), which experimented with the market mechanism and welcomed interaction with foreign entities, particularly after Deng's 1992 tour of the Special Economic Zones (*nanxun*). Government officials initiated reforms in the assignment system and devised new market-based methods to distribute labor to where they believed it was needed. They instituted "mutual choice" (*shuangxiang xuanze*) to allow graduates and employers, instead of state functionaries, to make decisions about where to work and whom to hire; opened job fairs to facilitate this exchange; supported face-to-face interviewing; and established talent exchange centers to manage the process of job change across sectors of the urban economy (state, private, and foreign). Job assignment offices on campuses were renamed "career guidance" offices, and university officials learned how to guide graduates into appropriate positions instead of assigning them.

These critical reflections and governmental shifts have produced a new form of governing that I call "late-socialist neoliberalism," shaping new subjects (urban professionals) and spaces (global cities) in China. I call this neoliberal governmentality "late-socialist"[14] (versus postsocialist or just neoliberal) because it exhibits multiple techniques, norms, and modes of self-formation, including socialist elements. Late-socialist neoliberalism is (at once) distinct from Maoist-era state socialism and the dominance of central state planning and the command economy, and from neoliberal regimes found in the United States and Europe. The social form of patriotic professionalism, for instance, weds neoliberal methods of labor allocation with a Maoist-era sensibility of the relationship between labor power and nation building.

A critical aspect of the governmental change in China was the adoption of more distanced techniques of governing that encouraged self-governance rather than state-directed planning. These techniques—such as individual job selections rather than state assignments, or the location of investment decision making in municipalities instead of in central agencies—differed from those of the high-socialist era, when citizens and cities had little autonomy to generate their own plans, to create new models for development, to pursue individual interests, or to accumulate family wealth.

In contemporary times, graduates must be well versed in what constitutes responsible choices; how to make those choices; and how to develop the self through the management of skills, knowledge, and potential rather than through allegiance to a strict set of Party rules or state-directed welfare distribution. This shift away from direct state assignments is an important aspect of the development of professionalism, for the new methods of labor distribution require a subject who differs from the high-socialist worker. Employment markets for college graduates—as well as the decentralization of urban planning—pivot on a respecification of social actors as autonomous in ways not possible under the centrally planned system of direct assignments (see Rose 1996b). In the process of learning how to make choices—and making them—active, enterprising subjects have emerged, what David Bray (2005: 179) describes as the transition from the "traditional employment mentality" to the initiative to "create your own rice bowl." Late-socialist neoliberal governmentality has cultivated active and enterprising subjects who are able to make choices about appropriate employment that develop the individual, the city, and even the nation—citizen-subjects who are the "counterpart to entrepreneurship, innovation and national competitiveness" (Rose 1999: 282). The professional employee, in other words, has emerged in place of the assignee.

These techniques have created a space that Li Zhang and Aihwa Ong (2008) term "a new social" in contemporary China, in which self-directed career planning, self-improvement through training and education, and self-cultivation of proper ways of acting (e.g., no spitting during the Olympic Games) have shifted the locus of development from central authorities to young professionals and the municipal governments that try to attract them. This new focus on the *self* (and on the local) exhibits a "reconceptualization of target subjects from objects of administrative fiat to autonomous agents with vested interests and rights" (Sigley 2004), albeit an autonomy that is meant to support national modernization efforts. As the new professionals I met embraced a self-enterprising ethos, they also talked about the importance of caring for their families and of developing themselves to help China prosper. Concern for the nation was integrated into their own individual career pursuits. Thus, even as individuals made their own choices about where to work, and even as explicit commitment to the socialist project was no longer necessary, post-Mao governing remained concerned with the "overall strength of the nation," relying now, however, not on ideology but on "the capacities" of people (Sigley 2004: 565). At the same time, practices that aim to enhance "the capacity and potential of individuals and the population"—what Ong calls "optimizing technologies" (2006: 6)—intersect with discourses of culture/ education (*wenhua*), quality (*suzhi*), and appropriate feminine and masculine activities (see Chapters 5 and 6) as well as other forms of regulation that lead to fairly stable social categorizations and to potentially "unruly" subject forms (Zhan 2005; see also Rofel 2007). Subject formation, in other words, is a complex and contested process.

In the following chapters, I examine various sites in the "microphysics of power," the detailed and multiple points and norms through which the governing of others and of the self occurs, and how these specific nodes are necessarily linked to questions of national strength and social collectives. To make sense of how neoliberal practices and socialist norms of national progress are able to come together in a relatively stable social formation, I take an analytical approach informed by the work of Michel Foucault and other governmentality scholars. In particular, I argue what at first may seem counterintuitive: that the promotion of choice, autonomy, and freedom are not naturally existing human characteristics but techniques of governing that specify the post-Mao professional subject.

Choice as a Technique of Governing: A Governmentality Perspective

Many analyses of post- and late-socialism present reforms in central planning as moments when people experience freedom from the state. These analyses assume that when the state retreats, individual agency is restored, and people have the opportunity to be who they really are. The focus of this study— the growth of employment markets and career options in a globalizing city— is an arena where narratives of freedom are especially strong and to which people often point as proof of the retreat of the state and the decline of governance in everyday affairs in China. This study also highlights the professional middle classes, a group that scholars have documented in cities across Asia as forming their identities through individual actions, especially consumption and lifestyle choices,[15] and as harboring the potential for political opposition as the state retreats from their lives.[16] These studies, however, frame their analyses around state-society power struggles and identification of individual agency, rarely analyzing choice or autonomy themselves. For instance, they tend to ask whether the arrival of autonomy and the private accumulation of wealth are the roots of a liberal political system in places that do not have such political traditions, and whether this liberalism will lead to popular democratic movements against authoritarian governments. This line of inquiry is based on a conceptual separation between state and society and suppositions about politics as direct opposition to the state. The assumption is that the state either intervenes in people's lives or it does not; if it does not, people have opportunities for political participation and opposition to the state.

In contrast, my study shifts the question away from the discovery of individual agency and possible opposition to the state to an inquiry into how modes of power and normative practices help produce the professional choosing subject. Shifting away from questions about overt political opposition does not mean I disregard questions of politics or resistance to forms of power. Rather, the point I am making is similar to the distinction Colin Gordon makes in his description of Foucault's concept of governmentality. Gordon notes that, unlike classical political philosophy, which was concerned with the "best government," "governmentality is about *how to govern*" (1991: 7; emphasis added).[17] Similarly, I am not asking whether the professionals would be better off with a liberal democracy and when they would demand it but rather how they have come to be self-enterprising subjects in a regime that has undergone a series of critical reflections about how best to govern in China. What I am trying to avoid are the assumptions about the evolutionary development of capitalism, civil society, and democracy that are embedded in many discussions of emerging middle classes.[18]

Thus, although it may be tempting to see reforms in socialist planning as the onset of freedom, such a perspective assumes that autonomous decision making and calculative choice, whether in job searches, home purchases, or love seeking, are natural human characteristics that exist a priori. In this book, I do not present the act of choosing as an already-existing condition within individuals that is expressed with the end of governance; rather, I interpret choice and autonomy as techniques of governing adopted by the post-Mao government (Hoffman 2006). As a technique, job choice may then be analyzed as a part of power relations, a mechanism of regulation, a device deployed to help encourage college graduates to be self-enterprising individuals, offering a more nuanced analysis of self-enterprise, opportunity, and choice than many studies of the middle class do. While middle-class consumption and lifestyles may be used to map contours of social change, studies of consumption per se not only underemphasize *production* in middle-class formation but also, by naturalizing the act of choosing, mask much about who these young people are and the mechanisms and rationalities that have led to the emergence of professionals.

A central argument in this book is that as we recognize the real and tangible changes in Chinese citizens' everyday lives, we also must understand how the very notions of freedom and autonomy are a part of the governing and subject-formation processes. Experiences of autonomy and choice interpreted in this way may be analyzed as mechanisms aimed to end the guarantee of dependency on the state and to promote post-Mao visions of national strength and modernity. The perspective that practices and strategies of freedom are not outside power relations and are not indicative of the absence of power draws on Foucault's writings about liberal governmentality and power/knowledge (e.g., 1991, 1997a). For Foucault, governing is about "the conduct of conduct" and refers to rationalities and techniques that seek order and economy and that shape self-governance. The specific argument about choice as a technique of governing also builds on the work of scholars who have extended Foucault's work on liberal governmentality and have argued that regulation and management of subjects happens "through freedom."[19] Freedom in this analysis is "a technical condition of rational government" that helps produce "entrepreneurial" and "competitive" individuals (Burchell 1996: 24, 23). My goal here is not to measure the degree to which people really are or are not free from the state. Similarly, Lisa Rofel argues we must be critical of hypotheses about how people are "casting off socialism [in China] to find their true inner selves" (2007: 6),[20] and Gary Sigley argues that the post-Mao state has "regrouped" rather than "retreated" (2006).

To understand how choice is part of the complex and sometimes contradictory subject-formation process, I turn to the everyday techniques and rationalities of governing in such domains as universities, job fairs, families, and urban spaces. As I describe in subsequent chapters, governing through choice crosses over state, market, and familial domains to help constitute and give meaning to professionalism and professional subjectivity. A governmentality approach is useful precisely because it focuses on rationalities and technologies and therefore allows us "to see forms of power that conventional state-centric approaches miss" (Greenhalgh and Winckler 2005: 205). An ethnographic analysis of choice across these domains offers insight into how governmental rationalities have specified urban professionals who see themselves as independent from state-planning organs and tied to the nation through the legacy of the socialist welfare system, dreams of China's prosperity, and practices of self-cultivation.

Neoliberalism in Late-Socialist China

Thinking of choice as a technique of governing presents interesting links between contemporary China and technologies of rule that are associated with "advanced liberal," or neoliberal, regimes, such as the United States. The work of British sociologist Nikolas Rose is particularly useful here: He argues that in advanced liberal regimes, governing occurs in more "distanced" ways and "through the regulated choices of individual citizens" (Rose 1993: 285; 1996b).[21] Distance, in his analysis, refers to the space "between the decisions of formal political institutions and other social actors" that fosters responsible and self-enterprising subjects (Rose 1996b: 53), what has been termed "socialism from afar" in China (Zhang and Ong 2008). These autonomous subjects are governed through their choices, which exhibit a degree of expertise, self-mastery, and self-maximization, such as choices about healthy living, continuing professional education, or responsibly managing consumer debt.

In addition, many definitions of neoliberalism identify "good" government as "the end" of state intervention into the economy and society, the promotion of the market mechanism, and the generalized fostering of entrepreneurialism. In numerous interviews I conducted in Dalian, people suggested that the market mechanism—and not the planned economy's job assignment system—was the most "rational" and "reasonable" way to distribute educated workers across workplaces and even cities. Particularly after China adopted the market "as a mechanism of government" in 1992 (Sigley 2004: 568), markets became a "cure" for problems (H. Yan 2003a: 499) and a kind of "test" (Foucault 1997a: 76; Hindess 2004: 26) or "regulative ideal" (Collier 2005b: 23) of good or efficient government.[22] In other words, the problematization of central planning led to the adoption of modes of governing—the marketization of labor distribution, the valorization of autonomous and calculative choices, the decentralization of decision making, and the emergence of self-enterprising subjects—that referenced advanced liberalism.

Nonetheless, it may be confusing to talk about "neo" or "advanced" liberalism in China. In fact, recently China studies scholars have been debating the evidence of neoliberalism in China, a place with Confucian, imperial, and socialist histories, but not a "liberal" political tradition per se. Wang Hui, for example, identifies the "sprouts" of "neoliberal ideology" when factions pushed for "market radicalization" and greater decentralization of power and privatization after the 1989 social movement (2004). Others, however, dispute that "neoliberalism" exists in China. Andrew Kipnis, for instance, takes issue with Pun Ngai's (2003), Hairong Yan's (2003b), and Ann Anagnost's (1997b, 2004) discussions of *suzhi* (quality) discourse as neoliberal, arguing instead that the ways social hierarchies are naturalized in China are not liberal. Although Kipnis's critique of the conflation of Marxist critiques of global capitalism and Foucauldian studies of neoliberal governmentality in China studies is important (2007; see also Barnett 2005; Song 2006b),[23] his analysis confines neoliberalism either to "systematic discourses" or "an ideology," producing an either/or analysis that dismisses the possibility of neoliberal technologies of governing combining with nonliberal elements. Moreover, the rejection of the argument that neoliberal elements exist essentially relegates China to a status of "other" and "different." In addition, focusing only on moral hierarchies and authoritarian aspects of *suzhi* discourses (e.g., Kipnis 2007; Hsu 2007) fails to acknowledge the importance of how market relations do affect subject formation—particularly through campaigns to raise the population's quality and the infusion of particular kinds of value into bodies and identities—as Pun's, Yan's, and Anagnost's work does.[24]

Rofel also questions the coherence of neoliberalism in China by extending Mei Zhan's (2005) notion of "unruliness" to argue that China was not simply "confronted with a uniform bundle of neoliberalism" when joining the World Trade Organization (WTO), for instance (Rofel 2007: 159). Rather, in negotiations over China's ascension to the WTO, she notes "an unstable social field of neoliberal interaction" and "strange hybrids that belie the idea that neoliberalism is a uniform set of principles" (2007: 166, 169). Such interventions are critical for moving beyond the addition of an "s" to the term "neoliberalism" to make it plural, the idea that "a singular type of neoliberal subject" (Rofel 2007: 2) exists, or the notion that China is "in transition" and thus "not yet" neoliberal (H. Wang 2004). Susan Greenhalgh and Edwin Winckler's work also pushes beyond simple understandings of neoliberalism descending on China in their study of reproductive-planning policies and the place of science in the constitution of autonomous and self-governing subjects (2005). Yet, in these studies, references to a "neoliberal capitalism," "*the interests* of neoliberalism" (Rofel 2007: 188; emphasis added), and a neoliberal subject "whose interests, desires, and choices *align with* those of a neoliberalizing market and state that have shaped those interests, desires, and choices to their own ends" (Greenhalgh and Winkler 2005: 244; emphasis added) do exist. Such perspectives imply that neoliberalism is always associated with one hegemonic, political project, a position I reconsider in this book.[25] Ong's work on "neoliberalism as exception" and "exceptions to neoliberalism" is helpful in pushing past simplified notions of variations of neoliberalism by analyzing how states in Asia have adopted neoliberal *and* authoritarian measures in one regime of governing. Ong's argument is noteworthy in that it foregrounds the complex and strategic governmental interventions that are not "reducible" to one particular political project but that, for instance, include *and* exclude specific segments of the population from "neoliberal considerations" (2006; see also Dunn 2008; Hindess 2004; Sigley 2004).

My project is not to define neoliberalism as a particular bundle of elements or as having one particular set of interests related to capitalism and class power. In the United States, for instance, the Left *and* the Right have adopted neoliberal "ways of doing things," to use Foucault's language, employing these techniques for various ends.[26] Much of the literature on neoliberalism in anthropology and geography, however, assumes that neoliberalism takes a particular form, with a "standard" bundle of policies and a particular political project (Hoffman, DeHart, and Collier 2006). Although groundbreaking in many ways, these arguments are limiting in others. Geographers, such as David Harvey (1989b, 2005) and Jamie Peck and Adam Tickell (2002), argue that neoliberalism—characterized as entrepreneurial city management, privatization, deregulation, and extension of market logics to the provision of urban services—has reshaped urban spaces and landscapes. Although Peck and Tickell, and such others as Neil Brenner and Nik Theodore, are interested in processes of neoliberalization and diverse neoliberal forms, whether "roll back" or "roll out" neoliberalism (Peck and Tickell 2002), as a "restructuring ethos" (Peck and Tickell 2007)[27] or as "geographies of 'actually existing neoliberalism'" (Brenner and Theodore 2002), they emphasize an overarching ideological element, what Peck and Tickell call a "new religion of neoliberalism" and a "metalogic" (2002: 33, 36). These definitions of neoliberalism take a political stand (particularly regarding global capitalism) that presumes an opposition, and perhaps incompatibility, between neoliberal projects of individual improvement and self-enterprise and notions of social progress, solidarities, and collective values.[28] Such an approach to the study of neoliberalism in cities presents it as a fairly coherent "top-down" package, as Clive Barnett also notes (2005; see also Mitchell 2004), and thus does not provide the conceptual tools to explain how specific neoliberal practices may combine with nonliberal norms and politics in everyday activities and in nonstate domains. Recently, however, new challenges to the assumed forms that neoliberalism may take have appeared through discussions, for instance, of variation and hybridity (Larner 2003; Brenner and Theodore 2002), a technical analysis of neoliberalism (Collier 2005b) and "global assemblages" (Ong and Collier 2005).[29]

By disaggregating the various components that constitute a regime of governing—a move governmentality studies offer—I analyze contemporary social forms and what is at stake in their emergence. I describe a new family formation termed "one household, two systems" in Chapter 6, for instance, that referred to the strategic deployment of family labor simultaneously in the state and private sectors by young professionals. Typically, the woman stayed in the state sector, and the man ventured into the world of private enterprise. This practice was the result of familial negotiations over how to enhance stability and manage new risks that were linked to the legacies of state socialism, spatialized gender ideologies, and the market distribution of goods. Additionally, I argue that in the new norm of professionalism, we see a combination of the neoliberal cultivation and actualization of autonomous choices with Maoist-era expressions of concern for the nation, wedding individual career development with China's future prosperity.

Thus, although I argue that neoliberal governmental technologies are evident in China, I want to emphasize that late-socialist neoliberalism differs in significant ways from the advanced liberal "formula of rule" described by Rose. This is particularly true in terms of the "supplanting" of certain norms of "service and dedication" by norms of "competition, quality and customer demand" and the extent of "the de-statization of government" in China (Rose 1996b: 56). The notion of patriotic professionalism, for instance, suggests that political norms cultivated in the Maoist era have not been fully supplanted by neoliberal ones. Ordinary citizens actively embrace an ethic of self-care that foregrounds individualized career development and social mobility enacted through the marketplace *with* politics reminiscent of socialist modernization that link work and patriotism and that emphasize the good of the nation as a whole.[30] Individual and autonomous employment choice is intimately connected with an understanding of labor power as being critical to socialist modernization projects. Similarly, in his research on urban budgetary practices in an industrial city in post-Soviet Russia, Stephen Collier argues that fiscal-planning reforms adopted neoliberal "technological mechanisms" but also that a "rationality of a market-type" intersected with other substantive ends found in Soviet bio-politics. This intersection meant that neoliberalism did "not imply the wholesale replacement of one form of social organization with another"; in other words, the adoption of the market mechanism in budgeting did not imply the "marketization" of society (2005b: 388; forth-coming). The emergence of patriotic professionalism similarly suggests that there has not been a "wholesale replacement" of Maoist revolutionary subjects with Westernized, middle-class individuals and that this social form does not simply represent the corruption of socialism by global capitalism.

Additionally, in advanced liberal regimes, the extensive privatization, deregulation, and marketization of everything from health care to insurance highlight the particularly de-statized space of these domains, the kinds of decisions that are made, and the individualized nature of expertise. Provisions of goods and services and decisions about them have been pushed outside the bounds of the formal government bureaucracy. In China, however, the late-socialist state conditions the meaning of post-Mao autonomy through regulation of the domains in which choices are made and the ways in which they are made. This conditioning is apparent in the consistent use of moral education to guide graduates into certain positions, university interventions into what is called an unbalanced marketplace, and the impact of the socialist urban-welfare system that associated the state with security for many urban families. As I explain in more detail in Chapter 4, even as Western liberal political theory has emphasized individual liberties and freedom from the state, in post–World War I *Ordo*-liberalism and Chicago School neoliberalism, the role of the state has been acknowledged as critical in arranging liberty and free competition. Wang Hui also argues that in "the Chinese version of neoliberalism," the state is critical to the emergence of neoliberalism, what he terms a "complex mutual dependence" between state policies and market ideology rather than "some fundamental conflict" between them (2004: 21).[31] Thus, while this ethnography moves across state and nonstate domains, it also accounts for the state as an active participant in late-socialist neoliberalism.

I turn to governmentality studies to help with this analysis precisely because such an approach allows for the conceptual flexibility to analyze the practices, technologies, ethics, and politics that combine in particular regimes. Few scholars have taken neoliberalism itself as an object of study in this way, distinguishing between the technical, political, and ethical elements that con-stitute a "way of doing things."[32] Indeed, Foucault explains that he "tried to analyze 'liberal-ism' not as a theory or an ideology—and even less, certainly, as a way for 'society' to 'represent itself' . . . but, rather, *as a practice,* which is to say, as a *'way of doing things'* oriented toward objectives and regulating itself by means of a *sustained reflection*" (1997a: 73–74; emphasis added). In other words, it is not an inevitable governmental system that defines neolib-eral governmentality per se but rather a rationality of "sustained reflection" that leads to particular practices. Analyzing these practices allows us to understand how neoliberal practices may combine with nonliberal, socialist, or authoritarian practices, for instance, without describing such combinations as contradictions, anomalies, disorder, or betrayals (see also Collier 2005a, forthcoming; DeHart 2010; Muehlebach 2007). In this book, I argue that patriotic professionalism and "one household, two systems" family formations are ideal domains through which to examine these often-undocumented social forms and to understand what is at stake in their deployment. Moreover, examination of their emergence pushes us to reflect not only on recent forms of governing, professional subjecthood, and urban spaces in late-socialist China but also on what we mean by neoliberalism itself (Hoffman, DeHart, and Collier 2006).

Contemporary Connections between Talent and the Global City

In many ways, the emergence of the post-Mao professional subject is an urban phenomenon. The careers these young people sought were middle-class, white-collar, office, management, and entrepreneurial opportunities found predominantly in urban labor markets and urban economies. Among new graduates existed a palpable urban hierarchy in which they assumed the best opportunities (*jihui*) were in the dominant cities of Beijing, Shanghai, and Shenzhen, although many hoped to stay in Dalian as well.[33] Employment decisions by professionals incorporated a spatial consideration that hinged not only on governmental rationalities of choice but also on the refiguring of urban places as hubs in the global economy and as locations of opportunity. Cities also embraced the idea that attracting talent (*rencai*) would be good for local development and economic growth.

As I explain in more detail in Chapter 2, I understand the emergence of active and enterprising professional subjects as being intertwined with processes that have led Dalian to pursue place-specific and border-crossing images as competitive strategies. Plans to become the "Hong Kong of the North," for instance, were developed locally, exhibiting autonomous decision making and self-enterprise by municipalities that echoed employment choice and career planning by young professionals. Urban place-making campaigns, such as the "Hong Kong of the North" or images of Dalian as a "green" garden seaside city, also were enmeshed in conversations about job opportunities for the professionals, thus not only resonating with job choice and practices of professional career development but also relying on those practices. Planners in Dalian have explicitly linked the success of open-door modernization with the kinds of workers, residents, and conveniences found in this city. At the same time, college graduates have been encouraged to become outward-looking professionals who train and promote themselves as skilled and talented employees, simultaneously helping the city develop. A "vocabulary of enterprise," in other words, links the decentralization of urban planning with the promotion of an "innovative spirit" in college graduates—that is, late-socialist rationalities of enterprise constitute places and people.[34] As part of what Cris Shore and Susan Wright (1997) call the "anthropology of policy," a central argument in this book is that acts of individual self-development and place marketing—even when they are touted as evidence of freedom from state control—are new mechanisms in late-socialist governmentality.

The analytical focus on how reform-era methods of governing specify particular kinds of spaces and subjects also challenges more naturalized correlations made between human capital and urban development in the urban studies literature. Much of this literature on the value of expertise, talent, and higher education for urban economic growth and national progress presents this correlation as a rational and even natural phenomenon. Although neoclassical economists previously emphasized "the accumulation of physical capital" for economic development, they now argue "that knowledge, training, and skill possessed by humans might be as important as, if not more important than, physical capital in the determination of output" (G. Chow 2007: 208; see also Becker 1994; Castells 1989; Glaeser 2005). Across Asia, economists have upheld the improvement of the "stock and quality of human resources" as a sign that a government is preparing its labor force for new engagements with the global knowledge economy (Chowdhury and Islam 1993: 19; Keeley 2007; Xiao and Tsang 1999; Siu and Lau 1998; Yusuf and Nabeshima 2006). Urban scholars also have noted the link between skilled knowledge workers, concentrations of professional and managerial producer services, and "global city" developments (e.g., Sassen 1991, 1998; Olds 2001; Yeung 2000).[35] This correlation has become particularly popular in the United States, with Richard Florida's arguments about the ascendancy of a new "Creative Class." Florida suggests that the creatives generate economic growth through the production of new ideas and technologies, and that the cities that can attract this class with cool neighborhoods and tolerant attitudes will prosper. Creativity, he writes, "is now the *decisive* source of competitive advantage," and thus municipal governments must build cities that attract such workers (Florida 2002b: 5; emphasis in original; see also Florida 2005). Although the celebration of talent permeates urban politics in many cities, it is critical to understand that what seems like a rational, commonsense, and natural form of economic growth, urban development, and class formation has emerged in China through historically specific problematizations of the Maoist-planned system, new articulations of the global knowledge economy, and a highly contested reworking of the relationship between the state and expertise. Examining the situation in China, in other words, provides an opportunity to think critically about urban politics that celebrate the creative class and the naturalized choices they make (see Chapter 2).

The contemporary emphasis on human capital for economic growth is, I argue, the current iteration of red-expert debates in China. In the high-socialist era under Mao, ideologically committed ("red") jacks-of-all-trades were promoted and trusted over politically suspect "experts." Those who focused on their individual (i.e., selfish) pursuits of expert and technical knowledge were considered politically unreliable and were relegated to the "stinking ninth" class position. According to Mao, technological and scientific knowledge "were not politically neutral matters," and their practitioners could have a "class character" and thus needed to be monitored and reformed carefully (Meisner 1977: 224; see also Greenhalgh 2008). This perspective on knowledge produced heated debates (or red-expert debates) within the Party regarding what was better for China's modernization and development—political commitment or knowledge and expertise.[36] The "technocratic move-ment" ushered in by Deng and his fellow reformers decreased reliance on those who were "red" and increased admiration for those with "expertise."[37] Deng was explicit that people should respect knowledge and talent (zunzhong zhishi, zunzhong rencai) and that education, particularly scientific and techni-cal education, was critical to the nation's development (Deng 1994e: 40–41).[38] China, he said, could not succeed "without skilled personnel and knowledge" (Deng 1994d: 20),[39] and if China "could get its education right, its human resources would be unbeatable by any country" (Hughes 2006: 32). The linking of science and technology with national development has been termed a "techno-nationalism" that promoted science and technology in nation build-ing and raised questions about how to adapt or adopt Western practices into Chinese culture and tradition (Hughes 2006; see also Deng 1994a; He 2002; Miller 1996; Y. Yan 2002).[40] Promotion of these human resources was rein-forced when in 1997 President Jiang Zemin "called for 'cultivating millions of high-suzhi [quality] laborers and skilled technicians to meet the demands of modernization'" (cited in H. Yan 2003a: 495) and as transnational agencies also called for "human development" and "investments" in China's human capital (UN 1999; Dahlman and Aubert 2001). The critical reflections on

Maoist governmentality that led to the valorization of talented human capital made it thinkable and reasonable to consider expertise, science, and technology as sources of economic growth and thus to connect urban development with this type of worker.

Desire for talented employees also was institutionalized in household-registration policies. Having a legal household registration (*hukou*) in a major city was a critical factor in job searches, and hiring decisions in Dalian's talent market often began with questions about where one had a registration. Developing a career and establishing a family with some security in one of these cities required a legal residency permit (*hukou*), influencing where job seekers went and what they did. College graduates nevertheless had more means to change their legal residency than former farmers seeking construction, household, and restaurant jobs in urban centers.[41] Rural migrants in particular have faced tougher policies in the name of controlling urban growth, suggesting that a kind of "variegated citizenship in which populations subjected to different regimes of value enjoy different kinds of rights, discipline, caring, and security" has emerged (Ong 1999: 217). Policies that attract talent and discipline migrants—that is, the contemporary reworking of the relationship between the state and expertise in this most recent iteration of the red-expert debates—have thus led to new norms of productivity, understandings of human resources, and noticeable new valuations of the citizenry. Although talent is coveted and cities compete with each other to attract and keep such resources, the socialist worker and rural farmer have been *de*valued. After the terms "*rencai*" (talented personnel) and "*zhuanye renyuan*" (experts) became commonly used in conversations about urban planning, many citizens felt it was commonsense and reasonable that *rencai* would and should have social mobility. Migrant workers selling products on city streets, working at construction sites, and offering other urban services, on the other hand, were often associated with crime and instability (L. Zhang 2001; Solinger 1999). Employers and young professionals regularly used such terms as "*wenhua*" (culture/education), "*suzhi*" (quality), and "*wenming*" (civilization) to distinguish between people and to help define an urban sensibility.[42]

This celebration of human capital for urban development and the devaluation of migrants and farmers are producing profound inequalities within and across China's cities. Reforms that have produced prosperous coastal sites, such as Dalian, and new middle classes have also produced sites of decline, a troubled "rust belt," and new forms of poverty.[43] Many in China have identified such shifts as a "rationalization" of the social structure, in contrast to what they term the *unnatural* and *irrational* class and gender polarizations of the Maoist era (see Chapters 5 and 6; see also Rofel 1999, 2007). The valorization of talent coupled with language about the rationalization of the social structure in recent years has, in many ways, naturalized new class distinctions, such as those between professional middle-class urbanites and rural-to-urban migrant laborers.

Yet, as I argue in this book, the fostering of talent in the global city should be analyzed as governmental strategies and assemblages (see also T. Li 2007), rather than as a natural evolutionary pattern or the arrival of truly free citizens and rational markets. In municipalities around the world, the celebration of talent has created new urban landscapes of high-end leisure-focused neighborhoods; it has been based on feelings of insecurity in the competitive global economy; and it has devalued certain workers and citizens while professionals and creative talent have been valued. Thus, an important aim of this book is to problematize the commonsense-ness of the correlation between talent and global city prosperity, and thus to denaturalize the resulting social-class formations (see Chapter 5).

Anthropological Fieldwork in a Global City

Fieldwork and research for this book have extended over a period of ten years, beginning with my first visit to Dalian in the summer of 1993 to learn more about the city's strategy to become the "Hong Kong of the North." The following summer, I focused more specifically on the new talent market in Dalian, which at that time was in a small space on the edge of a city park, just past some odorous public restrooms. This was followed by twelve months of research from 1995 to 1996. I lived at Dalian University of Technology, where I was the first foreign graduate student, and I worked closely with Professor Liu Zhongquan in the Sociology Department. This research was supplemented by six months of observation and informal conversations in Shanghai in 1996 and 1997 and shorter fieldwork trips back to Dalian in the spring of 1998, the summer of 1999, and the winter of 2003.

In many ways, Dalian's talent exchange center and talent market were my original field sites. I have seen this center grow from a small set of rooms to a large hall next to the library to a multistoried office building. During my fieldwork, I frequently went to the Sunday job fairs at the talent market to meet job seekers and employers. It also was an excellent opportunity for participant observation, since young people looking for work in a foreign company often approached me, asking what company I was representing and what kinds of workers I needed. I attended a series of major job fairs, conducted on-the-spot interviews, observed, and (in the case of the Spring Festival fair in 1996) had ninety-eight students (fifty-six men and forty-two women) fill out brief surveys about their job-hunting experiences.[44] Professor Liu and two friends helped me that day in an effort to minimize the impact of my American-ness.

Professor Liu also introduced me to researchers and workers in the city government who were responsible for economic development, planning, and rural-urbanization processes. Visits to their offices, materials they provided, and Professor Liu's own research on urbanization in Dalian were important sources of information. I also read histories of Dalian, newspaper articles about the city, and materials on Mayor Bo Xilai and his plans for the city and Mayor Xia Deren and his support for the IT industry and port facility expansion. People I interviewed also regularly commented on changes in the urban landscape, adding ethnographic descriptions to official representations of the city.

Although the talent market was an important site for me, it also was critical that I met professionals who were satisfied with their jobs or who used connections or the newspaper to find new positions. Sources for meeting other young professionals were numerous, but the most common was an introduction from others I had met, such as the owner of a private company who introduced me to a friend of his at the tax bureau, the manager of a factory who introduced me to his two college-graduate children, and the friend of a teacher whom I met the very first time I went to Dalian who called me and simply said, "I think we can become friends." She was right, and I spent a great deal of time with her and her in-laws. Five of her husband's aunts and uncles were college educated. These multiple methods were necessary for urban fieldwork (see also Smart and Zhang 2006). Although it is impossible to count all those I met briefly at job fairs, on buses, and in taxis (it was common to share taxis), the nonstudent (postgraduate) group of informants and friends numbered well over one hundred.

I also systematically interviewed two classes of graduating seniors at Dalian University of Technology (DUT; chemical engineering and English for science and technology majors); and had three classes from DUT and neighboring Northeast Economic and Finance University fill out questionnaires regarding their job-hunting plans.[45] As I always lived on campus, I was able to spend time with college students informally in addition to the more formal interviews and surveys I asked them to complete. In 1996, I also interviewed international finance majors at Northeast Economic and Finance University and project-budget majors at a nearby secondary specialized school (*zhongdeng zhuanke xuexiao*) under the authority of a provincial ministry.[46]

Interview questions included inquiries about educational and work background, families, future hopes, leisure activities, and living situation. Most often, we would talk about their professional lives, which inevitably led to conversations about their parents and spouses or girl- and boyfriends. The longer, more formal interviews with working professionals lasted anywhere from one to six hours and often overlapped with meals. I established emotional bonds of friendship with many that took us beyond the formal interview, talent market, or university setting. The participant-observation role I experienced when spending time with these professionals allowed me to learn more about their ideals, dreams, troubles, families, and working lives. With the extension of fieldwork into various city spaces and private homes and family time, I also was able to examine how these other domains were affected by the marketization of labor allocation and how the legacies of the urban-welfare package as well as gender and family norms shaped contestations over the meaning of middle-class professionalism.

Over the years, I met regularly with administrators at DUT who were responsible for career guidance and student admissions. I also conducted interviews with administrators at Northeast Economic and Finance University, Liaoning Normal University, and the secondary specialized school. Extended and multiple interviews were conducted with human resource managers or those responsible for hiring, such as the sixteen companies (two foreign ventures, five joint ventures, five state-owned units, three private companies, and one collective) that I focused on during 1995–1996, and I had numerous shorter conversations with those trying to hire workers (e.g., at job fairs) during all visits between 1993 and 2003. Often personnel managers told me of their own experiences as well, providing reflexive and insightful commentaries on how the laboring generations differed.

The college seniors I interviewed were approximately twenty to twenty-three years old, and the ages of the postgraduates ranged from their early twenties for the more recent graduates to their early forties for those who were married with families, or at least hoping to be soon. Those I originally met in the 1990s also got married, had children, became established in their careers, and changed jobs multiple times during this decade of research. I have referred to this group off-handedly as "reform-era babies," but it is a serious classification as well. Major political events in their lives included the series of student demonstrations in Tiananmen Square in 1989 and the subsequent crackdown and emphasis on patriotic education in the years following, the 1999 U.S.-led NATO bombing of the Chinese embassy in Belgrade, and Beijing's loss of its bid for the 2000 Olympic Games. Throughout their lives, they had seen an improvement in their families' standards of living as many people came to have some disposable income and new products were available for purchase. Air conditioners, refrigerators, televisions, and stereos were increasingly common in these people's homes, although the desire for products often outstripped their financial means.

What Follows

In the following chapters, I explore late-socialist neoliberalism in China and how these new ways of doing things have shaped global city spaces and urban professional subjects. In Chapter 2, I consider the respatialization of Dalian from an industrial Chinese city to a potential strategic site of global capitalism (e.g., as the "Hong Kong of the North") and how these spaces emerge in conjunction with subjects who are said to make such a city successful (outward-looking, enterprising professionals). Although the chapter's focus is on post-Mao urban-development strategies, the entrepreneurialization of place, and the localization of decision making, I also argue that colonial and socialist visions of modernity have framed the contemporary processes of global city formation.

In Chapter 3, I present evidence of the new practices and technologies of governing that have emerged with reforms in the university system and direct state job assignments. These practices included calls for job choice and employee mobility across cities as mechanisms to rationalize the distribution of and to enhance the development of talented human capital for national and urban growth. Choice and guidance rather than mandatory plans framed the graduates' employment experiences, producing new opportunities and new insecurities in the shift from assignee to employee. In the process, employment itself became a site of *self*-development and potential personal fulfillment (whether achieved or not) in the global city, a marked change from the Maoist-era notion of labor as part of the means of production owned by the state.

In Chapter 4, I explore how these new technologies of job choice and an ethos of self-enterprise have been wedded in unexpected ways with ideas of state strengthening and Maoist-era ideals and expressions of patriotism, leading to the specification of what I call "patriotic professionalism." As talent was upheld as a critical source of global city status, new norms of self-development and enterprise framed the young graduates' lives as they faced choices (*xuanze*) and opportunities (*jihui*) not available in the planned system. This chapter thus moves from the explication of choice as a technique of governing to questions of how that shapes subjectivity. I argue that the subject form of patriotic professionalism incorporates technologies that resonate with the Western liberal tradition as well as norms, politics, and forms of authority that are not liberal in nature.

The professionalization of employment and the rise of talented human capital in the global city are contested and uncertain processes, even as city marketing campaigns expressed their emergence as commonsense and natural. In Chapters 5 and 6, I explore some of these negotiations in more detail by moving into other social domains. Chapter 5 focuses on how the norms of culture/education (*wenhua*) and quality (*suzhi*) were infused into the hiring process. I argue that these norms reinforced the idea that people could change their lives by focusing on self-improvement and self-enterprise, redeploying Confucian ideas of self-cultivation and Maoist calls for constant self-study with neoliberal notions of entrepreneurialization of the self. Yet I also suggest that processes of class reproduction are being naturalized in China, limiting social mobility for many. Employers made links between an applicant's home environment and the idea of an embodied quality that was exhibited through ways of talking, thinking, and behaving, legitimizing and naturalizing these social distinctions and new forms of social inequality in the city. Recognizing this diversity and the tensions between these standards of behavior also illustrates how subject formation is a contested and heterogeneous experience.

In Chapter 6, I turn more directly to the dismantling of socialist urban services and provisions, particularly housing, and ask how this process is linked with gender regimes. I examine the "one household, two systems" (*yi jia, liang zhi*) family formation, in which one family member (usually the woman) stayed in the state system for security and benefits, while the other (usually the man) ventured into the world of private business and money, linking gendered notions of security with traditional distinctions of inside/outside as well as ideas about the safety of modern city spaces. Families and young professionals "calculated" the risks and benefits of working in the different sectors, fusing an economic way of thinking with gender regimes as well as anxiety around the restructuring of the socialist city.

In Chapter 7, I conclude the book by returning to questions of how we may analyze and make sense of neoliberalism in China, particularly in light of the global economic crisis. I argue that the analysis in this book may contribute to our understandings of the crisis due to its focus on human capital formation and production, rather than consumption, in self-formation and due to its governmentality perspective in analyzing transformations in the relationship between states and markets. I argue that while individual choices and enterprise are emphasized in China, these techniques of rule do not push governing into the nonstate realm as we see in the United States. The state remains an important participant in late-socialist governing—a governing I term "neoliberal"—through a premium on nation building, patriotism, and the legacy of a socialist state system that distributed goods and services to urban citizens. Building on the work of other governmentality scholars, in this book I aim to provide tools for analyzing neoliberalism in multiple sites. Moreover, I suggest that a study of subjectivity is a particularly fruitful domain for this endeavor.

2

Refiguring Dalian

The administration of Dalian's Free Trade Zone, a bonded area in the Economic and Technical Development Zone that is forty-five minutes from the city center, has published investment brochures for potential foreign investors. Similar to marketing materials found in cities across China and elsewhere in the world, these cultural texts offer legible images of reform-era urban coastal spaces. The image on the cover of one Free Trade Zone brochure from the mid-1990s clearly displays the repositioning of Dalian as a global city that is situated in national and non-Chinese networks of capital and culture (Figure 2.1). The cover's background is light blue, highlighting two main images and the words "Free Trade Zone Investment Guide" in pink. The first image appears to be a globe, set in stark blues and greens and bearing an imprint of China's coast opposite North and South America. The globe is situated so that Liaodong Peninsula is conspicuously placed in the center of the page. Hovering just above this imprint are several colorful lines that loop around the globe and congregate at Dalian, suggesting the city's translocal connections and its relevance to the global economy. The second image is a picture of a ship, steaming along one of the looping networks, aiming for the hub that is Dalian. In another brochure, Dalian is again at the center of the map image with lines that represent nautical distances to major

FIGURE 2.1   Free Trade Zone cover.
(Courtesy of Dalian Free Trade Zone Investment Promotion Office.)

ports around the world radiating out from it (Figure 2.2). Just below this image is another picture that also represents the hublike qualities of Dalian, with similar networked lines emanating from the city. Interestingly, in this second picture, the outline of China disappears in the background (Figure 2.3). It is as if the city exists on its own, a freestanding center for business and leisure that could serve not only northeast Asia but also the world.

These images illustrate that Dalian's recent transformation has much to do with the city's shift in status from a place within the socialist nation's landscape of production and politics to one that is enmeshed in domestic and transnational networks and spaces of global capital. In contrast to high-socialist practices that embedded cities and citizens in central, provincial, and municipal production plans, these new coastal centers highlight the increased autonomy the city has from central plans and its integration into

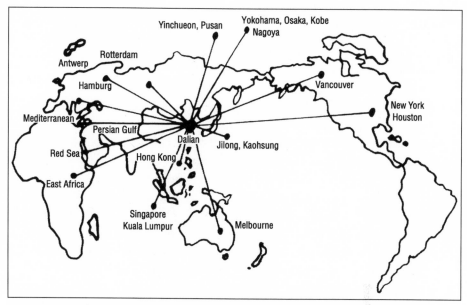

FIGURE 2.2 Dalian in map of spokes (major international shipping lines).
(Courtesy of Dalian Free Trade Zone Investment Promotion Office, translated and reproduced.)

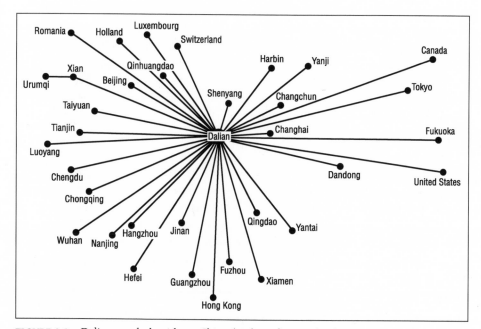

FIGURE 2.3 Dalian as a hub without China (air lines from Dalian).
(Courtesy of Dalian Free Trade Zone Investment Promotion Office, translated and reproduced.)

global networks and capitalist enterprises. This reterritorialization of Dalian from a Chinese industrial city to a strategic global site presents the city as a center of trade, finance, and tourism for northeast Asia and as an enterprising entity that actively generates such images. Also in marked contrast to the Maoist era, when Dalian was well known for its concentration of state-run heavy-industry units in power generation, oil refining, shipbuilding, and chemical and machinery production, this new urban space references new priorities on green city building and nonpolluting industries, such as pharmaceuticals, textiles, consumer products, software engineering, and call centers. Mayor Bo Xilai (1993–2000) adopted environmental and urban beautification practices to distinguish Dalian from other port cities in a highly competitive global market, to improve the quality of life for residents, and to attract more talented employees.[1] Under Xia Deren, the city has embraced the information technology industry, competing directly with such cities as Bangalore, India, for foreign direct investments (FDI). The repositioning of Dalian as an outward-looking location, strategically situated in a global network, also was about establishing the city as a site that nurtured outward-looking, globally oriented, and strategically situated professionals. As a *Dalian Daily* article notes, the economy may be "the first key element" of any modern international city, but "talented" human resources (*rencai ziyuan*) also are a key factor (*guanjian yinsu*; Shi 2000).

Current narratives that identify Dalian as a site of development, global attractiveness, and expertise are not completely new but echo earlier colonial projects of urban planning, port-city construction, and desired modern personhood. By examining Russia's (1898–1905) and Japan's (1905–1945) presence in Dalian as I do in the next section, we learn how the city, its population, and its skyline have been shaped by visions of a "better" modernity for many years. In addition, modernist planning, whether colonial, socialist, or capitalist, not only takes the city as a site of experimentation and transformation and a place in which to enact visions of progress, "better" communities, and possible utopias but also takes citizens themselves as subjects of social engineering (Bray 2005; Caldeira and Holston 2005; Holston 1989; Rabinow 1989, 2003). Urban planning thus is understood here as a "political rationality" that "informs the way urban areas are problematized, programs of government formulated, and technologies of government deployed" (Tang 2000: 360), shaping cities and citizens.

Considering the visions of modernity embedded in urban formations at distinct historical moments also underlines that "the urban" is not just a physical place in which actions occur. Rather than being a container, the urban is a series of processes that shapes places as well as people, exhibiting the "stretching out" or extension of social, political, and economic relations across space (Massey 1994: 88). These transformations "are always at some level struggles over the use and meaning of space and time," shaping "who does or does not do what, *where,* and *when*" (Pred 1990c: 12; emphasis in original). As regimes construct urban landscapes, not only do new material and imagined geographies emerge, but new social trajectories, subjectivities, and histories emerge as well, what Katharyne Mitchell describes as "the tightly interwoven relationship between socioeconomic change, urban spatial trans-formation, and the narratives and practices of contemporary regimes of gov-ernance" (2004: 5). Thus, instead of assuming direct connections between place and culture, it is important to recognize that "associations of place, people, and culture are social and historical creations to be explained" (Gupta and Ferguson 1999: 4).

These urban visions also remind us that "profoundly diverse materializa-tions of globalization" (Wu 2006: 3) and "differential pathways associated with global city formation processes" (Olds and Yeung 2004: 492) exist. Being defined as a global city does not require alignment with classic categorizations that emphasize the agglomeration of particular functions or population size (e.g., Sassen 1991). Rather, localized experiences of globalization, reorienta-tions of the economy and labor markets, re-spatializations of imagined worlds, and conscious attempts to model the city after other global sites are evidence that Dalian is a global city. Additionally, arguing that Dalian is a good site from which to examine globalization and the emergence of enterprising sub-ject forms suggests that non-Western cities, such as Dalian, that "do not reg-ister on intellectual maps" of global and world cities not only may be consid-ered "global" but also may be particularly important sites for generating ways to think about the urban itself (Robinson 2002: 531; Ong forthcoming). The use of models as a way to govern the urban in Dalian is one example (Hoff-man forthcoming), as is analysis of rationalities of enterprise as productive of spaces and subjects, which shape urban landscapes of prosperity and decline and self-enterprising professionals and unemployed youth. Global city spaces and desired human capital have a mutually reinforcing and constitutive rela-tionship, in other words; they are not pre-existing, autonomous entities but rather are mutually enabling social forms. My goal in this chapter, then, is to introduce the research site in more detail and to develop the idea that city building and subject making are related processes.

Past and Future Visions of a
Global and Modern City

Examining Dalian's colonial history highlights the historical depth of the city's global aspirations and attempts to be a site of beauty and social order. In addition, Dalian's contemporary late-socialist metropolis echoes these early efforts at modern city building, although now through neoliberal urban- and subject-making practices. Each iteration of the city—the colonial, Maoist, and late-socialist—may be read as a display of modernity and power and as built expressions of social and economic relations.

Earlier modernist and globally oriented visions were embedded in Russian (1895–1905) and Japanese (1905–1945) visions for Dalian as a major international port city (Zhu and Li 1988; Liu and Sui n.d.). While Russia coveted Dalian for the guarantee of a year-round, ice-free commercial port on the Pacific coast, Japan wanted control of the peninsula for the rich resources of Manchuria, and potentially Siberia, as an expanded territory for social and political experimentation.[2] Echoing the colonial experiences of south and southeast Asian cities, Dalian was fundamentally planned and developed from a small fishing village by these colonial regimes. Russia developed the first master city plan in 1899, built the first wharf in 1902, and constructed rail links to Harbin and from there to the Trans-Siberian Railway. Foreshadowing Mayor Bo's plans for Dalian in the 1990s, Russia emphasized urban beautification projects through construction of urban parks, civic projects, traffic circles, clearly defined commercial and residential zones, and references to Paris and the City Beautiful movement.

When the Japanese defeated the Russians and took control of Liaodong Peninsula in 1905, they also declared Dalian a free port and began to build the city into a major colonial commercial center and base for the South Manchurian Railway.[3] Japanese planners used traffic circles, regularized road systems, and imposing buildings to make their claims on the city, linking their regime with the modernist rationalization of space and thus with displays of power. A 1926 Japanese Tourist Bureau map of Dalian made this modern urban vision explicit: "One of the best laid out and imposing cities in the Orient, with many magnificent public buildings, fine streets and parks. . . . At the centre of the town there is a wide open space of ground laid out as a beautiful garden, and called the Central Circle, from which radiate, like spokes of a wheel, well paved and macadamized streets lined with fine shade trees on both sides." According to one Japanese observer in the mid-1920s, the planners and builders did an impressive job, leading to comparisons with other major urban centers:

> The city of Dairen [Dalian] as it stands today is at once the monument and the measure of Japan's ability as a builder of modern cities. . . . The general aspect of the city . . . is that of a European or American port. . . . Its modern occidental buildings, tall-chimneyed factories, and red-roofed residences climb from the waterfront up to the slope, because, like Seattle or Kobe, Dairen is built on the side of a hill. There is nothing of the immemorial East about it. . . . Dairen can stand alongside Kobe or Shanghai without a blush.[4]

Comparing Dalian to Kobe, Shanghai, Seattle, and Hong Kong[5] associated the city with internationalism, modernity, and high standards. Making connections between individual cities rather than their national homes is reminiscent of what have been called "global cities" in the contemporary era, illustrating that current iterations of global urban practices in Dalian have extended genealogies.[6]

When the Communists gained control of the area in 1945, however, their modernist city-building project reoriented coastal cities away from capitalist exchanges and border-crossing, global aspirations and toward the new capital of Beijing and redistributive frameworks. This reterritorialization established Beijing as the focal point for the country, centralizing authority and the unified national geography. The newly formed Chinese state took over spaces previously inhabited by the Japanese and challenged colonial power relations of exploitation, segregation, and capitalism. The monumental building that housed the South Manchurian Railway offices became the seat of the new socialist city government. What had been Yamagata Road, jutting off the former Central Circle and leading to the port, was renamed Stalin Road, and the park in front of the administration building was declared Stalin Square, illustrating attempts to shed colonial memories and to root the city in Communist ideologies. Officials also divided and distributed the abandoned yet elitist Japanese beach homes to several Chinese families as well as to some Russian ones,[7] and in the extensive 1958 city plan, "much land was allocated to factories" as industrial production took precedence (M. Li 2003: 41). In contrast to capitalist processes that drew people into urban centers, often to live in slumlike conditions, Maoist-era practices aimed to limit urban growth, to eradicate urban-rural inequality, and to equalize development that had disproportionately benefited coastal areas and dominant classes.[8] Private property was nationalized and redistributed among the population. The new urban landscape also showcased large central squares for political rallies and celebrations, such as Tiananmen Square in Beijing. Master plans for such cities emanated from the Soviet Union, but they also were built on practices from the Yan'an era (1935–1948), when Mao and his comrades experimented with localized production and self-sufficiency.[9] Dalian's image referenced in the Free Trade Zone brochures described above presented an image of the city that broke from this socialist vision and resonated with earlier urban planning practices and transnational linkages. The current re-emergence of Dalian's international significance, its goal to become the Hong Kong of the North and the center of the Northeast Asian Economic Circle, must be understood in relation to this past history of modern city building by colonial and socialist regimes. In the next sections, I examine how rationalities of enterprise, autonomy from central government planning, and attempts to prepare for the twenty-first-century knowledge economy have shaped the late-socialist city.

Contemporary Reterritorialization of Coastal Cities

The brochures described above suggest that recent reforms have helped produce a new translocal and global urban form in this site—a place where the year-round ice-free port has become an important urban "asset."[10] After the success of the Special Economic Zones (SEZs) in the southeast, which were the first geographic experiment of the open-door modernization strategy, the central government designated fourteen harbors in 1984, including Dalian, as "Coastal Cities" (Figure 2.4).[11] Official and popular documents referred to SEZs and Coastal Cities as "catalysts" for the development of interior regions, "classrooms" for learning new skills, and "corridors of development." Scholars and planners have used images of "mouths," "windows," and "hinges" in Dalian, where the mouth represented foreign access to the resources of the northeast and domestic access to things foreign, creating a "hinge" between national and international markets and cultures.[12] As one administrator in the Zone said to me on my first visit there in 1993, Siberia would become a Japanese development area, and Dalian would be the window for this trade. Dalian's role also would be as a model, partner, and liaison to its hinterland (*fudi*), the three northeastern provinces of Liaoning, Jilin, and Heilongjiang, helping them develop into "profitable and modern" areas as well. Echoing the 1926 tourist map, as a site for regional trade in the 1990s, Dalian's win-

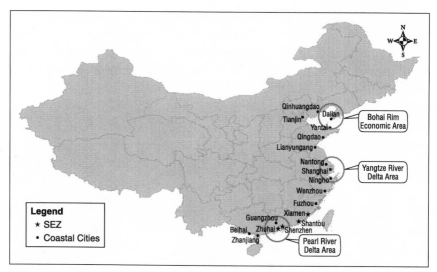

FIGURE 2.4   SEZs, Coastal Cities, and NETs (Bohai, PRD, YRD) in China. *(Created by Xiongjiu Liao.)*

dow status made the city seem more similar to other global port cities than to its own provincial capital of Shenyang.

Representations of Dalian as a hinge also led to discourses that described the city as a "center" and "hub" and in the middle of "circles."[13] For instance, planners referred to Dalian as the center of the Northeast Asian Economic Circle (*dongbeiya jingjiquan*), a geographical space deemed relevant to the city's Free Trade Zone as well (Figure 2.5). Although calls for a northeast-specific economic circle appeared in China in 1988, the idea of developing such "economic spheres" originated in Japan and Korea (Yahuda 1994: 254; Rozman 1998: 6). Dalian also has been described as the center of the Bohai Rim Cooperation Area, an "urban belt" that includes fifteen cities and districts around the Bohai coast and the Tianjin metropolitan area, drawing in the three provinces of Liaoning, Hebei, and Shangdong (D. Goodman 1989: 24; G. Segal 1994; Zhongquan Liu n.d.). Identification of the Economic Circle and the Cooperation Area created new translocal and regional geographies, fueling what has been termed the new "regional bias" of national development (Phillips and Yeh 1989: 130; see also D. Goodman 1989). These city regions have also been called "natural economic territories" (NETs). Other NETs that have received support from the central government are the Pearl River Delta and the Lower Yangtze development areas (D. Goodman 1989: 24).[14] (See Figures 2.4 and 2.5.)

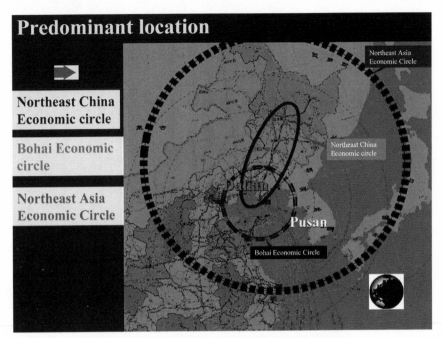

FIGURE 2.5   Presentation of Dalian's Free Trade Zone (2003).
(Courtesy of Dalian Free Trade Zone Investment Promotion Office.)

The new translocal and border-crossing urban geographies of Coastal Cities, Cooperation Areas, and NETs have created spaces of economic experimentation and special privilege through "zoning technologies" (Ong 2006). Construction of Dalian's Economic and Technical Development Zone (*jingji jishu kaifa qu*; hereafter the Zone), officially approved by the State Council in 1992 and one of the earlier official development zones in China, is a good example.[15] Promoting special infrastructure systems, tax benefits, special leases, and duty- and tax-free areas, Dalian's Zone is about thirty kilometers outside the city in what was Maqiaozi Village, an area similar to Pudong in Shanghai, where master plans leveled farmers' fields and constructed a "new city area," including the Free Trade Zone (FTZ), an international logistics center, and harbor.[16] These zones are well within the municipal administrative area of approximately thirteen thousand square kilometers, which includes the city proper, two suburban districts, three county-level cities, and Changxing Island, which as of 2005 has been developed as an industrial and shipping zone (Figure 2.6).[17] Although a half century earlier, Japanese citizens and entrepreneurs had fled the area when the Communists gained control of the northeast, with construction of zones in the 1990s, officials have

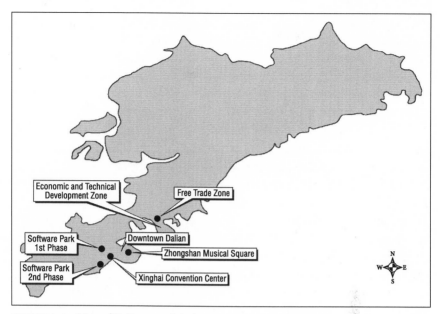

Economic and Technical Development Zone

Free Trade Zone

Software Park 1st Phase

Downtown Dalian

Zhongshan Musical Square

Software Park 2nd Phase

Xinghai Convention Center

N
W   E
S

FIGURE 2.6   Map of Dalian municipal area. *(Created by Xiongjiu Liao.)*

been inviting Japanese companies to invest in projects.[18] These invitations produced many tensions within the local population, reflected in a common saying that the municipal government was better at selling the country (*mai-guo*) than at loving the country (*aiguo*). New urban place-making practices "alter the collective memory embodied in the walls and streets of the city," but, as I was reminded by comments throughout my fieldwork and as Anne-Marie Broudehoux argues, a "city's cultural capital can never be manipulated as consensually as place marketers would like" (2004: 27; see also K. Zhang 2004). Official reorganization of the spatial structures in Dalian did not go uncontested, in other words, producing feelings of disjuncture and "symbolic discontent" (Pred and Watts 1992) as Japanese returning to the city did for some Dalian citizens (see also Zheng 2009).

Decentralization, Entrepreneurial City Management, and Models of Urban Development

Significantly, designation as a Coastal City, along with a decision a year later to allow Dalian to surpass the provincial government and report directly to the central government on economic and administrative matters, promoted locally sanctioned management and decentralized municipal development.[19]

Dalian was granted the right to report directly to the central government for economic issues rather than going through the provincial government. This, David Goodman explains, made the city "in effect [an] economic province" but notably only in economic matters, as political ones were still reported to the province (1989: 24). The decentralization of economic autonomy in particular was deemed necessary for local development, particularly development that was region-focused rather than Beijing-focused. Wang Hui even argues that the "decentralization of power and interests" (fangquan rangli) was the "core" of the social effects of post-1984 urban reforms (2004: 13).

This localization of urban management took many forms, including adoption of more entrepreneurial policies, place-marketing campaigns, and specific urban images. Models became a particularly important resource in the new competition cities faced, with Dalian's leaders marketing the city and its assets with images of the Hong Kong of the North, the Pearl of Northern China,[20] a Grand Dalian,[21] and an economic hub of northeast China and Asia. As in cities around the world, Dalian's municipal leaders faced new kinds of competition with other localities to attract foreign investments, tourist and leisure spending, and talented human capital.[22] With the decentralization of power, municipalities, like young professionals, have had more autonomy to generate their own models and images, even as state-generated modernization visions remained relevant. Contemporary modeling of urbanization "best practices" references state directives, such as Deng's reference of Hong Kong as a model of economic success and Singapore as a model of development and "good public order" that China could "surpass" (Cartier 2001: 210), as well as Maoist political rituals, such as the "Study Lei Feng" campaign, and Confucian teaching methods. Since 1949, for instance, Party officials have identified and honored model workers, model households, and even model cities for emulation, such as Dazhai for hard-working peasants and more recently Wenzhou for an entrepreneurial spirit.[23] Models may be generalized, referring to "the grand narratives of society," or focused, referring to "a specific task, or . . . area of information," such as urban planning (Bakken 2000: 177). Yet similarities in models at diverse historical moments do not necessarily mean their deployment duplicates earlier moments. Modeling, as a mechanism of governing, can be "quite flexible and open to a range of reappropriations" (Bray 2005: 36; see also Hoffman forthcoming).

In the early 1990s, and under the leadership of Mayor Bo, Hong Kong was the primary model of urban development in Dalian as the city attempted to gain recognition on the global economic stage, to obtain much-needed foreign capital investments, and to appear cosmopolitan to investors and residents.[24]

To build the Hong Kong of the North, urban researchers and planners talked about diversifying the local economy; promoting trade, finance, and tourism; and linking up with the international economy more directly. The city was promoted as a place with an abundance of highly educated and cultured workers who would not only help the foreign investor, the official discourse argued, but would also learn management and technological skills from these companies. The final goal was for these professionals to help China rely less on outsiders and more on its own human capital and assets.

In the context of these plans, Hong Kong represented leadership, advancement, and multinationalism. Cities and towns in the Pearl River delta region in southeast China often looked to the previous British colony as a mentor, partner, and liaison to other parts of the world economy. One Dalian resident claimed Mayor Bo promoted the image forcefully so the central government in Beijing would give the city more money and more autonomy to reach its goal. "It would have been too embarrassing," he elaborated, "if everyone knew Dalian wanted to be the Northern Hong Kong but then saw what existed. They (the central government) were forced by him jumping up and down and shouting out this model to give the city more."

Yet, as the 1997 handover of Hong Kong loomed and the central government emphasized Hong Kong's colonial history, Dalian reduced its use of this model. Hong Kong also came to be critiqued as too focused on money, similar to the way college graduates were critiqued for pursuing the highest salaries. "They only do business," one man assured me, "so it is a limited model of development for the city." Dalian, on the other hand, would become a well-rounded and beautiful city that would raise the level of the citizens. "This is part of the city's culture," he explained.

Mayor Bo turned toward Singapore and its Garden City vision as a new model for Dalian. Harkening back to Ebenezer Howard's Garden City ideal from the early 1900s (Howard 1965), Singapore symbolized urban control, green beauty, social order, and the lack of the "chaos" found in many overcrowded urban centers. Bo made a strategic decision to pursue more "sustainable" urban development that would green the city (luhua), clean up polluted waterways, and control the city's size and population growth as well. This model, expressed in the phrase "strive not to be the largest, but to be the best" (buqiu zuida, dan qiu zuijia), also contrasted with the excessive growth of places such as Shanghai and Beijing (Hoffman forthcoming). Instead, the growth he sought was in FDI (see Hsieh 1999).

By emphasizing the city's distinct advantages, these marketing campaigns turned the city into a marketplace item, essentially subjecting "place" itself to commodification. This not only transformed Dalian's skyline but, as with entrepreneurial city-management strategies seen elsewhere, also modified the city from a site of needs fulfilled by the state to a "source of energies" and potential economic growth (Dean 1999: 152).[25] The new intraurban competition for FDI has meant municipalities have calculated advantages and disadvantages in new ways, accepting new kinds of "risks in the pursuit of goals" as well (Rose 1998: 154). Not surprisingly, discourses of market competition's role in urban development have also permeated social life, commodifying aspects of life that were not subject to market rationalities under Mao. The end of job guarantees, the opening of employment markets, and arguments about the value of human resources for place-based development are examples of how young professionals have also "become visible" to networks and "pathways of capital" that are searching for new investments (Dirlik 1999). Strategies to make Dalian a "famous international city" (*guoji mingcheng*) like Hong Kong or Singapore explicitly valorize talented personnel over factory workers, knowledgeable professionals over farmers, and global links over local stagnation. With these new place-making practices, the entrepreneurialization of the city is linked with the entrepreneurialization of college graduates and their skills, talents, and attitudes, subjecting both to the exigencies of global capitalism in new ways. In the process, new geographies and histories of inequality also emerged as the influx of multinational capital, market exchanges, and urban renewal policies reconstituted citizens and generated new inequities.

Place Making and the Production of Inequalities

Place making and place marketing intersected in the renovation of Zhongshan Square (*zhongshan guangchang*), a round park in the middle of a large traffic circle in the center of Dalian.[26] Originally built by Russian urban planners, Zhongshan Square has remained a focal point of the city through the years (see M. Li 2003). In 1995, construction crews cut down the trees, removed most of the low-lying bushes, paved a large raised area in the center, and built little fences to keep people off the grass (Figure 2.7). The paved section in the middle became a platform for official functions, such as educational campaigns and patriotic school performances. Most evenings, waltz music was broadcast over the loudspeakers, and people gathered for dancing and chatting in the newly renamed Zhongshan Music Circle (*zhongshan yinyue guangchang*). Previously, the plaza was filled with retired men playing cards and letting their caged birds sing to one another, especially under the shade of

FIGURE 2.7 Zhongshan Musical Square. *(Courtesy of Lisa Hoffman.)*

the trees when the summer sun beat down. After this renovation, however, most of the trees were gone, and with them went the shade. At the same time, mounted police appeared on the streets, patrolling this now very open and easily surveyed public gathering space. As a tool of urban growth, the renovation refigured Zhongshan Square from a social space at the end of Stalin Road to a more class-specific site of regulated leisure activity along the renamed People's Road.[27] Young people flocked to the area for evening strolls and dancing, while some elderly people were not afraid to say how disappointed they were with the changes.

Such place-making practices have meant that land prices in the Zhongshan central business and shopping district skyrocketed, creating real estate differentiation that Maoist policies tried to mitigate (see Liu and Sui n.d.). The manager of a plastics factory explained that he moved his production facility to the suburbs and used his downtown land for a hotel and restaurant complex, making a significant amount of money for his unit. Similar to redevelopment projects in other countries, Zhongshan Square, a public space that had been valued "as a place for people to sit, read, and gather [became] a way to maintain real estate values . . . and a means of attracting new

FIGURE 2.8 Victory shopping plaza in front of the Dalian train station.
(*Courtesy of Lisa Hoffman.*)

investments and venture capital" (Low 2000: 180). In addition, use of the term "*guangchang*" (square, plaza) for places with commercial value and activity is highly complex and contradictory, since the term is "firmly associated with the memory of revolution and the politics of various historical eras" (Dai 2002: 215–216). The redevelopment of Zhongshan, Shengli *guangchang* (Victory Plaza), the shopping area in front of the train station, and Renmin *guangchang* (People's Square, formerly Stalin's Square) all embody these tensions (Figures 2.7 and 2.8).

The new design for People's Square uprooted the monument to the Russian soldiers who had lost their lives fighting in Dalian and shipped it to Lushun, the former site of Port Arthur and currently a naval base. In its place was installed a large stone fountain facing the municipal building. While music played, water sprayed up in the main round section, and people walked behind the water, remaining relatively dry. Families, friends, and young couples screeched and pushed as they made their way along the wall, beaming when they came to the other side. The rest of the lawn remained the same, and no one tread on the grass of "the first lawn square in Dalian" (*di yi ge coaping guangchang*). When I asked friends about this new construction, they explained Dalian was becoming a modern and beautiful city, just like the phrase inscribed in large characters at the port's entrance. The implications of this particular transformation—the removal of a statue of soldiers for a "leisure" fountain—are significant and, Dai Jinhua argues, not innocent (2002: 220). These commercialized and humanized urban spaces remained in tension with the revolutionary memories of high socialism, obscuring but not erasing the reality of social inequality in contemporary China (Dai 2002).

Although these localized development projects and "beautification campaigns" focused on spaces for the city's new middle classes, these processes also produced spaces of decline, such as the troubled "rust belt" in northeast China.[28] Dalian's municipal leaders actively tried to distance the city from the provincial capital, Shenyang, a city that exemplified the rust-belt region with its numerous bankrupt enterprises, extremely high levels of unemployment among industrial workers, and regular labor protests.[29] Instead, to attract investments, they created images and wove narratives of a city that was business friendly, environmentally pleasing, and well positioned in the larger regional economy, echoing earlier City Beautiful plans that aimed to construct lovely and prosperous cities. One interesting way the contrast between Dalian and Shenyang was made was through gender distinctions. A prominent woman in Dalian explained to me that the city government wanted to capitalize on the natural "feminine" beauty of the area. As a "beautiful young woman" (*piaoliang de guniang*), Dalian could take advantage of its natural scenery and geographic location in the region. In contrast, Shenyang, which she described as a strong young man, did not have the ability to "attract" investors and travelers.[30] Moreover, in contrast to rural areas and those associated with them, the city itself, Hairong Yan argues, has been "renewed as the privileged space of modern civilization and civility (*xiandai wenming*), gesturing toward elusive capital and development. In this discourse, it appears that *Modernity and Progress*, which themselves are the ideological effects of post-Mao modernist imaginary, are given their permanent residency in the city" (2003b: 585; emphasis in original). These pronouncements not only produced a dissonance for those who critiqued the city's "low level" and the new elite's conspicuous consumption, they also marked new social inequalities that emerged with these imaginative geographies.

Another important site of decentralized municipal authority that has produced new forms of inequality is the household-registration (*hukou*) policy. Municipalities now have the power to determine which households and how many households can settle their registrations permanently in the city, a decision previously carefully controlled by central authorities (Chan and Buckingham 2008). The *hukou,* job assignments, the socialist welfare package associated with an urban assignment, and the dossier (*dangan*) with information about each individual were powerful governmental mechanisms structuring the lives of urban residents under high socialism (and to some extent late-socialism). They also marked the urban as a particular kind of social space and revolutionary political project (Bray 2005).

The *hukou* system granted one the legal right to live in a specific place, dividing the population into agricultural (*nongye*) and nonagricultural, or urban (*feinongye* or *chengzhen*), households.[31] An urban registration, unlike a rural one, guaranteed access to the state welfare system, leading to serious structural differences between urban and rural life that some have labeled a caste system (Tang and Parish 2000).[32] All citizens were required to report any changes to the registration, such as a birth, death, or marriage, and to present the registration book to apply for a job, to get married, and to buy rationed items. Changes to one's registration place were very difficult, especially after tighter migration rules were issued to curb the "blind flow" of migrants to cities after famines resulting from the disastrous Great Leap Forward. Without multiple notices of permission, it became virtually impossible to move up the urban hierarchy to a city like Dalian.[33]

Yet even as people have moved to places where they do not have registrations in recent years, and even as cities have had the power to make decisions locally about who may settle their *hukou* permanently, inequalities in the system have been reproduced. Municipal policies, for instance, have tended to favor registrations for wealthy home buyers, business investors, and high-level professionals over migrant workers from rural areas. They hope to "attract more talent" by loosening *hukou* policies for certain workers (Hu 2003). This means, of course, that the "floating population" (*liudong renkou*) of rural migrants is still denied permanent residency in the city (Chan and Buckingham 2008). Differentiated *hukou* policies also have been incorporated into "sustainable" city-building policies in Dalian. Sustainable development, forcefully supported by Bo in the late 1990s, meant not only enacting environmentally friendly policies, such as increasing the amount of per-capita open green space, but also managing who would be able to become a permanent resident of the city. Dalian's municipal government adopted three policies to make sustainable development possible. The first was controlling population and improving the population quality. These improvements would come about through disciplinary measures of birth control and through more pastoral methods of trying "to encourage middle-level or senior technical talents to settle in Dalian." The second action was limiting capital construction and improving its quality. The third was accepting only high-tech and low-pollution industries (C. Liu 2000). Those with bachelor's, master's and doctoral degrees received preferential treatment when they applied to settle their household registration in Dalian. Starting in 2002 in Dalian, for instance, all four-year college graduates (*benke*) who could find a job (in any type of unit or company) could settle their registration in the city and obtain a local permit. By 2003, this privilege was expanded to include graduates with three-year degrees (*zhuanke*), although with some restrictions about settling in the city center. If the employer had the resources to manage the household registration, it stayed there; if not, the employees could leave their *hukou* at the talent exchange center (see Chapter 3). In explaining this new *hukou* policy, an administrator at the talent exchange center told me that "highly talented personnel are especially important for building Grand Dalian (Da Dalian). We have to compete with cities like Beijing and Shanghai and Shenzhen. Salaries are lower here, and many people move on to these other cities after staying here for a few years and getting experience. We have trouble keeping talent [*liubuzhu rencai*]." Ease in settling the registration in Dalian aimed to keep that talent.

The Local and the Self: Technologies of Urban Space and Subject Making

In this chapter, I have argued that links between the production of urban spaces and subjects are apparent whether during Japanese occupation, the socialist era, or the contemporary reform period. In the contemporary period, vocabularies of enterprise and practices of localization have been particularly salient in this linkage. We see this manifested in SEZs and new commercial plazas, as well as in young professionals, individual entrepreneurs, newly arrived migrants, and expatriates now living in Dalian. Their everyday lives and desires have shifted with the emergence of global urban landscapes, a process Allan Pred has called "the interplay of social and spatial structuring, the simultaneous making of histories and construction of human geographies" (1990a: 35; also 1990c). A good example of this is seen in He Yue's story, a senior at Dalian University of Technology in 1996. When I asked her why she wanted to stay in Dalian after graduation (she was from Daqing), she said, "I could have picked other places, but I like the city's atmosphere. There is good potential for development here, and it is the best city in the northeast. It has better future potential." She conceived of Dalian within a wide spatial network that included not just the nation's three northeastern provinces but also the development potential of these urban places within global networks. This new translocal spatiality, which extended beyond the more traditional socialist relationship between the central government and an urban center, informed He's sense of personal options and future plans. Place making and people making are, in other words, "intertwined" (Gupta and Ferguson 1999: 4); that is, "geography matters" in the subject-formation process (Massey and Allen 1984). The "new urban forms" discussed in this chapter thus do not merely reorganize existing geographies, for they also produce "new horizons of action" (Jessop 1999: 25) in which the young professionals live and make decisions, whether they move, leave China, or stay put in Dalian.

In this chapter, I have also suggested that reforms in high-socialist forms of governing had wide-ranging effects on the city. Job assignments to urban work units, strict residency regulations, and state distribution of such goods and services as housing and medical care have all been problematized and changed. This has altered the appearance of cities, practices of urban planning, ways one becomes a legitimate urban citizen, and patterns of job-housing-residency for college graduates. The decentralization of authority shifted new kinds of risks and responsibilities to localities and individuals as well. Critical reflections on the command economy, in other words, led to rationalities of enterprise and the decentralization of power, which emphasized the self and the local in new ways. As forms of power and regulation, these governmental rationalities refigured the symbolic and material spaces of cities and enabled college graduates to plan their own careers, imagine futures of material success, and take risks while also bearing responsibility for the consequences themselves. This newfound autonomy and decentralization also burdened places and people with new worries about unemployment, inequality, insecurity, and even homelessness.[34]

Existing debates in urban studies typically identify governance through decentralization, localization, and privatization as neoliberalism in the city. As I discuss in Chapter 1, these debates depict neoliberalism as a particular kind of political project that marketizes life, privatizes public goods, deregulates urban services, and ultimately disenfranchises citizens and reinstates class power. Although I find important connections between China and these Western examples in terms of the decentralization of authority, the entrepreneurialization of city management, the privatization of urban amenities, and the production of new forms of inequality, it is critical to understand that China is not simply "duplicating" forms of governing found in such places as the United States and Britain, whether at a local or national scale. As I argue throughout this book, the adoption of neoliberal techniques of governing, such as the decentralization of authority to the self and the local, may combine with other elements to produce unanticipated political and social forms. While China has localized much authority to municipalities, the state remains important in, for instance, campaigns aimed at raising the population's quality and the regulation of population flows. In fact, Fulong Wu (2003) argues that the postsocialist entrepreneurial city in China is a state project.[35] Even with the shifting of responsibility for jobs and housing away from the state and toward the individual, the state remains symbolically and materially important in urban life. The household registration (*hukou*), for instance, although having been revised, continued to influence where young professionals would live and who would hire them. Once families established legal residency in a city, they strategized about how best to access benefits that might still be available from the state, especially housing and health care subsidies, producing a new family formation known as "one household, two systems" (*yi jia liang zhi*; see Chapter 6). The renovation of public squares (*guangchang*), the building of newly stylized high-rises (e.g., *dasha*), and the beautification (*luhua*) of the downtown area correspond with attempts to raise the quality of the population and to produce proper citizens for a global city. Dalian's Singaporean model of a garden city and controlled growth coincided with reform-era imperatives to improve the "stock and quality" of the population while also maintaining control over the urban redevelopment process; planning objectives to humanize (*renxinghua*) the city connected easily with narratives of civility and strategies to build an "innovative city" (*chuangxin xing chengshi*) with an "innovative culture" (*chuangxin wenhua*; Dai and Bai 2006).

Another site of resonance with neoliberalism described elsewhere is in terms of the urban politics that emerge with the desire to bring talented human capital to the city. In order to attract high-level creative professionals, cities in the United States, for instance, have de-emphasized their industrial histories and instead supported new arts centers, downtown living communities, and diverse consumption opportunities. Many of the policies adopted by municipalities have used Richard Florida's coolness index ("cultural and nightlife amenities") and diversity index ("proportion of coupled gay households in a region's population") as guides for city building (Florida 2002a: 744; 2002b; 2005). Similar to the renovation of Zhongshan Square described above, these pro-development policies privileged middle-class consumption and elided the new forms of inequality that necessarily emerged in the process. British and American geographers have critiqued municipal adherence to such policies and to Florida's thesis in particular, precisely because it uncritically reinforced "neoliberal" urban policies and "naturalized as inevitable a prescribed set of urban transformations" (Zimmerman 2008: 240).[36] They argue that by focusing their energies on sites of middle-class consumption, city planners essentially ignored such issues as access to "opportunity structures" like credit (Hackler and Mayer 2008), "the nagging question of who [would] launder the shirts in this creative paradise," and questions of "ownership and control of property in the physical, bricks-and-mortar sense" (Peck 2005: 757, 744).[37]

In this chapter I have argued that global cities and talented citizens are mutually reinforcing social forms. Specifically, I have argued not only that reform-era governmental rationalities have shaped these new spaces and subjects but also that they are constitutive of each other. This analysis is distinct from "build and they will come" urban strategies that are based on the idea of an already-existing professional who makes individualized locational choices that are not tied to job opportunities or family considerations. Florida, for instance, argues that creatives make decisions based on personal enjoyment and quality of life, what Jamie Peck critically calls "itinerant hedonists" (2005: 766). My central position in this book, however, is that choice itself is not simply a state of freedom but should be analyzed as a mechanism of governing that shapes subjects who choose. Examining how places *and* people have been constituted by rationalities and technologies of enterprise and commodified in place-wars and interurban competition in China underlines that talent (or being a member of the creative class) is not an already-existing form of personhood and certainly that this is not a naturally existing form of subjectivity. Deciding where to live, in other words, "is not the result of atomistic responses to amenities," as Florida's thesis suggests (Markusen 2006: 1938), but emerges through complex interactions between—in this case—the legacy of the socialist welfare system, governmental technologies of "choice," practices of career development, and official directives to cultivate talent (*peiyang rencai*). The celebration of talent and the new hip neighborhoods, in my analysis, are mutually reinforcing and constitutive processes.

In the next chapters, I turn more directly to questions of subjectivity, governmental technologies, and the cultivation of talent. In Chapter 3, I consider reforms in the high-socialist job assignment system, and in Chapter 4,

I ask how new practices of choice have shaped the emergence of the enterprising and patriotic professional. The professional subject is also embedded in discourses of culture (*wenhua*) and quality (*suzhi*), as well as familial and gender regimes of the heteronormative, patriarchal family. This produces palpable tensions for young people, as they are highly steeped in narratives of the value of their human capital and the need for them to develop themselves so that China may also become strong on the world stage. Furthermore, the methods of population and labor management from the Maoist era (household registration, personal dossier, job assignment) and the legacy of the urban welfare package continued to frame decisions young people made, for even as the power of the older practices to control diminished, their significance has not disappeared (Chapters 5 and 6).

3
Cultivating Talent

On the fourth floor of the main building on Dalian University of Technology's (DUT) campus, directly behind a grand statue of Mao Zedong, was the graduate employment office (*biyesheng jiuye bangongshi*) where I first began a series of discussions on the changing role of universities in job placement. That morning in 1995, I listened to Director Xie Baihua explain through the cigarette smoke that his office engaged in "service work" instead of the implementation of central government plans. "Our work is now about graduates' careers and helping them with professional planning—not about assignments," he said. "The system we use now is called guidance (*zhidao*), rather than the mandatory plan." Eight years later, in an interview in 2003 that took place in DUT's new science and technology building that now housed the employment office, a university official reiterated this perspective, emphasizing that the previous system was about control, but now the emphasis was on service, guidance, and acting as a bridge between graduates and employers. The onset of the guidance system, also referred to as human resource management (*renli ziyuan guanli*; see Liu 2004), indicated important changes had taken place in the roles that universities and the government played in managing the transition to the working world. It also highlighted a post-Mao, reform-era focus on and belief in the value of particular kinds of human capital for national development. These changes created a new zone or space in which standards of appropriate professional desires were formulated through the intersection of new techniques of governing by the state, market practices of competition and choice, and graduates' expectations of fairness and potential social mobility.

Universities, which I identify as agents of state policies and directives and also as new sites of decision-making authority, fulfilled their task of supplying the market with appropriate professionals through a variety of new methods. These new, more distanced forms of state regulation included opening talent markets (*rencai shichang*), engaging in career guidance (*jiuye zhidao*), organizing mutual choice (*shuangxiang xuanze*), and implementing restrictions on where graduates could go. These new technologies of governing managed the population and human capital development in ways distinct from socialist planning. In this chapter, I examine in more detail how state-directed labor allocation was problematized and how the new techniques devised to govern urban educated workers were adopted. I begin with a brief overview of the assignment system (*fenpei*) and critiques that were made of this system during the reform era. These critiques are important, for they indicate a growing desire for college graduates and other talented personnel to be increasingly responsible for their own career development. In the following sections (and chapters), I consider the various technologies and microphysics of subject making that have helped frame who the new urban professional should and could be.

The Assignment System

To understand the significance of guidance, choice, and job fairs, it is important to have a sense of what existed prior to the reforms. In the high-socialist system, the state had a virtual monopoly on all graduates of higher educational institutions through the assignment system. Starting in the early 1950s and as part of the national "plan," college graduates, all of whom were supported by government funding, were assigned a position, usually for a lifetime and often separating him or her from loved ones. A key governmental objective was full employment, and education's purpose was to fulfill central production plans. The number of graduates needed in each major in the following five years was determined at high levels of the government rather than at the university level or by the students' own interests. The government paid for students' educational costs, and all graduates then went to work for the state—two conditions that changed in the reform era.

The experience of Song Yan's parents, who were sent to a small town several hours by train from Dalian, illustrates how the assignment system worked. Song is a young woman who changed jobs five times in one year after graduating from college in the mid-1990s. Her parents experienced the transition from school to work quite differently than she did. For Song's parents' cohort, universities reported the numbers of graduates and fields of study to the province. The provincial-level authorities reported this information to the central level, and national-level planning groups took the numbers and requests from work units to make assignment decisions. Plans were then sent back down to the local level for implementation by the universities and local governments (see Rai 1991: 174). The assignment system was top-down and bureaucratic, prohibiting input from the graduates or the work units.[1] As such, it was effective in placing needed personnel in far-away places and, along with the dossier (*dangan*) and household registration system (*hukou*), enabled the government to use geographic distribution as a form of social control and potentially as a punishment for political wrongdoings. The authority to distribute people around the country was important, as much technical and industrial development had been moved out of coastal cities in a bid to make interior regions more self-sufficient and to make key industrial sites less vulnerable to possible Soviet- or American-backed Taiwanese attack (see Naughton 1988). It also meant the educated elite, such as Song's parents, potentially would have to move to places far from urban centers and away from the more cosmopolitan lives they had hoped to have for themselves and their children.

For Song's father, the forced move with the job assignment to a non-urban area far from Dalian was personally upsetting and depressing. While he assured me that he and his wife felt dedicated to the country and their scientific work, they desperately wanted to bring the family back to the city. He used every possible method to get their assignments and residency transferred back to Dalian, which he ultimately did, yet he remained personally troubled about this change. As young people who had pronounced their commitment to the new society,[2] he felt they should have accepted their assignments with pleasure. Under such a system, labor was not a resource to be developed individually, as Song's father learned, but rather was part of the state-owned means of production and socialist welfare package (see Bian 1994; Davis 1990). This too changed in the reform era and was evidenced in how his daughter shifted between different jobs, eventually settling in at a foreign freight-forwarding company. Although she stayed at this position for many years, after getting married, she started her own business producing upscale bed linens and returned to the foreign company in the early 2000s as a relocation expert for incoming expatriates.

All college graduates, like Song's parents, were considered cadres (*ganbu*) and thus were managed by the personnel bureau (*renshiju*) rather than by the labor bureau (*laodongju*). This distinction was the foundation for the new labor markets that eventually opened, with talent markets (*rencai shichang*) managed by personnel bureaus and labor markets (*laodong shichang*) by labor bureaus. In the high-socialist era, the personnel bureau was responsible for people in clerical, technical, managerial, and engineering positions from universities, colleges, institutes, and schools, as well as decommissioned military officers (see Child 1994). In Dalian, many of the positions graduates received were in central- and provincial-level heavy-industry units in power production, oil refining, shipbuilding, and chemical and machinery production, fields "favored, protected, and subsidized by Chinese economic policies and structures" (Shirk 1985: 197; see also JPRS 1962: 127–132). The high concentration of such units in the city and surrounding area (many facilities originally established by the Japanese) also meant that Dalian had a decent concentration of technical personnel (*jishu renyuan*) during the Maoist era, even with policies that distributed graduates away from the coast. Assignments in Dalian also included textile- and food-product (aquatic, grains, oils) facilities or administrative, educational, health, or cultural units.

Although all work units were not equal, assignment to an urban state-level unit, which most college graduates obtained, basically guaranteed the graduate a wage, subsidized housing in the city, and other benefits.[3] In fact, an assignment to a unit and possession of a proper registration was the only way to get housing and other necessities in the city during the Maoist era. Thus assignments came with benefits of the socialist welfare package known as the "iron rice bowl." Other than when colleges were closed during the Cultural Revolution, getting into college and graduating with the status of a cadre who would work in a state unit denoted a guarantee of lifelong employment and stability. Along with the transfer of the graduate to a new workplace, his or her dossier (*dangan*), the file with personal and political information kept by schools and workplaces, and household registration (*hukou*) also were transferred. Schools and workplaces monitored an individual's behavior and noted any offenses or political deviations in the dossier. Black marks in the file could have made one a future political target and certainly would have affected promotions. Generally, dossiers had such details as background information, appraisals, assessments, punishments, work history, information on rewards, ranking, and Party status (Dutton 1992, 1998). The dossier and the *hukou* together became a powerful form of social and political control during the Maoist era and a hallmark of socialist China compared to Eastern European nations (Whyte and Parish 1984). Mayfair Yang argues that the combination of the work unit, dossier, and registration was a particularly effective way to regulate the population and produce citizens willing to accept hierarchical work assignments. Yang extends the analytical tools offered by Michel Foucault to the analysis of Chinese socialist relations and proposes that the socialist state ordered, regulated, and normalized citizens through practices of the redistributive economy. She argues that the state engaged in disciplinary techniques and forms of bio-power that rewarded certain behaviors and penalized others, establishing norms for social behavior and interaction, the effect of which were citizens appropriate for a world of hierarchy embedded in rhetoric of equality. The dossier, she writes, was a powerful normalizing force, because it generated a "general anxiety of not knowing what [had] been written and what could be written in one's dossier, and what future disciplinary use could be made of the dossier records" (1988: 413). Such techniques were intended to produce motivated socialist citizens for a planned economy of unequal job assignments and central distribution of benefits. Security of high socialism, in other words, was underpinned by state techniques of social control and normalization such that duty to one's country and socialist selflessness reinforced a system of centrally allocated jobs, salaries, housing, and household registrations.

Although groundbreaking in the field, Yang's work describes a process of state ordering during an era more openly committed to a planned economy. The dossier, for instance, has lost much of its effectiveness in determining one's professional life. Some young people I met abandoned their dossiers and moved to another city and job without official permission, and some companies turned to them only to verify graduation certificates and legal papers, not to investigate the applicant's "political behavior." This loss of effectiveness suggests new techniques were required to regulate and manage the population. Universities continued to rely on political education, but they also used monetary incentives to persuade graduates to take jobs in difficult and key industries. The transition from assignments to guidance (and techniques of governing, such as choice) suggests not that the state has disappeared but rather that it has regrouped as part of a broader shift in China from detailed state planning (*jihua*) to more macrolevel supervision (*guihua*; Sigley 2006: 503). As the market has been embraced and central planning has been rejected, the state has refigured itself to govern through techniques that are more distanced in their application than direct state plans were, changing the government of the self and of others and thus "what people are today" (Foucault 1988: 45). Reforms identified a number of problems with the assignment system and called for major changes in the way labor was motivated and distributed. Human resources (*renli ziyuan*) also took on a new meaning as foreign direct investment arrived and demanded certain workers and labor relations. Developing human capital became an issue of the "quality" of the population, wherein it was hoped that the "population burden" could be converted "into a human resource asset" (Tan 1994: 33; Greenhalgh and Winckler 2005).

Contemporary Red-Expert Debates

The current emphasis on expertise and professionalism must also be understood in terms of ongoing debates about desirable citizens. Although policies in the early years of the Communist regime underscored the value of expertise, and great efforts were made to include intellectuals in constructing the new society as they had been in the Soviet Union,[4] later political campaigns strongly critiqued the class position of those who had education and special knowledge. What emerged was the valorization of those who were politically committed and expressed their "red-ness," a system Susan Shirk terms "virtuocracy" (1982). The division of labor was a particularly important topic about which debates over stratification, redness, and expertise occurred. Despite the ubiquity of occupational specialization in socialist societies, Maurice Meisner argues that its acceptance in China "as the necessary consequence of 'modernization' did not come so easily or quickly as it did in the Soviet Union" (1989: 91). Particularly noteworthy is Meisner's point that Mao's dislike extended beyond specialization itself to a "general distrust of . . . experts (but not necessarily expertise), and professionalism" and that this distrust was not generated in traditional Confucian preference for the "amateur ideal" and a "generalist" but rather grew out of Mao's more populist ideals (1989: 92–93).[5]

Yet specialization appeared in China and can be traced to the country's reliance on a Soviet model of socialist industrialization and the unintended effects of the socialist rationalization of labor divisions. In fact, in 1949, China had only 50,000 scientists and technicians, but by 1952 there were 425,000, and by the mid-1960s there were 2.5 million (Meisner 1989: 95). Factional fighting over the red-expert distinction in the Cultural Revolution (1966–1976), however, led to a more generalized belief that higher education was producing an elite. This position then led to calls for part-study and part-work programs that would bring a new segment of the population into higher education, critiques of the wage-scale and work-grade systems that produced stratification, and attacks on occupational specialization by Mao. The emphasis on red-ness also led to attacks on teachers, suspension of the college-entrance exam, use of political recommendations for college admissions, and eventually the complete closing of universities from 1966 to 1972. The entrance exams were ended when Mao declared that "meritocratic practices, such as academic examinations and industrial skill hierarchies," could be the basis for continued class domination "in academic and economic institutions" (Shirk 1982: 18).[6] Gregory Chow argues that between this closing and the use of political recommendations for admissions rather than entrance exams from 1972 to 1976, "we can estimate roughly that at least 700,000 to 800,000 students of college age did not receive a college education for 10 years" (2007: 218).

These campaigns had profound effects on that generation of workers and students who were funneled into highly politicized class positions. Moreover, state policies, such as job assignments, ration coupons, household registrations, and dossiers, continued to structure how that stratification was experienced. College graduates, for example, had access to the iron rice bowl with their job assignments as cadres (*ganbu*), unlike other urban residents who worked in collective enterprises and unlike rural residents in general, which created an association of security with the state for college-graduate urban families (see Chapter 6). Yet the fact that the state determined where, for instance, Song's parents worked limited how that stratification would be expressed in social relations. Social mobility was not an open field during Maoist times, and distinguishing oneself from others on the basis of expertise, knowledge, and professionalism was politically risky.

In contrast, in the reform era, Deng Xiaoping made it clear that occupational specialization and, by extension, professionalism were necessary for modernization (Meisner 1989: 107). It was no longer a matter of bureaucratically allocating undifferentiated labor; specifications of skill, personality, background, and potential all factored into where workers went. Under Deng, intellectuals officially became part of the working class, recasting mental work as legitimate socialist labor;[7] professionals received more autonomy; and careerism was deemed acceptable—all in the name of national growth and prosperity.[8] Education and professional competence were important not only in the economy but also in the Party and civil service, so that many of the young people I met hoped to find stable jobs in the government as "experts." This contemporary celebration of talented human capital is the current iteration of red-expert debates.

A New Formula of Rule:
Challenges to the Assignment System and the Cultivation of Human Capital

After reforms began, people started using a market-based logic to critique the job assignment system for what were termed its costs, inefficiencies, contradictions, and irrational distribution of human resources.[9] The assignment system and the state sector were accused of monopolizing educated and trained workers and not allowing them to transfer between cities or units. Deng argued for letting talent "flow" not only so it could be used more effectively but also because without movement, ideas would become ossified (*rencai bu liu dong, si xiang jiu hui jiang hua*), hindering national and local development (Deng 1994d: 305). Markets, real and imagined, became the saviors in this logic, and labor mobility became "singularly celebrated" in the transition to the socialist market economy "as a new form of freedom" (H. Yan 2003b: 579).

As I note in Chapter 1, state units and civil-service offices also were accused of wasting talent and overstaffing, what has been called the "stagnation stage" of personnel management (Shuming Zhao 2005: 108). Although many positions were available for college graduates in the early 1980s, left unfilled by the Cultural Revolution generation that did not have the same educational credentials, by the mid-1980s, there were fewer positions and more graduates (Hayhoe 1996: 120; see also Bian 1994). Overstaffing thus became even more serious in succeeding years, leading to "dissatisfaction" among workers and "inefficient" use of human capital (Hayhoe 1996: 119–120, 174–181). A survey conducted in 1987 by the State Science and Technology Commission reported that "14.3% of technical personnel were 100% *efficient* in their role; 44.7% were 75% *efficient*; 30.25% were 50% *efficient*; 8.38% were 25% *efficient*; and 1.71% were not efficient at all" (cited in Tan 1994; emphasis added)—a new way to evaluate and value human assets.

In addition to the newly identified poor utilization of talent in state units, pressure mounted on the assignment system in the early 1980s because of the frequent mismatch of graduates and positions. Direct-state assignments often were not related to the students' majors (*duikou*), nor did they consider the individual's personality or interests. "This both wasted their training and made the students unsatisfied," said Director Xie, director of the employment guidance office at DUT. In his words, units were to blame for these newly articulated problems, because they "did not use talent well. . . . [T]hese workers were not respected for their value and were wasted." Schools also "did not think about what kinds of students and what level students society needed, they just trained them." And students had "no pressure of competition," making them "passive and not willing to study. . . . [T]he school's goal now," he continued, "is to let the market help solve these problems." In job fairs, employers faced accusations of waste head on by advertising themselves to prospective employees as "knowing how to use *rencai*" (talent), and publications describing the talent markets argued they supported the "rational use" (*heli liyong*) of talent (Yu 1999: 157).[10] A man hiring employees for a state-owned unit explained, "We need talented people for development. It doesn't matter what kind of enterprise it is. Everyone needs them. Talented people solve difficult problems. You can train them, and they help guarantee an enterprise's future development."

To address these newly identified problems of waste, inefficiency, contradiction, and lack of rational flow, in the 1980s, the Education Commission initiated a series of incremental reforms on college campuses. Attempts were made "to match" students with more appropriate positions and "to match" units with the kind of talent they needed. At first, units were given more choice in the hopes of easing overstaffing in unprofitable enterprises, and universities attempted to match students with the "right" positions. Rather than taking one assignee, work units began meeting with a few students at a time, offered new workers a year-long probation period instead of the traditional lifelong post, and even allowed reassignments if the original one was not suitable (Agelasto 1998). Only in the mid- to late 1980s were students allowed to participate directly in the process called mutual choice (*shuang-xiang xuanze*), and only in the early 1990s was there a further push to reform the assignment system so graduates could work outside the state system immediately after graduation.[11]

Although notions of efficiency and calculated costs are naturalized in Western capitalist commonsense, this particular articulation of the problem in China should not be taken lightly, for it signifies important changes in the way the state sought to govern its citizenry and people sought to govern themselves. We may think of these new methods of governing as techniques, mechanisms, and devices that produce new standards of behavior (e.g., a professional who is globally oriented), new understandings of a work ethic (e.g., one that is profit oriented and self-enterprising), and new assessments of value (e.g., valorization of urban talent over rural migrants). We then may understand how challenges to the assignment system were linked with the production of subjects deemed necessary for reform-era modernization, subjects who actively participated by developing themselves in the name of individualized success, local development, and national strength. The phasing out of the assignment guarantee and the phasing in of job fairs and resume writing, I argue here, are evidence of new devices and technologies of neoliberal governmentality that specify particular kinds of post-Mao subjects.

Guidance, Choice, and Autonomy as New Technologies of the Self

The appearance of practices of choice and guidance indicates new mechanisms and devices of governing have been introduced. These new mechanisms assumed new standards of behavior—people had to know where to go to make job choices, what to consider when making them, the repercussions of their choices, and the symbolic capital associated with these choices. This is not to say that people made no choices under Mao, as they certainly did, but the command economy structured life in ways quite different from today. In fact, as noted above, the system of dossiers, household registrations, and job assignments helped produce subjects amenable to a redistributive economy (M. Yang 1988). As such, we can begin to understand how new practices of choice or job assignments helped specify new subjects of government. Investigating experiments in new systems of labor allocation for college graduates thus offers us an opportunity to examine how choosing subjects emerged.

The earliest reforms in the assignment system began in 1983 with experiments at four universities: Shanghai Jiaotong University, Xian Jiaotong University, Shandong Marine University, and Qinghua University in Beijing. The two main universities discussed here are DUT and Northeast Economic and Finance University (Finance University). DUT is a key university directly under the State Education Commission (SEC), and Finance University is under the Finance Ministry. The year 1985 is particularly important, as it marked the ratification of the Decision on the Structural Reform of Education, which covered numerous aspects of higher education from setting new admissions policies to ending student stipends (CPC CC 1985).[12] Job allocation plans continued to exist, however, for the policy was not to eliminate assignments and all regulation of educated bodies, but to "rationalize" the system (Agelasto 1998: 264; Paine 1994: 130).[13]

Reflecting national trends, between 1985 and 1989, Dalian's Personnel Bureau initiated the new supply-meet-demand system, gave more autonomy to universities through recommendations and direct contact with the receiving units, and allowed students and units to meet. As noted above, units were allowed to take graduates on a twelve-month trial basis and return the graduate if they were not happy with him or her (DRJ n.d.). Only in the late 1980s did students also gain autonomy and begin to experience choice directly with two-way or mutual choice (*shuangxiang xuanze*), which started in 1988 (Agelasto 1998: 265).[14] The 1993 Outline of China's Education Reform and Development furthered the decentralization of decision making to universities, the 1995 Labor Law verified short-term contracts and the right for enterprises to find their own employees, and reforms in 2003 ended "jobs for life" for public employees, what Shuming Zhao argues "has been one of the biggest restructuring efforts in the field of employment in China" (2005: 115). This shift from a fairly strict adherence to centrally produced state plans to a more locally produced and university-administered guidance and macro-adjustment system created important changes in how educated urbanites entered the working world and related to their labor power. A man hiring for a state-owned company explained to me in an interview, "With the assignment system, you couldn't choose who your workers would be. They were neither what you needed nor were they appropriate. But through the advertising [*zhaopin*] system you can solve this problem. The mutual choice system is more flexible. . . . [D]ifferent kinds of people can make their own choices. Supply and demand is working here. The individual has power to choose a job that provides the opportunity for them to expand and use their abilities." Decentralizing the labor allocation process from central planning bureaus to universities, graduates, and the hiring units created a process where governing occurred through more distanced techniques, relying less on coercion and more on "persuasion, education and seduction," as in other advanced liberal regimes (Rose 1996b: 50). It is precisely through these practices of guidance (*zhidao*) and choice that new standards of professionalism were established and contested by all those involved. Not only did state rationalities about how the country would develop change in post-Mao times, but the modes of regulating and governing the citizenry also shifted. Choice, rather than direct distribution, shaped subjects' needs, desires, hopes, and actions, producing more self-enterprising individuals.

Dalian's Municipal Talent Market: A New Site of Subject Making

An important site or space for negotiating the meaning of professionalism was the talent market and job fair. The earliest form of these centers, which were known as talent exchange centers (*rencai jiaoliu zhongxin*), appeared in 1983 (in Shenyang; Davis 1990: 90). Dalian initiated new guidelines in 1989 that called for the expansion of mutual choice and job fair exchanges with

FIGURE 3.1   Job fair at Dalian University of Technology, 1996. *(Courtesy of Lisa Hoffman.)*

the opening of a municipal talent market (DRJ n.d.).[15] The markets provided a place, managed by the municipal personnel bureau, where those with higher education and special skills could meet with employers and sign short-term contracts. They were aimed at those already in the working world, since in the 1980s college graduates still had a responsibility to move into the state sector for some period after graduation. As state-sponsored students, the state expected them to stay within the state sector, unless they, or their new employers, wanted to pay the state back for their educational costs. Later they also became important sites of new graduates' job searches. If someone found a job and needed a place to keep his or her papers (e.g., work history for insurance and retirement purposes, dossier), the centers could legally do this as well (DTSC 1995). This was primarily a service for individuals working in smaller, private companies, since those who worked in large organizations, such as state-owned enterprises, universities, or the civil service, kept their employment records in the workplace. The main purpose of the market was, and continues to be, to facilitate the job-search process for companies and for those seeking employment. Municipalities held city-wide job fairs, and universities held fairs limited to their own graduates (see Figures 3.1 and 3.2).

The first time I attended a Sunday job fair for human resources or talented personnel in Dalian (summer of 1993), I was surprised to listen to company

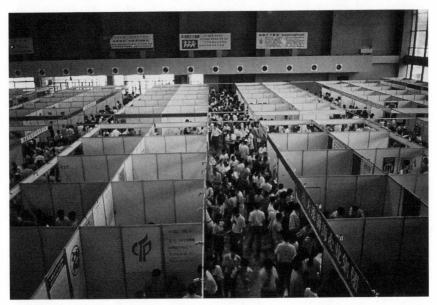

FIGURE 3.2 Job fair run by the city government. (*Courtesy of Lisa Hoffman.*)

owners and personnel managers describe the kinds of employees they wanted to hire. It was one thing to read about reforms in China's planned economy and quite another to stand in the middle of a room and listen to those who fashioned themselves as employees and employers try to sell themselves to each other. This early talent market in Dalian was marked by a small sign that read "*rencai shichang*" at the top of a set of stairs in a complex at the corner of a city park (Figure 3.3). At the end of a hall was an open room with information posters on the walls. To the left was another hallway with several offices housing administrators from the municipal personnel bureau who managed the talent market. People looking for work stood in the open room with small notepads and eyes fixed on the postings on the wall that listed job openings. At the Sunday job fairs (*zhaopin huiyi*), company representatives sat behind tables with descriptions of who they wanted to hire posted on the wall behind them. Job seekers would approach the tables to ask questions and to participate in the new practice of interviewing. The weekly job fairs attracted young graduates looking for a first job, retired workers looking for second careers, unemployed or underemployed people with education or special skills, and dissatisfied workers who sought higher salaries, better benefits, and the chance for personal development.

FIGURE 3.3   Signage for the "talent market" (*rencai shichang*). (*Courtesy of Lisa Hoffman.*)

By the fall of 1995, Dalian's employment center and talent market had moved to a much larger building near the municipal library. To get to the weekly Sunday job fair, I had to walk through a used-car market that was held every week as well. Taxis, the ubiquitous white minibuses, Cadillacs, and even red sports cars were jammed together in the narrow passage that led from the main road to the building. Other cars still managed to drive through, so walking to the building often felt like swimming upstream. Distinct from two years prior, in 1995, job seekers purchased tickets before they entered the main hall and carried resumes as they approached company and unit representatives. In addition to the main hall, the building had side rooms and a second floor with several large cavernous spaces that could be used for special events, such as the annual fall job fair, the Spring Festival graduates' fair, and the summer graduation fair. In the same fashion as before, companies set up desks in these rooms and posted descriptions of desired employees on the walls. Typically, these postings advertised how many people they needed; position titles; and required education level, knowledge base, and experience. Some companies even specified age, gender, and height, which was especially common for public relations (*gongguan*) positions, aimed at attractive, tall, young women. Examples read: Manager, 5+ years' experience, 35 years or

大连市人才市场委托招聘登记表

年　月　日

单位名称　（必填）		单位地址（必填）		邮　编	
营业执照号（必填）		注册资金（必填）		所有制性质(必填)	
联 系 人　（必填）		电话（必填）		是否公开单位名称	
传　　真		电 子 邮 件		是否公开单位地址	
单 位 简 况					

人 才 需 求 情 况

职　　位	性 别	人 数	年 龄	学 历	职 称	其　　　　他

FIGURE 3.4　Form filled out by employers at the municipal job fair. *(From Dalian City Talent Market.)*

older, male; Secretary, 3-year college degree (*zhuanke*), 20–25 years old, female. Job seekers filled out standard application forms with their names, addresses, ages, schooling levels, majors, job experience, and the like and attached a recent photo; the forms were similar to those that the talent service center had employers use (see Figure 3.4). It did not take much time to expand beyond the confines of this building, however. After a severely overcrowded Spring Festival fair[16] in 1996, the personnel bureau decided to move the summer graduation fair. It was held in Dalian's new Xinghai Convention Center, which was Mayor Bo Xilai's flagship attraction. These fairs and the job hunt in general, which included reading newspaper advertisements and relying on personal networks for opportunities, had become common practice by the mid-1990s. When I visited the next home of the exchange center in December 2003, it was in the Human Resources Building (*rencai dasha*), a newly built modern office building near Jiefang Square (Figure 3.5). By this time, the talent service center offered cubicles for company representatives to use when interviewing potential applicants, and windows were in place for separate functions, such as insurance, retirement, and dossier and *hukou* services.

FIGURE 3.5 Municipal talent market, 2003. *(Courtesy of Lisa Hoffman.)*

In addition to state-owned units pressured to use these talent markets, township and village enterprises, foreign companies, and private ventures all used these sites as places to meet potential employees and to fill posts. Dalian's municipal government held the largest and most expansive talent market, but each district in the city and the development zones held their own fairs as well. Newcomers to the city typically visited such a site, as did the Dalian graduates I met who ventured to other cities to look for work. It was common knowledge where the talent markets and the labor markets were, and often one would see postings and announcements about upcoming events, such as the annual fall job fair. Nevertheless, as a young dentist once said to me, "I didn't believe I could find a job in the talent market until I went with a friend. I thought people just used connections to find jobs. But when I graduated I went there many times to have a look, although I never did find anything suitable [*shihe*]." By the early 2000s, the weekly markets had become the site for small and medium-size companies to find employees, while larger firms (foreign and domestic) used newspaper ads and Internet sites, such as hrChina.com and 51job.com.[17] The government also has encouraged municipal talent service centers to launch employment Web sites, to standardize their services, and to regulate private job agencies to help promote "the rational allocation of labor resources" (China's Employment Situation and Policies 2004).

My practice was to walk through the job fairs and approach those looking for work and those looking for employees. A typical exchange was similar to the one I had in 1996 with two older women who represented a township enterprise. I asked them how they tended to find their employees and what they were looking for when hiring. In this case, they found employees through the talent market and, as I learned from a more extensive interview the following week, through family connections. One woman explained that they asked about a person's educational background, work experience, and abilities. Job seekers typically asked them about benefits, salaries, and whether the company could help them settle their household registration (hukou) in Dalian. They could not and thus were reluctant to hire an "outsider." "They would not be a stable employee," she explained. "If they don't have a proper registration, they may leave, and that is not good for the company."

Exchanges with job applicants followed similar narratives of what was wrong with their current positions, what they were looking for, how hard it was to find a satisfying position, and what compromises they would willingly make. For instance, I met a man who had graduated in 1986 who explained he was from Dalian but had gone to Heilongjiang Province to work. His parents used to work at Dalian's TV station, but they had moved to Heilongjiang as well. The situation there was not good, he explained, and he wanted to return to Dalian: "I've already been here for two months looking for work. I am doing some temporary work [his specialty was computer-aided design], but that does not solve my household registration problem. I need to solve it." Another man a few years older who graduated in 1984 approached me to see what company I was representing. After learning my purpose, he told me that he stayed at his first job doing equipment management, which he received through government assignment, for ten years. In 1993, he found work in a foreign company at one of these fairs, but now he was looking to change again: "I have done this work for two-and-a-half years, and I have not had a lot of development in this position. I want to get into the business and management side so I can make my own decisions and decide on my own work." Similar to other young professionals I met, he embraced the reality of relying on himself and seeking out new opportunities (jihui). A young woman I met at the talent market in 2003 echoed these narratives. She told me about her move to Shanghai to work in an office and how disappointed she was with that experience. She had returned to Dalian to find a position that would develop her skills and provide her with a good opportunity. Although she hesitated about trusting a small company again, she remained enthusiastic about her potential and her job search.

Campus Job Fairs: Universities Shepherd Graduates to Market

Universities also held their own fairs. On-campus fairs differed from municipal ones in that they were run by a specific university, were open only to that university's students, and, in the case of DUT, drew units from across the country. These units predominantly were large state-run enterprises, which used to receive DUT graduates through assignments. In 1996, DUT held its campus fair in March, just after the Spring Festival holiday, but school officials moved it up to February in 1997, one of the earliest in the country. They argued an earlier job fair gave DUT graduates a greater advantage in the job hunt (DUT 1997), evidence of an increasingly difficult job market for their graduates. Recent articles continue to highlight the problems graduates face when seeking satisfying and appropriate positions, especially as the numbers of those entering college increased after 1998 (e.g., Cody 2006; see also Table 1.3).

The morning of the first day of the campus fair I attended, DUT's vice president told company representatives who had come to hire his school's graduates that the school wanted to establish "fair competition." This was followed by a plea for the work units to help the university do this kind of work and to "understand the market, our role, and your needs." Fair competition would be enhanced through the fairs, which provided an opportunity for students to learn more about a unit before agreeing to work there and for the units to evaluate the abilities and background of the students. Theoretically, if the students were competitive enough, they could go anywhere in the country through this kind of market system. Such an argument selectively overlooked that students were distributed nationally through the assignment system as well. It also showed that a school's reputation mattered—the famous schools attracted better employers. Yet, a DUT employment officer noted, this also meant the students faced greater competition and pressure to uphold the school's reputation once working.

Later in the day, after this early-morning welcoming ceremony in a large campus lecture-hall, we walked to a nearby middle school where the actual fair was held. Company representatives, divided in classrooms by geographic area and industry, sat behind tables and waited for students to come to them.

All had posters behind their tables, similar to the arrangement at the city-wide fairs, stating the majors they wanted, how many people they needed, and if they required men or women. The rooms with companies from Dalian and such joint ventures as Sanyo (which needed primarily engineers and technicians) were crowded, but the room with units from Shanghai was virtually impossible to enter, highlighting the geographic hierarchies influencing graduates' employment strategies. Those doing the hiring, however, did not seem anxious to find people during these few days. "It is hard to say if it is easy to find appropriate new employees here," one man said. "Sometimes we bump into them at these fairs. It doesn't matter if we find any people now though." Students, however, complained about the fairs and that they expected better choices. As I arrived the first morning of the two-day fair, I heard students calling to each other as they poured in and out of the middle school's entrance. One young man asked his friend what he thought as he walked out. "Just okay," he responded. "There aren't any good companies or work units here."

That afternoon, I ran into a friend in the hallway who took me to talk to a classmate of his who had just signed a contract. This young man was wearing a suit and tie, while most of the other men donned white shirts and dark blue pants. A government agency (*zhengfu jiguan*) from a medium-size city near Dalian had hired him to work in their foreign economic relations and trade department. "I should have a chance to develop there," he explained. "We talked for several hours in these rooms, and then they hired me. They picked me because my major is important to their office; I have both chemical engineering and English together, you know." The salary, at only 400 RMB per month (a low wage in 1996; the average was around 1,000 RMB per month in 2003), was not so important to him, "because my family can help," but the unit did promise him rent money. His main concern, however, was the household registration, which would move to this city with him: "It is not as good as a Dalian registration, or one in Beijing. So, I am still looking for a better position." Changing jobs after signing a contract was against the mutual choice rules, and he could be fined or forced to go to the first position, or both. When I talked with him a few months later, he brought me up to date on his situation. He had taken part in the provincial exam for government work and was offered a job in the Bureau of Foreign Trade and Economic Cooperation. Because it was a provincial-level office, the school allowed him to break the original contract, and the first agency wished him well at the higher government level.[18]

After this fair, I met with Director Xie and inquired about his perception of the results. He acknowledged that only 302 out of the 1,464 students for whom the school was responsible[19] signed contracts, and of these, only 21 students (7 percent) were female. Twenty-two percent of the students at this technical university were female. In 1995, 35.4 percent of all university students in China were female, a number that increased to 42 percent by 2001 (China Statistical Yearbook 2002). The majority of the more-than-200 units that came to DUT's fair were state owned, with only 6 joint ventures and 30 group companies participating. Despite the low number of signed contracts— in fact, lower than the year before—Director Xie was happy that 23 students signed contracts in smaller towns (*zhongxiao chengzhen*). "They could imagine the potential development there," he boasted, "and were willing to live in such cities for better salaries and housing options." The university's newspaper, however, reported that only about 20 percent of the graduates found "appropriate work," because their hopes were too high, they did not understand how to look for work, and their blindness was so great (*mangmuxing hen da*). The press reinforced the messages young people received from their college employment counselors, encouraging them to have realistic expectations, to be willing to go to more remote places, and to be content working in the state sector. When I spoke with the office's director in 2003, she reiterated the idea that graduates' expectations were too high, the university had to get supply to meet demand, and they needed to help prepare and to guide graduates into appropriate positions through market exchanges. To help do this, they had established a fairly detailed Web site for students (http://career .dlut.edu.cn) to complement the office's regular newspaper publications.

Many of the new graduates were disappointed with the options they had and were direct and forceful about feelings of unmet expectations for training opportunities, career development, and potential social mobility and status. This dissatisfaction, however, is distinct from discontent with the planned system. Under the planned system, everyone expected assignments. In contemporary China, young college graduates looked at themselves and their self-perceived sets of skills and imagined what they and their families might become (see also Duthie 2005; Fong 2004, 2007). The sentiments expressed to me also were different from what Deborah Davis (1990) describes in her work on satisfaction or lack of satisfaction in the state sector of employment once reforms allowed people to change jobs, even though many units would not let their employees leave (see also Zhou, Tuma, and Moen 1997; Walder 1995a). The population Davis describes was embedded in the state sector and Party hierarchy through their work, which is different from the young graduates and professionals discussed here.

Finding satisfying and "appropriate" employment was not an easy process for many graduates, and university employment offices tried to help them with suggestions about how to write letters to potential employers and how to act in interviews. They told students, for instance, that handwritten characters in a letter could express the students' ability much more than typed ones. DUT administrators helped students with the content of the letters as well, explaining that it should be different for the different units. Before the campus job fair, students were reminded not to ask about salaries or benefits, "because units were opposed to that." Assuming that students knew little about what they should be asking or doing and little about how to sell themselves in the new marketplace, teachers and administrators stepped in to guide them in their experiences of mutual choice and instruct them on how to dress and act as they thought cultured, socially responsible educated professionals should. In line with Party calls for cleansed campus environments in the mid- and late 1990s, women were cautioned not to wear too much makeup, and young men were instructed not to smoke or to be too informal, which included not wearing flip-flops. A Central Committee document specifically stated schools must "resist the infiltration and effects of negative and decadent thinking, restrain low and vulgar cultural tastes and irrational cultural tendencies, and lead the campus cultures and atmospheres in the direction of healthy and tasteful development" (CPC CC [1994] 1999: 95–96). While campuses worried about the "low and vulgar" cultural influences that might permeate university boundaries, more market-oriented publications stressed the importance of one's professional appearance. A publication available at the Shanghai talent market, for instance, offered advice to job seekers regarding how to prepare for interviews, including a reminder to go to the washroom and check one's physical appearance one last time before the meeting. Bodily practices of personal appearance were enmeshed in the ability to conduct oneself as a proper urban professional, an increasingly desired sensibility. These fairs were an important way university employment offices redirected their efforts away from bureaucratic assignments and toward new types of normative techniques.

At the same time, universities continued to receive directives from central and local authorities on where graduates *should* go. This meant school administrators needed to convince graduates—who made their own decisions—to work in certain industries and in certain locations. In 1996 and 1997, a significant majority of the graduates from DUT entered state-affiliated units without being directly assigned. This percentage, although still high, did decline in 1999, the vice director of DUT's employment office noted, because of "market needs" and graduates' willingness to go to private and community-run companies. However, it remained approximately 50 percent even in 2003.[20] The story told here is not necessarily about how young professionals turned away from the state and the state economy, in other words, but rather about how entry into the labor force through the medium of guidance was a cultural and political experience.

Cultivating Professionalism: Admissions and Curriculum Reforms

The cultivation of professionals for the knowledge economy relied on an expansion of tertiary educational and training opportunities in the city (see Table 1.3). This included reforms in the admissions structure and the curriculum, with the goal of "training students in creative spirit, practical abilities, and entrepreneurship" (L. Zhou 2006: 91).[21] A significant change occurred when universities began to accept self-paying students (zifei) who covered their own expenses, chose their own majors, and found work by themselves upon graduation since universities considered them "outside of the plan."[22] Their entrance scores were lower than those of the traditional category of state-sponsored students (gongfei) but were considered high enough for acceptance. These scores were on the national unified college entrance examination, which Deng supported as the primary criteria for enrollment in 1977 rather than recommendations and class background. The growth of self-paying students in Liaoning over the years reflected a university's need to find alternative sources of funding and Deng's encouragement of such students during his famous 1992 tour of southern China (nanxun).[23]

Another route to college for students whose scores were not high enough for state-sponsorship and whose families were not wealthy enough for self-paying enrollment was through the committed or predetermined program (dingxiang). These students, many of whom came from smaller cities and more remote areas that had trouble competing with larger cities for the now-mobile college graduates, agreed to study certain subjects, often unpopular majors, and return to their hometowns upon graduation in exchange for university admissions and educational expenses. Universities were under strict orders to insist that committed students complete their contracts with the government and return to the remote areas after graduation. Local governments heralded committed students as fulfilling their duty to the nation

by willingly—and voluntarily—agreeing to serve in difficult places after graduation. Nevertheless, many of these students used every method possible to
find other positions and change their residency to urban areas. Schools also
accepted students sent by their units or by the municipal or provincial government for training (*weituo peiyang*). Like the committed students, unit-
sponsored students had their expenses paid by an enterprise to which they
returned after graduating.

The inclusion of self-paying and unit-sent students forced universities to
manage two systems at the same time until 2000, when the last class of students with state sponsorship graduated. One of the systems was the direct,
mandatory plan (*zhilingxing*), which governed students for whom the university was responsible for arranging employment and whom the university
sponsored financially. The other was the guidance plan (*zhidaoxing*), which
governed the self-paying and unit-sponsored students who were not guaranteed positions and were not considered the university's direct responsibility.[24] Self-paying students went directly to the market, unit-sponsored students returned to their former workplaces, and state-sponsored students were
the ones whom the universities felt responsible to shepherd through the
practice of "mutual choice."

Although state-sponsorship was the traditional form of enrollment, even
these students paid partial tuition by the mid-1990s. In 1994, forty schools,
including DUT, started the tuition-paying system for entrants, charging fees but
still paying the bulk of the costs for the students (see M. Zhang 1998: 245–
246). With 1997 admissions, however, the two systems were melded into one
through a policy of "merging tracks" (*binggui*) where distinctions between state-
sponsored students and self-paying students disappeared, forcing students, Luo
Xu argues, "to adopt a different attitude toward study and career, looking—not
waiting—for possibilities and opportunities for their future" (2004: 797). At
that time, all students had to pay a regulated fee (*shoufei*) and go through the
market to find work, making the shift to guidance more complete.[25] DUT had
made the shift to a tuition system earlier than Finance University, however,
since DUT was under the SEC and Finance University was under a ministry.

The passing of state sponsorship in favor of a more money-oriented
admissions policy was not without its critics, however. "Tuition-free education for college students will soon become only a fond memory of the past,"
Cui Ning (*China Daily* 1997) lamented, "as the remaining 368 free colleges
and universities in China begin charging students fees this year. Among the
1,032 colleges and universities in the country, 664 stopped providing free
education last year and implemented the tuition payment system." Moreover,

with the combination of tuition fees and the end of guaranteed job assignments, rural families have questioned the social mobility value of higher education (Rosen 1997: 252).

Schools were aware that the majority of students who could afford the self-paying status were urban residents, not rural. To keep higher education affordable, fees were not to exceed 25 percent of actual education costs. At DUT and Finance University, this meant yearly fees for 1997–1998 ranged from 2,000 to 2,700 RMB, depending on one's major, and in 2003, a university official said the fees went as high as 5,000 RMB. The more popular majors were more expensive (see also Rosen 1997, 2004). Schools also tried to remedy financial burdens with work-study programs and no-interest loans that became scholarships if the student did well or if he or she were willing to go to a remote area after graduation. Rather than sending students to the countryside to "learn from the peasants," as happened during the Cultural Revolution, universities offered monetary incentives by forgiving loans if one took this route and volunteered to go to a remote area to use one's skills.[26] The state still expected schools to produce patriotic professionals, but how that was accomplished differed from Maoist methods in important ways. Reforms in the assignment system, admissions and fee changes, and the concomitant celebration of talent in the global city must be understood in relation to the post-Mao turn away from red-ness and toward expertise, Deng's pronouncement that education should be linked with modernization and development, and an emphasis on "education for quality."

Experiments in curriculum changes aimed to make college training more "relevant" to the economy, more suitable for a government wanting to ease its own labor and welfare burden, and more market oriented and innovation based for transnational labor markets.[27] In critiquing the "mode of student training" for the planned enrollment and job allocation, the minister of education argued that "students thus trained had a narrow specialty and knowledge range, and poor adaptability to social change. Limited training goals also hampered their individual and diversified development" (L. Zhou 2006: 88). Reforms aimed for more flexibility and relevance for student majors, creating "an environment where students have greater choice and autonomy for self-development" (L. Zhou 2006: 88).

Finance University administrators, for example, determined that their majors were too narrowly defined, a remnant of the Soviet-influenced system, and should be reformed to help students in the job market. Students specialized in one of thirty-eight different fields, such as international finance, international investment, taxes, and international enterprise management.

Attempts were made to predict where the economic trends were leading the country and thus what kind of graduates the school needed to produce. As mediators between the market, or what they perceived to be market demand, and the graduates, universities shifted from implementing state plans to anticipating market demand. A woman at the student affairs office explained that their graduates had had a particularly difficult time finding jobs in the mid-1990s, and the university needed to address this problem:

> By the time a student graduates after four years in school, the market demand for that major has already passed. This happened in the banking field first. It was very popular, and so many students wanted to study these majors, but the positions in the banks filled up, leaving many finance majors with nowhere to go upon graduation. . . . So, instead of placing students in a major for four years, they will spend two years with basic courses, and then for two years they will study "marketable" majors. Insurance is a good example. Unlike international trade, which has slowed down and has too many graduates, there will be a lot of growth in the insurance industry in the future, and jobs will be easy to find. The best students will be allowed to choose their specialty first, allowing them to determine marketability and suitability for them as individuals.

DUT pushed their curriculum reforms a bit further to create what they called more "comprehensive" graduates with majors that matched "the needs of society." Some of the fields were offered for only two or three years, while others had a history of eight to ten years. As foreign trade increased dramatically in 1985, DUT responded with a new major in 1987; it combined studies in the sciences, trade, and a foreign language, which made the graduates very marketable and more comprehensive in their talent, a change from the limited range of courses previously taken by any one individual in China. The major was sponsored by the provincial governor, and all graduates were supposed to stay in Liaoning for several years of work after graduation. The chemical engineering–English major students I interviewed were in this program. A number of them stayed to avoid the penalty, but others chose to pay a steep fee or found ways to negotiate a reduction to leave the province to find work elsewhere.

Other new majors that appeared at this technical university were foreign trade, public relations/modern secretarial studies, and international industry and commerce relations. Responding to market-place popularity, in the 1990s, DUT decreased the number of students in applied physics, applied mathematics, and environmental projects, while increasing the number in industrial electrical automation, computers, construction, production-process automation, and machine design. Statistics from the graduating class in 2003 indicated that the top three industries for DUT graduates were the IT industry (26.7 percent), construction (23.9 percent), and manufacturing (19.3 percent). Institutions that used to train civil servants and factory technicians for state-planned allocation not only found ways to get graduates jobs without assigning them but also altered the training itself. Interdisciplinarity, comprehensive knowledge, innovation, and flexibility were new norms framing reforms in higher education.

Insecurities and Uncertainties of Post-Mao Professionalism

Although the new system offered more options and autonomy, it also meant the government had pulled back on its guarantee of work after graduation. Unemployment, simply put, was now a possibility and by 2001 had become "severe" for college graduates when the expanded enrollments from 1998 began finishing their studies (Hu and Sheng 2007: 38).[28] In 2009 and facing a global recession, graduates confronted an even tighter market as college enrollments increased further during the 2000s. Estimates projected that approximately seven million new graduates would be looking for work in 2009. Graduates have been encouraged to work "at grassroots levels" and in places "with tough conditions," to start their own companies, and to "be flexible" (China's Employment Situation and Policies 2004; see also Table 1.2).

These insecurities are not new. The early days of assignment reforms were quite controversial on campuses, setting the stage for tensions and negotiations between officials and educated citizens in the reform era. During the Cultural Revolution, parents worried their children would be sent to rural areas, but in the reform era they worried about their children's security in a new way. Would they be able to find work in a stable enterprise as they made their own decisions about what was most suitable for them as individuals? Moreover, many young people did not "know" how to look for work or how to develop their careers, prompting an East China Normal University (Shanghai) lecturer and his colleague to publish "the first book on careers guidance in Mainland China since 1949" (Zhang and Qu 1988;

Wei-Yuan Zhang 1998: 2). The ambivalence young people felt about the world in which they lived demonstrated how the shift from assignee to employee signaled a general shift in the governmentality of urban China.

Social debates on the "mismatch" between expectations and employment options were common. Graduates often were critiqued for having desires and hopes that were "too high" in relation to their abilities with the expression "*yan gao shou di*"—literally, "the eyes were high and the hands were low." Popular commentary in journals and newspapers about why people changed jobs often divided the reasons into good categories (e.g., further study and development) and bad categories (e.g., desire for higher salaries and perpetual dissatisfaction).[29] "We must tell students not to have high hopes" an employment officer at DUT said, "and that most jobs are still in the state sector." Although "choice" is often glorified in the press, the marketization of labor allocation and the pulling back of state guarantees has ruptured socialist ethics of labor security and basic health coverage, producing anxiety and insecurities for many, while also leading to new kinds of calculative, "economic" decisions (see Chapter 6).

One DUT graduate's family was suspicious and worried about the unstable life she might face by finding a position in the employment market. Sun Feiling explained that her parents worried she could not take care of such an important matter on her own and that the company would not honor the contract, leaving her without a job. She found a position with a company that could help her settle her household registration in Dalian, provided housing, and offered her opportunities to advance her spoken English. Nevertheless, her parents felt uncomfortable:

> My parents aren't really willing to let me go out, they want me by their side, but they support me because it is for my career, which is important. Still, they worry about this job. They worry that if I don't have connections to help me, then I may have some trouble. They really can't believe that I can find a job on my own. A few days ago, my mom called and said she is worried about the job because she still doesn't think the contract I signed is valid enough to get the job.

Her family, focused on high-socialist security rather than post-Mao rationalities of enterprise, worried about her ability to establish a stable life. Sun, in contrast, felt comfortable in this setting of individual decisions, calculations about what would bring her future gains, self-reliance, and potential difficulties. Later in our discussion, she explained she wanted to find a position where she could develop herself: "I don't know what the future will be for me. I have a lot to learn. . . . I have no blueprint for my future. I want to test myself. I am not sure of my ability. I want to test myself in society, and later I will decide." She conceived of her individual life as an enterprise (as discussed in more detail in Chapter 4), a continuous project of developing her human capital; an extension of, as Colin Gordon states, "the idea of one's life as the enterprise of oneself" (1991: 44). These practices of self-development referenced market-based notions of entrepreneurialism as well as "the language of classical 'self-cultivation' (*xiuyang*) in which one strives for excellence and perfection," albeit also including "values like risk-taking (*maoxian*), innovation (*chuangxin*), competition, and independence" (Bakken 2000: 61).[30]

As these young adults were weaned from the (nostalgic) security of a socialist urban welfare system and promoted as young self-sufficient yet patriotic professionals, they renegotiated what risks they were willing to assume and what was too much for them to bear. This reassessment became more acute after college enrollments expanded in 1998, meaning that a college degree was more common and thus the assessment of one's ability became even more important. Feelings of ambivalence ran through the lives of the graduates as they fashioned themselves for a highly competitive labor market and tried to fit their expectations into the reality of supply and demand in a socialist market economy. As the most highly educated human capital in a rapidly changing social and economic landscape, college graduates expected quick social mobility. Universities, tasked with making the students' relationships with the state less ambiguous and ambivalent, tried to direct the energies of their graduates toward national goals. Administrators blamed students for their feelings of dissatisfaction, claiming it meant their expectations were too high rather than the offerings too paltry. Prevalent in the 1980s when reforms began, such accusations of excessive expectations were heard again in the 1990s (Pepper 1995: 18.31). By the early 2000s, the Ministry of Labor and Social Security "adopted seven measures, involving job training, job counseling, information service, and unemployment services" to reduce graduates' unemployment and to avoid the "waste of human capital" (Hu and Sheng 2007: 48). In the face of even greater competition for existing jobs, graduates more recently have been encouraged to be self-employed and to start their own businesses. The insecurities they experienced were an important aspect of young professionals' subjectivity as they negotiated themselves into the practice of mutual choice.

Guidance and Choice as New Techniques
of Subject Formation

The zone of engagement between the state, the market, and young people that has emerged with reforms in the job assignment system is a critical arena for the emergence of professional subjectivity. Guidance and mutual choice framed job seekers' experiences as they negotiated their way through state interests, employers' hiring practices, gendered family ideologies, and their own dreams for the future. In doing so, they made decisions about what it meant to be educated workers and how they would relate to their labor power. Changes in the job assignment system altered the way in which the socialist state was involved in this subject formation process, but they did not eliminate the state's or the nation's presence. As students made independent decisions, they did so in consideration of complex rules about *hukou* transfers as well as feelings about how they could help China prosper—as talented human capital.

In this chapter, I have argued specifically that guidance and mutual choice may be analyzed as techniques of governing. These new ways of distributing human resources thus are forms of power that have helped shape an enterprising, and often patriotic, professional subjectivity. Thus, I suggest we analyze guidance and mutual choice in the universities not as an inevitable freeing of educated labor but rather as mechanisms of governing in late-socialist urban China. These new ways of governing incorporated techniques and ethics from the Maoist era, such as the household registration and national modernization goals, as they also contended with the expansion of nonstate sectors of the economy and intensified local manifestations of globalization. The 1998 Higher Education Law explicitly notes this integration of socialist understandings of labor and duty with the fostering of talent. Higher education, the text says, must "train senior specialized talents with innovative spirit and practical capability," but it also must "promote" and "serve" "socialist modernization" (Articles 4 and 5, chap. 1). It is the incorporation of these neoliberal technologies of governing with socialist politics that is the specific focus of Chapter 4 and that I argue produces the social form of patriotic professionalism.

4

Patriotic Professionalism

On a cold December morning in 2003, a colleague and I went to the building at Liberation Square that houses the offices of Dalian's talent exchange center. When we arrived, guards at the main entrance checked our credentials before allowing us to enter without buying a ticket. We wound our way around people in the lobby who were talking with others, reading newspaper job listings and company promotions, and watching opportunities scroll down on a large electronic wall screen. On the left was a small bookstore with materials about how to find an appropriate job, how to develop one's management skills, and how to study for an MBA. Although a familiar scene, this marble-floored building was a far cry from the city's first talent market tucked away in a park, which I had visited ten years earlier (see Chapter 3). As we walked up the stairs to meet with the director, we passed a large billboard that read, "Distribute human resources perfectly; build the talented highland of the North."[1]

Dalian, like cities around the world, touted knowledge workers as important sources of development and as assets when soliciting new investors, development projects, and residents. Company directors, human resource officers, and municipal planners all told me that they needed "talented workers" for their various projects to succeed. In fact, the talent exchange center's director told me that day in 2003 that officials worried because Dalian had trouble keeping the now independently mobile talent. The city, however, would not restrict the flow of talent as was done with stringent household registration (*hukou*) policies under high socialism, nor would it assign workers to specific workplaces to keep them in Dalian. In previous chapters, I explain how such direct governmental regulation and ordering of the population were identified as "problems" in the reform era, ushering in new ideas about how to distribute people across the country (i.e., through the market mechanism), new definitions of the desirable citizen, and new ways of cultivating the talented and quality employee.

In Chapter 3, I argue that choice, one of these new ways of doing things, should be analyzed as a technique of governing rather than as evidence of the end of governance. Many descriptions of the end of direct state job assignments emphasize the idea that individuals are able to let their true selves blossom with new choices. Studies of consumer choices by new middle classes across Asia, for instance, have highlighted the self-making aspects of personhood with those choices (e.g., choices about fashion, relationships, home decoration, and conspicuous purchases).[2] In addition, much literature on attracting creative, innovative, knowledge workers to a city represent these workers as freely choosing individuals.[3] Spending time with college students and young professionals in Dalian, however, made me realize that the very act of choosing was not a natural pre-existing state of the self but rather a cultivated form of personhood.[4]

Through ethnographic evidence, in this chapter I consider the kind of subject that is specified by choice. I argue that in learning how to make choices, college graduates adopted a self-enterprising ethos as "a way of being and of behavior" (Foucault 1997b: 286) that focused in particular on the idea of self-development (*ziwo fazhan*) through their careers. In becoming a choosing subject, independently made choices referenced the self in ways that resonated with and were distinct from the Maoist-era and Confucian practices of self-cultivation (see Chapter 5). In the first half of the chapter, I examine young professionals' narratives about employment, self-development, and career planning, a noteworthy contrast to their parents' cohort experience of labor power as part of the state-owned means of production. In the second part, I argue not only that the production of choosing subjects was about self-enterprise in the new century but that this ethic of individual choice intersected with practices and modes of governing in universities and municipalities.[5] For instance, graduates faced fees and fines if they broke contracts or went to cities where they did not have household registrations, and they were regularly exposed to directives from the government and university officials about responsible decisions. University career counselors, for instance, worked to guide (versus assign) graduates into appropriate positions that would help fulfill society's and the country's needs. In the young professionals' narratives, we learn how autonomously made decisions reflected a sense of responsibility not just to self-advancement but also to the nation.

The professional subjects that emerged through, and in tension with, these technologies were at once autonomous from state-planning organs and intimately connected with the nation through expressions of affinity for China's modernization and progress and through an understanding that their labor power could be used to support the country. In this chapter, I examine how individual career planning and self-focused development have linked with collective projects of making China strong and with norms of social and national obligation, exhibiting what I call "patriotic professionalism." Patriotic professionalism is not a subject position filled with great conflict for these young people; it is an often overtly unacknowledged social form in which they find individual freedom from state planning and a continued state presence in the experience of autonomous employment choice.

Another way to think about the combination of autonomous choices, self-managed career advancement, and state rationalities about the value of human capital development for the nation is to think about how China is adopting neoliberal techniques of governing. As I explain in Chapter 1, by taking a governmentality approach, I define neoliberal techniques as including use of the market mechanism to distribute labor and autonomous decision making by individuals who calculate costs and benefits. In general, neoliberal reforms are based on the idea that state intervention into the economy and into society is a significant problem of socialist planning. The problems of state planning must then be addressed so that more "efficient" forms of governing may be implemented. Markets and the practices of choice required in them are suggested in neoliberal reforms as good techniques to distribute educated personnel to where they will be used effectively.

In addition to a reliance on the market mechanism, neoliberalism is commonly associated with promotion of self-management and self-government rather than state management. Unlike direct state assignments, job fairs require self-activated choice by job seekers and those hiring new employees. Adopting an entrepreneurial attitude and a self-enterprising ethos has been encouraged by teachers, family members, bosses, and coworkers in China.

The new generation of knowledge workers and aspiring professionals emerging in this process finds career planning and strategic pursuit of workplace-based training to be normal and commonsense activities.

Yet while China has implemented "neoliberal" techniques of governing and governmental rationalities, they are not the only mechanisms in play. Some, such as talent markets, are neoliberal in form, but others are at times authoritarian, Maoist, and even reminiscent of late-imperial calls for state strengthening or redeployments of Confucian practices of self-cultivation (Chapter 5; see also Suisheng Zhao 1997).[6] The particular focus here is on the wedding of markets and choice (neoliberalism) with an ethos and politics of national duty through labor (socialism). The concept of patriotic professionalism thus challenges traditional social-science assumptions about the kinds of social forms that emerge with neoliberalism, for it exhibits elements from multiple forms of governing. Specifically, it challenges the assumption in standard social-science definitions of neoliberalism that identification of neoliberal ways of doing things also implies adoption of a political ideology that eschews social values of problem solving and solidarities and embraces private values and individuality (e.g., Brenner and Theodore 2002; Brin-Hyatt 1997; Peck and Tickell 2007). It is precisely these predetermined assumptions that I aim to unpack in this book, for embedded in patriotic professionalism is an unexpected combination of neoliberalism and socialism.

Enterprising Professionals: Choosing Self-Development

To understand this wedding of neoliberalism with Maoist socialism, we must first consider the enterprising nature of the professionals and the calculative choices they make. In the following examples, college graduates explain how they became choosing individuals. They made career plans, listed priorities for the jobs they wanted, and experienced face-to-face interviews with potential employers. Undergoing interviews, engaging in "mutual choice" with employers, setting career goals, and making step-by-step future plans are all new modes of understanding the self. These practices work through "an exercise of the self on the self by which one attempts to develop and transform oneself, and to attain to a certain mode of being" (Foucault 1997b: 282). These practices shape norms of professionalism that are firmly rooted in governmental rationalities of self-governance and self-enterprise and a "pragmatic" ethos about "how one lives" (see Xu 2004; Rosen 2004). Their narratives also help us understand how they have become individuals who choose.

As I explain in Chapter 3, by the late 1990s, going to job fairs and writing resumes were commonplace and anticipated activities by the new graduates. Thus, when I asked them about their job-search processes and hopes, they had ready narratives about their plans and dreams. Liao Meili, a female graduate at Dalian University of Technology (DUT), is a good example. She had found a position with a tourist agency in Beijing, a highly coveted location, and explained to me how she planned to develop her career:

> I have this plan—to go into a stable corporation, get experience, and then go to a joint venture or a foreign company . . . because there the competition is more severe, and I will be able to develop myself more. . . . I want to devote myself to [the new job] and see what I can do for it. Sometimes people complain the [state] units are too old and the habits can't change, but this is a new unit [where she will work]. I think I will stay longer than five years. I want to develop in the same corporation and do it from the grassroots. It is better for personal development. Now I have this plan, but I don't know about the future.

Development of relatively long-term plans for individual growth that included progression through different companies and workplaces was common for many of the young people I interviewed. Zhang Long, a schoolmate of Liao's, also offered a plan for what he wanted out of work. His, however, emerged as a list. First, he wanted to use his major; second, make a good salary; third, find a place where his potential for development would be good; and fourth, find a way to stay in Dalian. "I don't care if the work is stable," Zhang said. "I want to use all of my abilities and have a good salary, well at least a reasonable salary. If that means I have to change jobs a lot, I don't care." Listing priorities for a new job, as Zhang did, and constructing career plans, as Liao did, were new devices—the microphysics of power—that framed a personal sense of self through practices of choice.

In a questionnaire I conducted with International Finance majors at Northeast Economic and Finance University, a majority of respondents used strikingly similar language about finding work where they could "use their studies" and develop themselves while working. One young woman wrote, "This kind of job [in international finance] is very popular right now, and the field has the potential to develop." She also commented that she liked the system of mutual choice, because it gave her room to make her own choices, and at the same time the hiring unit was choosing her, she also could choose them. Job seekers spoke, in other words, as talented employees or human

capital—and not assignees—who wanted personal and professional development in work. Their narratives of finding positions that matched their majors
(duikou) where they could get good experience (duanlian ziji) and where
their abilities could flourish (fahui nengli) were more than just descriptive of
their dreams. Such narratives of the professional exhibited a "style of reasoning" that indicated reform-era rationalities of market competition and
self-managed development were possible.[7]

Employers also referred to recent college graduates as a distinct cohort
with notions of self-development and enterprise incorporated into their
working lives. This was made explicit when I was visiting Li, a man in his
thirties who was the personnel manager at a large Sino-U.S. joint venture
production facility in Dalian. Commenting on such workers, he said, "These
young people are not the same as the white-collar workers in state units, in
terms of their lifestyle, their behavior, and their thinking. They are younger
and better educated. They will develop, and we don't want them to leave our
company." A well-dressed man in his thirties who owned his own company
reinforced this idea in another interview when he said, "Young people today
are not the same as before. Before, no one asked questions about the company's situation. Now, however, they are interested in their individual benefits
and their development opportunities. Some do just ask about money, but
others want to know if they can develop here." Interactions with employers,
especially in the interview, were particularly salient moments when norms of
individuality and enterprise for the professional subject emerged.

The job fairs in general afforded the company representatives and the applicants opportunities for deliberate self-presentation. Tang Liping, who found
a position in a Sino-U.S. joint venture, described her interview experience:

> I heard they needed an assistant [to the manager] from a friend, so I
> sent my materials to the manager. Then I went for an interview. They
> introduced the company, and I introduced myself, my major, and my
> hobbies. . . . They asked me what I thought about salary and working
> conditions, and I told them that the salary is not most important and
> that working conditions and development of the company are most
> important. Also, it is very important if I can use my knowledge and
> improve myself. . . . I think the company will develop and grow. . . .
> [In five years' time], if I am still at this company, I will not be the
> assistant to the manager. I want to be the manager or a business pro-
> fessional, or maybe have my own trading company and be an inde-
> pendent company.

Tang also claimed that she wanted only one-year contracts with the company in case she decided to leave. She had confidence that her contract would be renewed if she worked well: "If the work is suitable for me and the personal relations are good, then I will stay. If it is not suitable and I am not happy, then I will go."

One DUT graduating senior, Chen Xiuping, had gone to the talent market in Beijing three times before finally finding a position in his home town of Shenyang with a Canadian-Chinese communications firm. He first met the company at the Spring Festival job fair, where he gave his resume to the personnel manager and vice general manager. As a state-supported student in a special provincial program, he was required to work for the provincial government after graduation unless the company was willing to cover the costs of his education. This firm was so interested in him that they said they would be willing to pay his education fee to the university. "This was the first one willing to pay for me," Chen said. He explained what happened at the fair:

> There was an interview for about twenty or thirty minutes. They asked me to introduce myself, and then they talked about the development and future of the company. All of this was in English. . . . I asked about the background of the company, as I hadn't heard about it before. I learned it is a global company. When looking for a job, you must note how devoted they are to doing business in China. I paid attention to the company's development in China, whether they made up their mind to invest in China, because sometimes they make fake investments. I also asked about the industry and the treatment in the company, like salary. If you work several years, they will provide a no-interest loan to buy a house. Medical care, I don't know if they provide it, but I can buy that myself. I don't care if the company gives this. From their attitude, I think I would be an important man in the company. They know they want me to work there, and they are willing to take special care of me. It is a good company. . . . Just three days ago, I decided to take the job.

The focus for these young graduates was squarely on their individual career plans and the autonomy they had from state plans. As subjects, specified by post-Mao techniques of interviews, mutual choice, and resume writing, they faced and constantly talked about opportunities (jihui), choices (xuanze), and insecurities neither available nor experienced in the planned system. Their desires also resonated with workplaces that tried to distinguish themselves from the inefficiencies of the planned system that hoarded labor or disregarded skills.

A critical aspect of this process was the shift from the understanding of labor power as a national resource to a source of individual and self-development. Under the previous planned system of high socialism, labor power and skills were not "owned" by the individual (Bian 1994: 51). Rather, they were part of the means of production owned by the state (Bian 1994: 96), and returns on one's labor power "were realized only in the state's production, but not on the individuals" (K. Cheng 1998: 23). Instead of referencing students' personal interests or abilities, something that would have been considered selfish and bourgeois, job assignments aimed to equalize development across the country (deemphasizing coastal areas) and to eliminate exploitative labor markets and unemployment. The acquisition of skills in the Maoist era was "for the improved performance of the organization or the fulfillment of political objectives of the central or local party leaders" and not for individual fulfillment or personal career specialization and advancement (Davis 1990: 89; 2000a). Labor power was not an individual resource to be sold in the marketplace or even to be developed for personal growth, nor was it about the "efficient use" of labor (Davis 1990). Job assignments were expressions of national duty and socialist nation building; work was not to have been about self-focused development. The political riskiness of individual career planning and skill development are exemplified in Liu Shaoqi's statement: "It is the worthiest and most just thing in the world to sacrifice oneself for the Party, for the proletariat, for the emancipation of the nation and of all mankind, for social progress and for the highest interests of the overwhelming majority of the people" (cited in Bray 2005: 60).

By the mid-1990s, however, there was a decided shift away from this understanding of labor power and toward the idea that it should be developed for and by the individual, what Amy Hanser (2002a) refers to as "job specificity."[8] Cai Li, a young woman from Wuhan who hoped to work in Shanghai, talked about the differences between the laboring cohorts, exemplifying this new individual focus and concern for self-improvement. Her parents had had the opportunity to return to Shanghai, their original hometown, in the early 1990s. But, she explained:

> They said no, because the job would have been harder than what they had. . . . They don't want to change. . . . If I were them, I certainly would move to Shanghai. If life is okay, then it is okay, but there is no chance for more improvement. They are used to this, and their

children are grown up, but to my brother and me, there still are a lot of opportunities available that we can try. I am not afraid of failure. I may have failure in Shanghai, but I am ready to face my possible failures. I don't know what I will confront. This is the main difference between the generations.

She went on to say that if the institute where she would be working as a translator gave her a good chance to improve herself, and her abilities and knowledge were used effectively, then it was likely she would stay there for many years. If not, she would go. Unlike her parents, who came of age in the era of traditional socialism, this young woman believed in the idea of career mobility as a source of self and social growth.

The notion of developing and training the self through work was not alien to China's socialist path, but the kind of self-development, career advancement, and family prosperity sought by the young and aspiring professionals I met was distinctly different from that of the Maoist era. Employment for talent (*rencai*) was a site of potential growth—for themselves, their families' lifestyles, their employers, and the nation. Cai, for instance, embraced the idea of individual choice, even if it meant that she had to face the possibility of failure that she could blame on no one but herself. "I don't know what I will confront," and "I am ready to face my possible failures," she said. That she did not fear the shift of accountability from the state to the individual exemplifies how neoliberal rationalities of self-responsibility are embedded in reforms in the job assignment system as well as everyday forms of self-governance. Similar to—although not the same as—prevailing rationalities in U.S. and British neoliberal regimes that encouraged people to "enterprise themselves," these reforms governed in a more distanced way, requiring the formation of subjects who were both autonomous and responsible. As an expert, this subject sought work that would build on existing knowledge and skills and would position the individual for future career success. It was through the very practices of making choices and feeling free in those decisions that the post-Mao professional subject emerged—an active and responsible subject deemed necessary for China's late-socialist development.

Nevertheless, these autonomous choices must be understood within the context of late-socialism, for market choice was experienced in relation to national progress and often was presented to the young professionals as being within a particular scope. A critical tension, in other words, has developed around the role of the state and the experience of autonomy, albeit one that does not produce pronounced internal confusion for the young people I met, a process similar to what Yunxiang Yan has termed "managed globalization" (2002). State directives are at once about autonomous decisions and about guidance by influential figures (e.g., teachers) to make appropriate decisions that will satisfy society's needs. Fostering individual, enterprising professionalism was a national project, framed within collective, socialist politics as well as specific regulations that shaped the scope of market practices and experiences of choice.

Guiding Choices: Conditioning Autonomy

New graduates were guided into appropriate positions and their autonomy was conditioned in a number of ways. Appropriate jobs included ones that aligned with the individual's personality, a position in the city where the graduate had a legal right to live, and employment that would help support China's development and thus the country's stature in the global community. Thus, even as the market gained status as a solution for problems generated by central planning, in China many recognized that it also harbored the evils of exploitation and oppression. To help the market gain maturity as a socialist market economy, active political intervention interacted with the new professionals' autonomy from state plans. This meant that as graduates learned they could not depend on state institutions or state plans for work, they also learned that state functionaries (along with other actors) and policies conditioned and guided the choices they made. This conditioning is apparent in interventions into the unbalanced marketplace and the use of fines, scholarship points, and publications to encourage socially responsible—but autonomously made—decisions.

As I explain in Chapter 3, in the early to mid-1990s, Dalian's Personnel Bureau was explicit about ending the job allocation system and promoting the market for distributing personnel. Yet documents also indicated a need for macro-adjustment (*hongguan diaokong*) policies and a restatement of a "basic guarantee" for all. The bureau worried about the "unbalanced development" of the market and lack of fair competition, justifying macro-government participation (see also X. Wang 2003). For instance, statistics showed that female graduates, ordinary students (*bufen yiban qunzhong de zinu*; i.e., children from families with no "good" connections), and students of certain majors were not able to find work easily. If the government threw them into the market carelessly (*bu wen bu wen*), the bureau argued, "it would not be good and would damage the reputation of the Party, advantages of socialism, and the safety of society" (DRJ n.d.: 4). Macro-adjustment aimed to alleviate fears of instability, which also regularly referenced the "chaos" (*luan*) of the Cultural Revolution; thus, as reforms were implemented, practices that could limit a "loss of equilibrium" were emphasized (Bakken 2000: 41).

Interventions also aimed to remedy the negative effects of what the bureau identified as immature aspects of the market in China. When the two-track system of admissions was still in effect, local personnel bureaus would provide assignments to students in the plan who had not found work by the end of the year in which they graduated. The universities would send their household registrations and dossiers to their hometown personnel bureaus, which would then identify positions for them. Students, however, often rejected such assignments, because they assumed they were dead-end positions. In the late 1990s, Dalian responded to these worries with a guarantee that posts would match students' majors and would not be in unprofitable units (*kuisun*).[9] The phrase "within a definite scope," which referred to the scope of mutual choice on campuses, also draws our attention to the way the state tried to manage and to order the distribution of talent throughout the country without assigning people. As a school drawing on a national population, DUT, for instance, was required to send its graduates across the nation in a reasonable (*heli*) manner, echoing past enforced state plans of geographic distribution. The notion of justified intervention—a policy that combines neoliberal and socialist governmental forms—was embraced in the early 2000s when top leaders explicitly promoted job creation and "employment expansion" as "fundamental to the livelihood of the people" (Hu and Sheng 2007: 46). The idea that it was justified—and reasonable—for the state to be an active manager of the market and society is also seen in President Hu Jintao's call for a "harmonious society" (*hexie shehui*). Concern with harmonious relations, potential social unrest, and growing inequalities is a notable change from previous years' more narrow focus on "economic growth" (see also Lee and Warner 2007).

DUT also used strict rules about household registration transfers to Beijing and Dalian to ensure that graduates did not congregate in these two cities. Too many graduates going to these major urban centers meant DUT's distribution of its students was irrational (*bu heli*). Fees associated with a lack of scholarship points made residency transfers to these two cities expensive, creating an incentive for graduates to return home.[10] To avoid additional fees for the transfer to Dalian or Beijing, DUT graduates each had to have a minimum of six academic scholarship points. Each semester, students could earn these points based on their class rankings, where first place equaled five points, second three points, and third two points. Points were awarded in each major according to academic accomplishments (80 percent) and behavior (20 percent; based on teachers' recommendations). Previously, restrictions on transfers covered fourteen major urban centers, but the school reduced them to Beijing and Dalian in 1996. If the students lacked points, they had to pay 1,000 RMB for each missing point, going no higher than 6,000 RMB for the six points required, which was prohibitively expensive for many students. The vice director of DUT's employment office explained in 1996 that the State Education Commission monitored where each university's state-sponsored graduates went.[11] In 2003, the director of the office noted that although the point system was no longer in use on campus, the largest and "most desirable" cities (e.g., Shanghai and Beijing) continued to restrict *hukou* transfers based on educational attainment. The report on DUT graduates' employment for 2003 also noted that 51.5 percent of the seniors wanted to go to Beijing, Shanghai, Guangzhou, or Shenzhen, but only 18.8 percent actually found positions in those cities; 41 percent remained in the three northeastern provinces; and even though only 3.8 percent hoped to go to smaller towns upon graduation, 23.7 percent in fact were headed to such locations (DUT 2003; DUT 2004).

In the late 1990s, graduates of agriculture, teaching, and medical schools faced many more restrictions in the job search than did graduates of DUT or Northeast Economic and Finance University (see also Kurlander 1998). Open mutual choice did not exist at such schools, because the government wanted to be sure these graduates would be reasonably distributed around the country. Since 1993, graduates of Liaoning Teacher's University in Dalian had been allowed to seek units on their own, but they were required to work for the government (i.e., not a company). The school considered some majors, such as history, so difficult to place, however, that they permitted them to look for jobs outside teaching. The only way to get around an assignment that a state-sponsored graduate did not want to take was to pay the school a "training fee," as illustrated by Chen's case above. I met a vibrant young woman who found a job as an executive secretary in a joint venture and paid 10,000 RMB to avoid going to her assigned teaching position. Claiming her family never could have afforded the fee, she saved it herself while working part-time in college.

Zhang Long, another young man who graduated from DUT's chemical engineering–foreign language combined program in the late 1990s, explained how he negotiated paying back his fee after moving to Shenzhen, where an aunt helped him find a job in a state-owned company. Zhang was part of a special undergraduate major that required him to stay in Liaoning Province to work. If he did not stay, he was required to pay 5,000 RMB to the university. Through campus gossip, Zhang knew that six students from his class were leaving the province, and not all were paying the fee. "One student paid no money because he went to a trade office in Beijing, and he has a good background. His father is some VIP in the provincial government. This makes me feel unbalanced; it is unfair," Zhang said. "A couple other students who went to Beijing only had to pay 3,000, so I wanted to see what I could negotiate." When he asked the director about how the other students were paying only 3,000 RMB, "they explained that those students were going to a famous state-run unit which sent sponsored students [wei-tuo peiyang] to DUT every year. . . . I commented on my company and said it was famous, too, but the teacher said our university seldom sends students to the south. They weren't interested in setting up a relationship with them" (i.e., they did not need to worry about guanxi [connections, relations] with his company). Through connections, Zhang was finally able to get his fee reduced to 3,000 RMB, although he would not receive a receipt and would have to tell others he paid the full 5,000 RMB. "I don't think they will pay it," Zhang said of his current employer. "Perhaps if I had a receipt and wanted to bargain with them to keep me, I could get them to reimburse me."

Universities implemented a variety of other measures to make sure graduates found appropriate positions for themselves as individuals, local development, and national needs. They included collecting information from employers and creating database systems of companies/units and available positions, publishing job-search newspapers and guides, recommending students for appropriate positions, and engaging in curriculum reforms (Chapter 3). DUT also sent their officials directly to workplaces to ask what kinds of personnel they wanted, a further important distinction from the bureaucratic distribution of labor. By the early 2000s, they regularly invited previous graduates to tell students of their experiences and government leaders to explain what people in the city thought of college graduates. In terms of texts, DUT published a small paperback entitled *Helping with Your Career* (*Bangzhu ni jiuye*) that included suggestions regarding how to make a job decision and explanations of the multiple and often confusing restrictions.[12] In the chapter on successful career choices, readers were reminded that human resources were valuable, they should not make "blind" choices, they should think about their personality (extroverted or introverted) and how it would fit with a particular kind of workplace and position, and they should consider what was required for different career paths. Readers were also reminded that their own development should take "society's needs" into consideration and that career development was not only about the individual (Tang and Wang 1992: 62–101). Elsewhere in the book, the authors explained the differences between enrollment types as well as how one could break a committed contract (e.g., by going to graduate school).

Another recent publication written to help graduates choose a profession listed several characteristics of a career, including its being a way for each individual to serve society as well as his or her position. Other items identified a profession as a way to develop each individual's ability, a stage for realizing life's worth, and a significant part of any person's life (Zhongren Liu 1999: 4–6; see also Wei-Yuan Zhang 1998; Xin Zhang 1997). DUT, like other campuses, also published its own monthly employment newspaper with articles about specific restrictions, letters from people who already graduated and had advice to offer their schoolmates (e.g., to go to the small towns), and updates on campus visits by companies.

Universities found themselves in difficult positions, as they had to produce a supply of educated professionals desired by the market and the kind of patriotic economic subjects desired by the state. Student expectations also remained high as they listened to rhetoric about how the nation needed talent (*rencai*) to modernize, and their frustrations increased as they watched others with less education establish careers and accumulate wealth and prestige. Teachers and administrators had to prod students to take what was available, because they wanted to avoid high unemployment rates and because it could be construed as patriotic to do so, although an administrator at DUT I met in early 2003 sighed and said, "We need more opportunities for the graduates." She also explained that development for the city and for the individual could happen only if society's needs, workplace needs, and graduates' desires intersected properly. Guidance, in other words, was not only about following residency and admissions rules; it also encompassed an ethical element that defined how people participated in the market.

University personnel, especially those in the newly named graduate employment offices (*biyesheng jiuye bangongshi*), understood that they had active roles to play in this process of choice. No longer implementing mandatory plans, school administrators were encouraged to guide students to learn about themselves as individuals while also being "aware of their social responsibilities" and "not promoting selfishness or egoism" (Wen 1996: 276, 217). Moreover, "innovation" was not to be for "showing off." Rather, students needed to understand that this kind of work had to be integrated with "a sense of responsibility to the state and the Chinese nation" (*People's Daily* 1999; see also CPC CC [1994] 1999). Director Xie Baihua at DUT (see

Chapter 3) echoed these sentiments when he said in an interview that in addition to thinking "about their personality, their uniqueness, what kind of work is appropriate for them . . . and the conditions of the company . . . [students] must also think about what the country needs and what the situation is like in that local place. They cannot only think of their own ideals." Reinforcing these ideas, in a recent statement, President Hu said that the young should learn to "love the motherland" as a key virtue of "socialist honor" (with harming the motherland being a signal of "socialist disgrace"; Olesen 2006). Thus, similar to the Maoist era, messages of national loyalty continued to be central to shaping the workforce.

Yet moral education that promoted feelings of nationalism should not be equated with propaganda, a pejorative term in the English language that likens state ideology to brainwashing. Instead, the kind of patriotism expressed by educated urbanites helped establish standards of respectability for professionals in society at large. As norms, they were important techniques of self-formation. Considering these methods and how students reacted to them helps clarify the ways in which young people came to understand what it meant to be urban professionals. It also helps us appreciate how making choices is not a natural human state but rather a cultivated form of personhood.

These practices also highlight how the late-socialist governmentality I describe in this book incorporated multiple technologies of governing into the subject-formation process. Through restrictions placed on students and employers, the state worked to set standards of behavior they expected from responsible citizens while at the same time retreating from the allocation process and relying on a more distanced form of governing. Students were expected to return to their hometowns, go to key state units "in need," abide by school deadlines for the job search, and take jobs that matched their majors. Even into the late 1990s, school officials could reject any positions students found if they did not meet these terms, making these more distanced techniques of power effective forms of discipline.[13]

To argue that the state remains an active participant in late-socialist neoliberalism is not a contradictory statement. Although in early classical liberalism, people wrote about the naturally existing spheres of economy and society and argued that the state needed to stay out of these spheres for them to function properly, in neoliberalism, or advanced liberalism, the market is not so much a natural sphere as it is an "institutional" arena that needs to be maintained by government policies (Burchell 1996: 21–24; Lemke 2001: 195). Members of the Ordo-liberal position in post–World War I Germany that formed around the *Ordo* journal and economists in the Chicago School in the United States acknowledged the role of the state in generating liberty and free competition. As Thomas Lemke explains, "Unlike [the] negative conception of the state typical of liberal theory in the eighteenth and nineteenth centuries, in the *Ordo*-liberal view, the market mechanism and the impact of competition can arise *only if they are produced by the practice of government*" (2001: 193; emphasis added). The idea that markets are institutional and historical entities is built into the neoliberalism of post–WWI Germany as well as the advanced liberalism of the contemporary United States (and its current rearticulations with the financial crisis) and late-socialist neoliberalism in China. Thus, to argue that the state continued to condition the very choices professionals made (e.g., through specific restrictions in the job-search process, patriotic education that promoted national strength, and the legacy of the socialist urban welfare package) does not contradict China's implementation of neoliberal practices.

In addition, the focus here on the microphysics of subject formation pushes us to consider that patriotic professionalism is not an exception to a general neoliberal rule but is in fact a generative form of neoliberalism. Liberal rationalities of governing adopt "both liberal and 'illiberal' techniques" (Hindess 2004: 28), depending on the segment of the population and the social domain, and also may work through processes of "exclusion" (Mitchell 2004). Gary Sigley uses the provocative term "liberal despotism" to describe contemporary China, for he argues that "authoritarian and illiberal measures are constitutive of the way in which a liberal arts of government operates" (2004: 563). College graduates in China were assumed to make responsible choices and thus could be governed through their freedom, but rural-to-urban migrants faced more authoritarian measures, such as restrictive household registration policies in the city, making it difficult if not impossible to get permanent residence.

Narratives of Patriotism and Professionalism

Many personal narratives wed a neoliberal self-enterprising ethos with an explicit concern for the welfare of the nation, particularly China's standing on the world stage. Throughout the research process, people told me that young workers should not think only of themselves as they made decisions about where to work: Their employment choices had to be informed by a sense of social and national responsibility, too, such that they were exposed to "two subjectification regimes"—neoliberal and socialist (F. Liu 2008; also Xia Zhang 2008). Central-level pronouncements made it clear that fostering a talented employee pool for the global knowledge economy was critical for reform-era modernization and local development. Concomitantly, many of the young professionals were explicit about how the choices they made were about furthering their own careers and making China strong and competitive. Yet making China strong and expressing patriotism did not require one to work for the state or to proclaim an allegiance to the Party (see also Duthie 2005, 2006).

Wen Shubang, a senior at DUT when we spoke, is a good example of how human capital exchanges framed the educated citizen as a potential source of national strength who learned about him- or herself through choices made autonomously and yet responsibly. Wen was eager to tell me about his upcoming position and sat attentively on the edge of the chair, with his elbows on his knees. He began by proudly stating that he had a position in a state-run foreign-trade office. "I heard they needed someone in this office, but the application period was already closed," he explained. "I went to talk to them anyway, and because my scores and accomplishments in college are better than others, they were still willing to hire me." Many graduates coveted this type of position, for it offered training opportunities, help with transferring one's household registration to Dalian, and some degree of security, as it was a part of the trade ministry. The salary, however, was just average. "A high salary helps a lot, but it is not that important now," Wen said, as he rationalized why he should be satisfied with the pay he had been offered:

I am just starting to work. I hope I will get a lot of training, and wealth, but it is not practical to want too much, because I am a new worker. If you go to a private company, the salary may be higher, but there are not as many opportunities for training there. What I need to see is if my salary meets my accomplishments after a year or two. . . . Many units wanted to hire me, including a foreign company [Federal Express]. I could have chosen a job with a much higher salary, but I didn't, because the jobs weren't related to my major. If I go too far beyond my major and my knowledge is too broad, I won't be able to advance my career. I won't know enough about anything, so what does it solve if only your salary is high? Going to a state-run unit is my own choice, and, anyway, I should work for the country [yinggai dui guojia fuwu]. Later, I can go to a private or foreign company.

His assertion that he had a responsibility to work for the country is in many ways reminiscent of old slogans, such as "Long Live Mao," that signaled a nod to "sacrifice for the nation" politics and highlighted the reproduction and reenactment of high-socialist practices in China. Yet contemporary decisions that Wen and his classmates made were quite different from those of the cohort before them. They struggled with the choice of working in a state, private, or foreign enterprise. Graduates also had to maneuver between wanting to fulfill individual dreams, confronting the reality of possible unemployment, and managing family pressures and duties—all while meeting their sense of social responsibility. Seeking career-development and training opportunities and credentializing oneself in a marketplace that valued market-oriented and transnational skills did not mean young professionals identified themselves as separate from or in opposition to the nation, no matter where they worked. Many were, rather, patriotic professionals, harboring neoliberal ideas of self-development as well as late-socialist understandings of duty to the nation. Wen embodied this responsibility in his rationalization of his average wage and in his conviction that he should be serving the nation.

The concept of patriotic professionalism allows us to see how ideas of autonomous self-development and collective imperatives of responsibility to the nation may be incorporated into a single subject position without causing personal turmoil.[14] The dreams of recent graduates and young professionals to go abroad to work, to study for an MBA in the U.S., or even to have the opportunity to train in a foreign company's office often were embedded in conversations about China's strength, echoing edicts from the Maoist era about the relationship between labor power and building the nation. Pan Qing, a young graduate who found a job with a large Korean trading firm, explained that she wanted the position because the company was "world famous," and she could "get experience" there. When I asked how long she thought she would stay, she answered, "In fact, I don't like this company, because I think I am a traitor to my country. When people are young, they think their goal is to get money from foreigners for China, but now it is the other way around"—that is, foreigners were taking money out of China. Her long-term plan was to go to the United States for an MBA, followed by finding work in trade. Announcement of this plan rolled off her tongue immediately after she criticized foreign companies in China, though she avoided any mention of the "foreign-ness" of the MBA. "I want to do something to prove that Chinese people deserve recognition," she said. "This is another reason why I want to go to the U.S. They have better education there, and I want to compete with them." For young women like her, these were not contradictions.

One of Pan's classmates who found a position in a state unit and with whom I spoke several days later explained why her "destiny" was "to work for the state and not for a foreign company":[15] "The foreign company can provide good conditions and comfort, but you give your talent to a foreigner, and they earn money from China. Maybe in five years, I will work for [a foreign company], but in ten years, I will be working for the state. Maybe I will continue studying as a post graduate in five years. . . . I will definitely work for a foreign company for two to three years, but not for a long time." She continued that state-owned companies should learn from foreign ones, because they were attracting so much of the young talent in China. "In a foreign company, you can never be boss, though—the highest level you can reach is executive manager. You just work for a foreigner, not for yourself." She admitted that many of her classmates did not agree with her argument that people should ultimately work for the state rather than foreign companies. Yet her narrative was filled with ambivalence about what was most important—working for the state, finding the best career opportunities, or earning a high salary. In fact, she had looked for a job in a foreign company but could not find one.

This confluence of responsibility to the self, one's family, and the country indicates a dynamic and complex interplay between the party-state and "popular nationalism" (*renmin minzu zhuyi*; Gries 2004). After protests in Tiananmen Square in 1989, patriotic education was emphasized at all levels, with concentration on the "excellent tradition of the Chinese nation" as well as "socialism, collectivism, self-reliance, hard struggle, and nation building," such that some have argued socialism was "reduced" to patriotism (also known as "the raising of national production"; Hughes 2006: 57, 31). Post-1989 nationalism also grew out of a "'de-romancitization' of the West" and a general support for state articulation of patriotism (Suisheng Zhao 1997) that was reinforced when China's bid for the 2000 Olympic Games was denied (H. Wang 2004). Caring for the nation, however, did not demand that one sacrificed one's professional future for the nation and adhered to a particular ideological position, as during the Maoist era. In the reform era, patriotism was about fulfilling one's potential as human capital, engaging the global world, and thus fostering national development.

In June 2005, two popular U.S. news magazines highlighted the incorporation of patriotism into acts of "free" career choice. *U.S. News and World*

Report began its "The Rise of a New Power" article about China with the following vignette:

> Richard Qiang could be an archetypal American. The son of blue-collar workers, Qiang thrived in school and graduated with a law degree from prestigious Fudan University. Then he landed a job here with . . . a New York law firm with dozens of corporate clients. . . . Only one thing distinguishes Qiang from a yuppie in Chicago or San Francisco or Manhattan: He belongs to the Communist Party. Like many ambitious young Americans who get involved in politics, Qiang's motives are pragmatic. *He hopes to work for the government someday,* helping craft China's budding legal system. Party membership is one way to open the right doors. (Newman 2005: 40; emphasis added)

Time magazine, on the other hand, featured a young man (twenty-four years old) who ran a "patriotic website" that got "30,000 hits a day." The article noted, "Strident nationalism is particularly pervasive among Chinese urban youth. Even as they sip Starbucks lattes or line up at the U.S. embassy for student visas, they bridle at what they view as *an attempt by the rest of the world to suppress a budding superpower.* 'America wants to keep China down,' Kang says. 'We should all be friends. But America must accept China as a friend on an equal footing'" (Beech 2005: 40; emphasis added). Imperatives to be responsible and to care for the country were important modes of subjectivization for the young professionals, affecting how they conceived of their present and future selves, while also echoing lessons in patriotic education texts. In this configuration, a young person could sip lattes and work for a foreign company while also standing up for China in the world, building on a history of protests and anti-imperialist campaigns from the Opium Wars to the Boxer Rebellion to the May 4, 1919, movement (Suisheng Zhao 2004; see also Y. Yan 2002). During anti-U.S. demonstrations in front of the embassy after the 1999 NATO bombing of the Chinese embassy in Belgrade, student chants evolved, for instance, from "Do not take GRE and TOEFL, but fight American imperialism with all our energy" to "Take TOEFL but not GRE, and fight American imperialism in our spare time" to, by the end of the demonstrations, "Take both TOEFL and GRE, and fight American imperialism by entering its rear area" (D. Zhao 2002: 904). Taking the exams and pursuing graduate work in the United States was not about betraying the nation but a project of self-enterprise that simultaneously supported the nation's progress.

Similarly, job fairs, resume writing, and face-to-face interviewing have become important devices in contemporary state strengthening and modernization—though now not through self-sacrifice but through the fostering of an individual's skills, talents, and expertise. It is precisely this combination of ideas about self-managed development and expressions of patriotism, either by working for the state or by making oneself and the nation strong, which offers evidence of a new ethics of subjectivity. The professional subject has emerged through the wedding of neoliberal governmentality with Maoist notions of duty recast in terms of reform-era economic goals.

Responsibility to the nation also often intersected with responsibility to one's own family, reflecting what Pan et al. (2005) refer to as "the master frame of 'family-nation'" in China. Wu Kaizhuang's situation helps explain. When I first met him at the city's job fair, he had recently returned from Germany and was looking for a new job. Wu lived with his parents in their small apartment almost an hour's bus ride from the center of town. He longed for the chance to go abroad again or at least to work in a foreign company. He prided himself on his language abilities and eagerly awaited any magazines or papers I had to offer. The German assignment, however, had been disappointing; the company failed, and he was not able to fulfill the dream he had established for himself. Immediately after returning to Dalian, he found a job with a large Sino-U.S. joint venture. His father strongly opposed the long commute this job required and the thought of another failure for his son in a "foreign place." In fact, in one of our early conversations, Wu said that his father told him if he worked for a foreign company, he would not be permitted to take time off to care for him if he got sick or if he died, resonating with what Vanessa Fong (2004) calls "filial nationalism." In other words, if Wu worked for a foreign company, his father feared that he would not be able to fulfill his filial duties. Wu told me, "I had to think of what my father said. I couldn't hurt his feelings." So he declined the position and returned to the market. He eventually found work in a tax-service company officially registered as private, though in reality it relied heavily on the subsidized labor of government employees.

As college graduates learned they had to extricate themselves from the legacy of state dependency and that labor was not only a national resource or part of the socialist welfare package but rather a site of potential individual development that should be accessed through choices made autonomously, they also learned that this autonomy had to be handled and these choices had be made in responsible ways. Maoist ideas about serving the country and duty to the nation became responsibly making employment choices. This new regime of self-development suggested a self-enterprising subject that was at once autonomous from state-planning agencies and still tied to the nation through strategic expressions of patriotism, whether in the form of working in a state unit, protesting the NATO bombing of the Chinese Embassy in Belgrade (what Dingxiang Zhao [2002] calls a "momentary outrage"), or attending pro-China rallies as counterpoints to pro-Tibet demonstrations during the 2008 Olympic torch tour. Independent job choices have been infused with Maoist-era politics of nation building and values of loving the nation as well as reform-era views on economic development, self-enterprise, material gains, and potential social mobility. Late-socialist neoliberalism, then, included active state participation. Recognizing the nation's presence in the very choices professionals made does not contradict China's current implementation of neoliberal practices, for state participation in fact has a long history within the Western liberal tradition. Yet as the experiences and desires of these aspiring professionals exhibit how neoliberal techniques of market allocation, individual choice, and self-enterprise are framed by the conditioning of the marketplace as well as deep emotions of caring for the nation, it is important to understand that this is not a seamless process.

Much anxiety, tension, and ambivalence is evident in people's everyday negotiations over the competing demands in their lives, tensions and issues I turn to in the following chapters. These young professionals desired social mobility and expected it as citizens with a high cultural level (*wenhua shuiping*) and talent, but they also were acutely aware of how their salaries did not allow them to purchase a home, or how their positions had lowly titles, or how their jobs reflected poorly on their understandings of middle-class masculinity or femininity—or how they could not find an appropriate position at all and remained unemployed. Graduates' desires to acquire experiences and even credentials that they determined would enhance their chances at social and professional mobility sometimes coincided with, but also sometimes contradicted, government expectations that they would adhere to upholding the nation. Thus, while the wedding of neoliberal techniques with Maoist-era principles is a critical and often overlooked aspect of the subject-formation process, additional forms of authority and systems of ordering have shaped the emergence of professionalism in late-socialist China. I now turn to debates about quality (*suzhi*), culture, nature, and gender in Chapters 5 and 6.

5
Turning Culture into Profit

I t was a beautiful August day when I went to talk with two personnel
managers at a large, three-party Sino-Japanese real estate joint venture. Its offices were near the beach, and with a little hunting I found
them on the second floor of a back building that had a great breeze off
the water and a wonderful view. The managers and I spoke at length
about how they made hiring decisions for office and service positions in
the company. Wu Xueming, a fashionable woman in her mid-thirties and
slightly younger than her male colleague, elaborated on their impres-
sions of the new graduates: "The ones who just graduated don't understand society enough. They think they have a lot of ability and can find
satisfying work. That is a mistaken thought. They have some *wenhua*
[culture/education] and knowledge, but they are not necessarily good
workers. Maybe their educational level [*wenhua shuiping*] is high, but
maybe they are not good workers. This doesn't represent their effectiveness. We need to see if their *wenhua* can become profitable, but they don't
understand this."

Similar to perspectives from other personnel managers and university administrators, Wu easily made a connection between profits and
wenhua—a term that referred to someone's formal educational or schooling level and to other distinctions of civility, composure, and class status,

a polysemous term that makes the English translation "culture" inadequate.[1] The linking of profits and education/culture exhibits important shifts in the politics of profits and the meaning of *wenhua* in contemporary China. Profits, which had been derided as exploitation of the working classes under Mao Zedong, have now been embraced as a form of success as well as a require- ment for enterprise survival. At the same time, *wenhua,* which as formal education had been castigated under Mao as a source of class oppression, was reassessed in the reform era and upheld as an important resource for China's future prosperity. As I argue in previous chapters, reform-era modernization logics have posited that the nation needed educated (*you wenhua*) and tal- ented people (*rencai*) to prosper and to compete effectively in the knowledge economy (*zhishi jingji*). In other words, *wenhua* referred not only to how educated and cultured someone was but also to what was now deemed a critical input into the production process: educated human capital. Wu's comment exhibits this market-oriented valuation of education and talent for the global city.

Intimately linked with these post-Mao discourses of *wenhua* is the concept of *suzhi* (quality), another key normative concept for young professionals. Like *wenhua, suzhi* has been associated with ideas of education and proper behavior and has been incorporated into governmental educational and pop- ulation programs in particular ways. Specifically, in the 1980s and 1990s, governmental directives increasingly used the term "*suzhi*" in educational reforms and in the one-child policy campaign, both of which aimed "to raise the quality of the people" (*tigao renminde suzhi*).[2] In contrast to Mao's claim that national strength would be found in revolutionary fervor and an abun- dance of people, post-Mao cultural critiques located the potential for reaching modernity in the population's quality, not its quantity (Anagnost 1997b: 119; see also Greenhalgh and Winckler 2005; Greenhalgh 2008). Ann Anagnost's influential work (1997b) has explained how the perceived low quality of the population was identified in the reform era as a reason for China's past failure and limited development. In the first decade of the reforms, Chinese "culture" also was blamed by many for China's lack of development, leading to "an anguished search for the cultural impediments to an unequivocal transcen- dence of China's 'backward' status in the global community of nation-states" (Anagnost 1997b: 78; see also Barlow 1991b; J. Wang 1996).[3] This lack of development has meant that rather than material poverty itself, the quality of the person—that is, their own self—had become "the object for improve- ment," reterritorializing "culture and subjectivity . . . into the field of Devel- opment," what Hairong Yan terms "neohumanism" (H. Yan 2003a: 500, 511).

Resonating with arguments in previous chapters about the shift to the self as a site of enterprise and development, in this chapter, I consider the implications of hiring practices that assessed subjects' accumulation of *wenhua* and *suzhi*.

Concepts of *wenhua* and *suzhi* are central to the emergence of the urban professional in China for several reasons. First, as I argue throughout this book, in Dalian—as well as other cities in China—those with high education/ cultural levels and high quality levels are explicitly celebrated. Second, discourses of *suzhi* and *wenhua* coalesce around ideas of self-improvement and self-enterprise, which, as I discuss in Chapter 4, are linked with national progress and modernization. Governmental programs, officials, and citizens all regularly commented on raising the *suzhi* and *wenhua* levels of the population to foster national development. Human improvement, in other words, "is not an end in itself, but is geared towards the very aim of Chinese reform" (Bakken 2000: 60). Third, not only have cities been advertising their human capital resources to others but certain characteristics of the "quality" employee have been directly linked with the urban, the modern, and the cosmopolitan— and thus *not* with rural places and laboring populations. Being a quality employee involves embodying urban, educated, and "well-brought up" sensibilities—"a kind of ideal personhood associated with urban modernity" (Fong 2007: 86; see also Duthie 2005; Murphy 2004; Schein 2001; H. Yan 2003b; Zheng 2007). Finally, this analysis of how *wenhua* and *suzhi* are integrated into hiring practices alerts us to what is at stake in these processes, specifically how these distinctions may be naturalized, and thus how the resultant class formations may seem reasonable and natural themselves.

Although much anthropological work on *suzhi* has focused on campaigns to raise the "low" levels in the rural population and "laboring masses" (H. Yan 2003a: 494), here I am interested in how urban graduates have been celebrated as sites of high levels of *suzhi* and *wenhua,* even as they have confronted difficulties in finding satisfying and appropriate jobs. Despite the small numbers of college graduates in the overall population, they exhibit symbolic power for the nation. Young professionals work to cultivate specific skills and abilities that reveal their high levels of *wenhua* and *suzhi,* ranging from technical knowledge about production processes to fluency in a foreign language to the ability to persuade a delinquent client to pay overdue accounts. These skills were cultivated in a wide array of social fields, including the home, university, and workplace, creating a tension between the notion that one could increase one's *wenhua* and *suzhi* levels (and thus change one's condition by oneself) and ideas about the inculcation and absorption of those skills in the home environment.

The norms of *wenhua* and *suzhi*—and the idea that high levels of each were desirable and necessary—are embedded historically in practices of self-cultivation in China.[4] Although these practices emerged with contemporary logics of late-socialist governmentality, they also referenced Confucian literati ideals and Maoist calls for constant study. Even though some aspects of Confucianism are highly hierarchical and fatalistic, there is also a strong sense that people are "malleable and educable" (Judd 2002: 20) and that becoming a cultured scholar requires self-cultivation (*xiu shen*) through study of the Confucian Classics, painting, poetry, and proper behavior. Maoist revolutionary practices also incorporated ideas of self-study and self-criticism into political campaigns, urging people to become better and more "well-rounded" socialists (see Jacka 2007; Kipnis 2006). Although the contemporary focus on self-cultivation references these traditions, it also explicitly embraces market-based economic growth through higher education and the study of science and technology.

A particularly important aspect of contemporary deployments of self-cultivation, then, is the idea that the individual and the family could make changes. Yet, if one failed, did not succeed financially, or remained unemployed, the assumption prevailed that "it would be one's own fault" for not having "grasp[ed] the vastly available opportunities today" (F. Liu 2008: 200). The shift in responsibility from the state to the individual did not mean, however, that governing was absent. Rather, the responsibilization of the self is a form of regulation, a technique of governing that specifies more active and autonomous subjects who pursue education and training, plan careers, invest in their skill base, and also cultivate the next generation to be creative and innovative workers who will help China compete in the global economy.[5]

When we examine the everyday hiring practices between employers and young professionals, it is apparent that there is much that the autonomous, active subject cannot change, particularly as people have adopted discourses of the "rational" and "natural" to explain why people ended up in certain jobs. Employers, the ethnographic evidence emphasizes, regularly referred to a potential employee's home environment and family background when assessing his or her suitability for the new job. Association of specific skills with the home space legitimized the acquisition of these skills as a kind of natural process, particularly for embodied aptitudes, such as speaking skills and appearance. Natural in this usage is the taken-for-granted character of embodied expressions of culture and power rather than biological characteristics per se. Appeals to natural social distinctions were understood in contrast to the Maoist era as well. Comments about the growing "rationalization" of social divisions were always compared to what people identified as the overly "politicized" and "irrational" Maoist social structures. Similarly, many suggested that gender distinctions and new expressions of masculinity and femininity were more natural than the "unnatural" and unreasonable silencing of gender differences during the Maoist past in particular (see Chapter 6; see also Rofel 1999). A tension exists then between belief in self-directed improvement and the naturalization of social distinctions that made it difficult for young people to capitalize on their own entrepreneurialization.

As government officials, university administrators, and personnel directors all made the connection between *wenhua* and potential profits, graduates and young professionals assumed it was legitimate and rational for those who studied to be able to convert their educational capital into economic and social gains. Many graduates felt that society finally was granting educated people and professional experts their due respect. Graduates I interviewed literally used the term "rational" (*heli*) to describe reform-era advancement opportunities, even as many commented that this rationalization had not been fully realized yet. "The reforms are very rational," a DUT graduate assured me, "so there is more and more competition. It is very hard for those with lower *wenhua* levels, but it is fair." If their goals were frustrated, interviewees blamed it on "irrational" (*bu heli*) aspects of the labor market, such as reliance on connections (*guanxi*), a lack of information, and an overemphasis on family background, rather than critiquing the legitimacy of the link between their cultural/educational levels (*wenhua shuiping*) and potential profits. "Now people are practical," a new graduate told me. "They face the reality that they have to join in the competition. We have to earn our bread by our own struggle, but material things and money are limited. If you want to earn more, you must work harder than others. That is fair. Most people have realized it. It is commonsense now." Framing *wenhua* and profitability together, in other words, made sense to many people, making Wu's statement, quoted in the chapter's opening paragraph, not only thinkable but also reasonable in contemporary times. In other words, people made "truth statements" about the reasonable-ness and natural-ness of contemporary social distinctions—and thus the conversion of *wenhua* into profit. Ability-based social mobility fit into a logic of late-twentieth-century modernization and development where it was "not just natural, but inevitable" (Moore 1986: 170) that individuals would be in pursuit of money and professionalism, and high *wenhua* and *suzhi* levels could be translated into profits for an individual or economic growth for a city. As people negotiated new connections between profits and *wenhua*, a new "regime of living" emerged that was concerned with "an understanding of the good," which also impacted subject formation (Collier and Lakoff 2005: 23). Not only was this regime a space in which negotiations of professional subjectivity occurred but it also provided "a possible guide to action" (Collier and Lakoff 2005: 23) in hiring practices and shaped new class formations as well. Technologies of subject making and norms of embodied *wenhua* were central to decisions about who would be working in which jobs and thus to prospects for social mobility, but they also were fundamentally ethical problems about how one should live.[6] Luo Xu, in fact, argues that among university graduates, a concern with "why one lives," a question popular in the 1980s, shifted to "how one lives" in the 1990s.

In this chapter, I consider how in the hiring process the assessment of education/culture and quality were highly contested, with results that potentially limited young professionals' ability to profit from *wenhua*. Taking *wenhua* and *suzhi* as norms that incited people to invest in themselves in particular ways and that disciplined people who did not possess or embody the correct levels, we may understand that the formation of talent in the global city was not a seamless process. Labor power for talent (*rencai*) had become a form of capital that graduates hoped to convert into other forms of capital for the company, individual, and family precisely because of reform-era discursive practices of *wenhua* and *suzhi*. Yet the unequal conversion of educational capital into other forms of capital was a common topic of conversation and indicated that education alone did not guarantee immediate compensation in the form of high salaries and well-respected jobs (see Hsu 2007).[7] The ability one had to accumulate wealth and prestige as a new employee also referenced less-mutable qualities, such as gender, appearance, family background, family connections, and household registration—whether one was from the city or the countryside.

The mutual-choice hiring process—analyzed here as a mechanism of power—enabled employers to normalize post-Mao professionals around these understandings of *wenhua* and *suzhi*, highlighting the tensions between constitution of an autonomous, choosing subject and naturalization processes that restricted the possibilities of self-generated improvement and career planning. Subject making, in other words, entails being made and self making (Ong 1996: 737), potentially creating and reproducing inequalities and class distinctions.[8] As social boundaries are hardened as rational or natural, social mobility and individual development goals may be frustrated. Articulations of *wenhua* and *suzhi* in the hiring process have framed the meaning of professionalism, the definition of "desirable" talent in the city, and potentially the distribution of and access to resources that shape new social class formations.

The valorization of high cultural/educational levels, a high-quality population, and talented human resources suggests not only that these are critical
norms in the constitution of professional subjectivity but also that they are
foundational points of truth in the rationalization and naturalization of new
inequalities and class positions in the city.

Assembling Culture and Quality in Contemporary China: Limits on the Conversion of *Wenhua* into Profit

In this section, I examine the contemporary usage of the two normative concepts (*wenhua* and *suzhi*) and how they have been integrated into the hiring
process. The term "*wenhua shuiping*" (cultural/educational level) came up in
numerous conversations with personnel directors, newly graduating students,
and those already in the working world, indicating it was an important factor
in the making of these post-Mao professionals. Although commonly used to
describe formal educational credentials, it was not always clear what "*wenhua*"
meant in these exchanges. Many personnel directors also mentioned a prospective employee's quality (*suzhi*), abilities, suitability, family background,
residency status, and gender when commenting on someone's *wenhua* level.
To appreciate the dexterity of the notions of *wenhua* in China today, it is helpful to think about Raymond Williams's discussion of the English term "educated." He argues it referred both to formal training and to the raising of
children, "as in *properly brought-up* which can be made to mean anything a
particular group wants it to mean" (1983: 112; emphasis in original). In many
ways, the term "*wenhua shuiping*" radiates this same ambiguity. The term
"*suzhi*" (quality) is also quite malleable and flexible in everyday usage[9] and,
like *wenhua,* exhibits a tension between familial aspects and experiential/
educational ones. The meanings associated with both terms have changed
over time, further complicating debates about what they convey.

In outlining the genealogy of *wenhua,* Ping He argues that the concept has
included a set of ideas that depicted human civilization and excellence, a
way of governance identified with Confucianism, and particular patterns of
self-cultivation and embodied being in the world (2002: 73–92; see also
Bakken 2000). In modern times, new ideas were associated with the term
"*wenhua*" that linked it with a national "essence" and significantly with political ideologies and projects (He 2002: 73–92). Mao, for instance, was explicit
about culture and the sciences having a class character, connecting pre-1949
education with bourgeois, individualist, and ruling-class ideologies. Those

educated before liberation[10] often were the targets of criticism during such campaigns as the Anti-Rightist Campaign (1956) and the Great Proletariat Cultural Revolution (1966–1976). During the Cultural Revolution, *wenhua* itself became an object of class struggle, with students attacking teachers and other authority figures, burning books, and destroying material objects associated with the bourgeois and exploitative views of past philosophies, religions, and teachings. Educated people found themselves on the bottom of the Maoist class-status system (the "stinking ninth") that sought to eradicate "feudal" and "capitalist" forms of exploitation and oppression and aimed to raise the national stature of peasants and workers. In contrast, Deng Xiaoping embraced education—and science and technology in particular—"as a core element of progress and national survival" and "the most important 'force of production' to be developed" (Miller 1996: 5, 62). Thus, the comments I heard about people's *wenhua* levels referenced a wide range of ideas: socialization in the family, the utilization of one's training to support collective projects (whether capitalist or socialist), and formal school study, including the contemporary rearticulation of Confucian literati ideals.

Therefore, the reform-era focus on *wenhua* seems to grow out of a number of circumstances. First is the current reappraisal of its role in the nation's development. In contrast to the Maoist era, the state and global capitalists relied on educated people and those with certain kinds of high-quality manners and ways of speaking. There have even been calls for more leaders to obtain "comprehensive" educations, promotion of a technocratic elite in the Party, and directives to increase the number of college and graduate-level degrees in the Party. Although some see this call as a "recreation of the imperial system" (Bakken 2000: 64), I argue it is critical to consider how meanings shift as one governmental technique is redeployed in another historical moment. Imperial exams and the system of placing literati officials across the country are not the same as the contemporary emphasis on education, knowledge, innovation, research, and creativity for global competitiveness.

Second is that *wenhua* no longer is the locus of violence and ideological battles that it was during the Cultural Revolution. *Wenhua* remains a point of social-class distinction, although not one based on oppositional class consciousness but rather on a series of distinctions that are closely related to one's quality. Even though the official language of class struggle is unspoken in the reform era and has been replaced by discourses of civilization and culture, social-class distinctions have not disappeared (Anagnost 1997b, 2008). In addition, relying on one's social and economic position as an expert or professional is a new way of achieving individual and family social mobility in late-socialist China.

Contemporary understandings of *suzhi* also encompass multiple and often ambiguous meanings, learned and naturalized characteristics, and structural and individualized aspects. Scholars have argued, for example, that although *suzhi* has been used to refer to "inborn characteristics" in the past, in reform-era education and population campaigns it has been used to emphasize the social aspect of quality-raising projects and the structural causes of low-quality levels—that is, aspects that may be changed collectively rather than individual failings (Kipnis 2006, 2007).[11] Others have emphasized continuing tensions between these meanings, arguing that the term *suzhi* is "amorphous," that it "refers to the innate *and* nurtured physical, intellectual and ideological characteristics of a person" (Murphy 2004: 2; emphasis added), and that "what *suzhi* is eludes precise definition" (H. Yan 2003a: 496; emphasis in original). *Suzhi* has been used to comment on the body and its hardware as well as someone's intellect, morality, education, and psychology (H. Yan 2003a: 496; Kipnis 2006: 304; Murphy 2004: 2), characteristics that could—and must—be enhanced through study, parental inputs, and self-cultivation.

Based on how employers in Dalian equated aspects of *wenhua* and *suzhi* with embodied characteristics, I suggest in this chapter that the sense of "innate-ness" remains relevant in the reform era. Because these norms have been associated with the home environment where class reproduction is naturalized, the resulting distinctions take on a naturalized character. In addition, because *suzhi,* like *wenhua,* has multiple meanings, its usage slips across educational factors and other structural issues to ones that are naturalized, either because they are embodied or because their acquisition is located in the home. In this way, these terms reflect Pierre Bourdieu's argument (1984) that it mattered where and how one's education/culture was acquired. Bourdieu distinguishes between cultural competence acquired in one's early childhood environment and that acquired through formal educational training. Through these experiences, cultural and symbolic capital is accumulated, which then has the potential to be converted into other forms of prestige and power.

"Background" was integrated into decisions about whom to hire for a position in Dalian in two general ways—as family background and connections (*jiating beijing*) and as the applicant's own societal work, educational experience, and achievements (*shehui beijing*), which resonates with Bourdieu's distinction. The ability to reason or to talk in a certain way, for example, often was attributed to the employee's home environment, while his or her knowledge of import and export regulations would be associated with the employee's educational and work experience. The ability to take advantage of one's formal educational training (i.e., turning *wenhua* into profit) was not equal for everyone; it mattered where one acquired one's *wenhua*.

Narratives about who was desirable and what kind of background mattered varied between enterprises, however. Personnel officers of foreign-owned and joint venture enterprises with resident foreign managers, for example, claimed they emphasized the applicant's social background (*shehui beijing*). They portrayed their workplaces as rational places that avoided corrupt *guanxi* (connections) practices found in older state-run units. The older units, especially government agencies, were portrayed by job seekers and other employers as supporters of the back-door process whereby only strong connections could get one a job. Yang Chengbai, the personnel director at a major Sino-U.S. venture in the Economic and Technical Development Zone, said, "We don't care too much about their parents, but we do care about their *shehui beijing*. Where are they working, which university did they go to, what is their work experience? . . . If they change work too many times, we are not willing to hire them." His company's professed rational interest in skills and education were not without their own cultural overtones, however, as exhibited in the following comments: "They [the applicants] should have two to three years' working experience, good English, computer skills, and good communication skills. More men have these requirements. Women, they need to have the ability to manage documents, to deal with statistics and plans, to communicate and deal with the detailed work. Men, on the other hand, like to be challenged and to have responsibility to make decisions." Although he claimed the foreign partner's hiring policies prohibited him from looking at family background, naturalized ideas about gender differences found their way into his concepts of competence and ability (see Chapter 6).

Comments from He Jian, a young man whom I met at one of the weekly municipal job fairs when he was hiring people for a collective enterprise, provide a good example of how family background (*jiating beijing*) was incorporated into decisions. When we met for coffee the following week, he explained how he found the people he needed for open positions:

> From the first impression, I start to mark down what I think of them
> [while he is still at the city job fair] and later meet with them again.
> I look at them individually at the talent market—are they outgoing

or quiet? Do they like to talk? Their language can express their ability, too. When they come to the company for a longer talk, I ask about their family situation. What do their parents do? How many people are in their home? If their parents are professors or doctors, or if they are the oldest child, I like it. The oldest child can eat bitterness [*chi ku*; withstand hardship]. They are like a social stratum [*shehui jieceng*] of their own. If the parents are professors or doctors, *then they have a high cultural level*; they have knowledge of the world and have met a lot of people. The language they use is important, too. Also, they use reason to think about problems, and the level of their thinking about problems is related to their parents. (emphasis added)

As someone who himself did not get a four-year degree, He did not see the traditional four-year bachelor's degree (*benke*) as the most important criteria, but that did not mean he disregarded an applicant's *wenhua* or *suzhi* level. For him, the home environment had much to do with an applicant's abilities and potential as a desirable employee. A remarkably similar focus on the household came from Lu Jiulong, a sixty-eight-year-old Dalian man who managed a large Singaporean forwarding and shipping office. "Where their parents work and what they do is important, because you can see their long-term level," he said. "For example, if their parents are doctors or professors, *then this has a connection or relation with their own level*" (emphasis added). One's upbringing in the home naturalized certain desirable criteria, shifting the potential for development away from the control of an active, self-enterprising young professional.

Wu, of the real estate joint venture, explained how they dealt with family background: "We ask what work their parents do and how many brothers and sisters they have. For instance, if their parents are divorced, it may influence them. Also if their parents are high officials or they have a lot of money, then maybe they are not willing to do common service work." Many of the positions available to recent graduates were not considered challenging and did not require a great deal of training, as was the case with the kind of service workers this company sought to hire. Yet graduates had high expectations of development and good salaries, creating disappointment quickly. University administrators took specific measures to alleviate this tension, as did such companies as this joint venture, which decided graduates from wealthy or powerful families could possibly be liabilities in the office rather than assets. Unlike most stories about how an elite background was worked into the hiring equation, at this company it was a disadvantage.

Nevertheless, this woman welcomed students whose *wenhua* levels were high, particularly graduates of four-year programs. On their own, however, cultural assets did not necessarily have value; rather, they needed to be turned into profitable returns for them to have meaning and worth. One form of capital needed to be turned into another. Lu from the shipping company echoed this feeling. When applicants asked about the salary, he would answer them by saying he did not know what they were worth yet. Once he could see how well they did as a worker, he would determine their salary level. By the early 2000s, more formalized conversations and published articles emerged about talent not only being defined by educational credentials. "Someone could have graduated from Qinghua [a very prestigious university in Beijing]," a professor said, "but that does not mean they are *rencai* [talent]. It is not according to their title or accomplishments. . . . They need to be quick learners and creative to be useful talent for the country." Innovation, creativity, and entrepreneurialism became explicitly articulated characteristics of the desirable employee.

In everyday practices, palpable tensions exist between official discussion of *suzhi* and *wenhua* and people's experiences of them. First is the tension between self-generated improvement and the naturalization of *wenhua* and *suzhi* distinctions, which takes improvement possibilities out of the hands of the individual. Second is the related tension between the objectification of talented labor in job fairs and the specification of active, autonomous professional subjects in the reform era. In interviews as well as printed materials, such terms as *chanpin* (product) and *zhiliang* (quality, for objects) were used to talk about college graduates. To explain why universities continually experimented with majors and curriculum reforms, a young woman working in Finance University's student recruitment office proclaimed, "Students are now more like products [*chanpin*]," which Professor Liu Zhongquan from DUT quickly followed with the comment, "And they need to be packaged up a bit." Packaging up these budding professionals meant regulating their desires and making them desirable to prospective employers, processes that worked through the norms of *wenhua* and *suzhi*.

Similarly, when I asked a representative from a large, state-run unit at the DUT job fair about mutual choice, he said, "This system is much better [than assignments]. We can meet them, talk to them, interview them, and understand the student more. . . . We hired everyone we needed at this fair, a lot of students came here. . . . Their *suzhi* is higher here, their quality [*zhiliang*] and ability [*nengli*] are better, so more units are willing to come to this school."

Both "*suzhi*" and "*zhiliang*" mean quality, but there is an important distinction between them (see also Kipnis 2006; Murphy 2004). *Suzhi* usually refers to a *person's* quality or level (e.g., character, morals, education, ability), while *zhiliang* refers to a *product's* quality (e.g., design, durability, technological level, quality of materials). A DUT publication also used this term, stating that units had higher quality (*zhiliang*) requirements for workers now, particularly in foreign-language ability, practical experience, and political quality (*suzhi*). Use of *zhiliang* to describe graduates was noteworthy because of its "improper" use and because it signified an objectification of graduates by employers and universities. Late-socialist reforms objectified the young professionals *and* specified more active and autonomous forms of personhood, as I outline in previous chapters.

Despite the varied meanings and histories of *suzhi* and *wenhua,* they existed in tandem in the reform era, for both terms are intimately tied to governmental rationalities on engaging the global economy.[12] If citizens' *suzhi* and *wenhua* could be improved, they would be more attractive to global capital investments and would be able to generate more profits. Considering the ways those hiring young professionals incorporated these norms into their decisions suggests a specifically contemporary understanding of human capital as economic assets in China.[13] This reinforces my arguments in Chapter 2 about how Dalian officials represented talent as a resource that would attract foreign and domestic businesses to the city, essentially turning *wenhua* into profit for the municipality.

The microphysics of power approach I take in this book, however, emphasizes that multiple domains regulate, normalize, and specify professionalism. Within these domains, we also see a variety of mechanisms, norms, politics, and ethics from neoliberalism, Maoism, familial regimes, and gender ideals. Thus, market-based techniques of governing should not overdetermine the subject form—a reason I also caution against using the term "neoliberal" to modify "subject." Identification of a neoliberal subject assumes too much about professional subjectivity in contemporary China, making it difficult to conceive, for instance, of how neoliberalism and socialism are intertwined in patriotic professionalism, or the referencing of literati and Maoist ideals of self-cultivation in market-inflected uses of *suzhi.* Arguing that human resources were evaluated in economic terms thus does not negate other aspects of *wenhua* and *suzhi,* but it does alert us to how reform-era governmental rationalities have defined the norm of a desirable worker. My analysis thus avoids presenting the state—or the market—as all powerful and as defining the value, ethics, and politics of work/labor. Rather, this analysis aims to account for the multiple forms and sites of normative regulation that have shaped the meaning of urban professionalism.

Another aspect of an applicant's quality that was incorporated into hiring decisions was the notion of character (*pinzhi*), which employers noted to determine whether the job seeker would cheat the company (see Kipnis 2006). This criterion, along with moral character (*renpin*), was mentioned by almost all of those hiring employees. Descriptions of what a good character entailed often pointed to such traits as loyalty and honesty—moral aspects of one's *suzhi* that in theory could be improved by the individual but that also tended to be associated with the family in everyday usage. A young manager at a state-owned hotel said that a good character was like wanting to work hard and to do one's best for one's teachers. "If you have ability, it has no use if you don't work hard. You can look at them talking to know this, to see if they are hard working or not," he said. He contrasted a hard-working person with ability to what he identified as the more typical state-enterprise employee who had no ability but had connections and thus could not be fired. Wu from the Sino-Japanese venture said her company could tell what a person's character was like from the way he or she talked and answered questions. "You can't see all of this beforehand though," she said, "so we have a trial period. But university graduates' character usually is very good. This is important in the service industry." She did note, however, that they had to let someone go, because "here they should wear certain clothes, but she wore *tuoxie* [plastic sandals] and clothes where we could see her stomach."

Several months after my first interview with the manager at the state-run hotel, we met again. He still felt plagued by his difficult working situation and emphasized that what was most important was honesty, even if it meant saying you did not like something. To explain his meaning, he said, "So, going to university is more important, and their family background, like being teachers and *zhishifenzi* [intellectuals]. Those in business, well, I don't really like those people. I like people who have studied [*dushu de ren*], because they are more honest. . . . [I]f individual entrepreneurs [*getihu*] have money, it is not interesting. They can buy anything, but if they suddenly have money, it is not interesting. Yet if highly educated people have money, then I really like that." A high *wenhua* level, in other words, corresponded to a high *suzhi* level and a trustworthy, loyal character. These characteristics were also naturalized, however, by being associated with one's family background.

In her study of narratives of class and status in the northeast city of Harbin, Carolyn Hsu (2007) notes similar ambivalence over the accumulation of wealth by small entrepreneurs (*getihu*), people whose quality was considered "low," and the wealth gained by businesspeople (*shangren*) who were associated with knowledge, talent, and education, and even the status of "'Confucian merchants,' or successful scholar-businesspersons" (Y. Yan 2002: 23). In the 1980s, there was a significant policy reversal from the Cultural Revolution era, when reforms made individual private enterprises legal. Opening a street stall to sell belts or a restaurant to sell noodles and dumplings remained a risk, however, since many worried that political winds could shift again. Urban tales circulated that those who did dare to open their own enterprises had criminal backgrounds, or at least no education, for they would be the only people willing to take such a risk.[14] Even in the late 1990s, wealth accumulated by small businesspeople in private companies was often critiqued for being "gained at the expense of national wealth" (Hsu 2007: 135). Businesspeople identified as more "moral" in their dealings, on the other hand, had education, culture, quality, modern and scientific knowledge, and, interestingly, they were said to have "served China's national interest through his or her success on the global market" (Hsu 2007: 141).

Preference for new employees who came from families of professors and doctors, who attended college, and who were eloquent and articulate speakers points to the possibility that those who were not from the correct background and who did not embody post-Mao conceptions of *wenhua* and *suzhi* faced increased barriers to social mobility. Even within the college-graduate population, differences based on urban or rural origins, family connections, and parents' occupations existed. Universities revised majors and curriculums to make their graduates more marketable, but they were unable to change family backgrounds.

Those looking for work also faced limits based on the power of their family's connections (*guanxi*), another significant hindrance to calls for self-improvement. Students from the countryside or more "common" families especially claimed they did not have the same opportunities due to their inability to capitalize on family connections in urban areas. An articulate young woman from a smaller city in the south simply said, "My relatives are all common people. They do not have power, so all they can do is offer me information." A schoolmate of hers commented that, compared with his classmates, he did not have a good job, because he had no "background." In other words, he had no family relations to help him find a job. Those already employed, such as a man in his early thirties, echoed these feelings. He complained that "fair opportunities" were hard to find, even for someone with good abilities and qualifications, and thus sometimes a person had to rely on "a friend's help."

Young professionals had high expectations, but they also acknowledged "irrationalities" in the mutual-choice system, including the use of connections, the lack of open information about job opportunities, and even the fact that it mattered where they came from (household registrations and family backgrounds). Frustrated expectations and incongruence between employers' desires and their own skills tempered excitement over the possibilities for personal development by many. Potential professionals expressed hopes over having the fruits of their talented labor power "returned" to them after seeing their parents' generation of life-long, assigned employment in state-run units, but they also acknowledged the limits to their possible social mobility. Worries over their future fates echoed concerns of earlier eras and produced a contradictory nostalgia for what was seen as the security but also lack of opportunity that was associated with state assignments (see Chapter 6).

Yet even when people were not successful in finding a satisfying job, professional norms have been established through distinctions of wenhua and suzhi as young educated people have been fashioned by and have fashioned themselves for mutual choice. As such, discourses around these norms were mechanisms of governing that deployed market-based techniques, norms of enterprise from the knowledge economy, and socialist ethics of collective projects, along with contemporary rearticulations of Confucian literati ideals and practices of self-cultivation.

The Naturalization of Class

This examination of how wenhua and suzhi have been integrated into the hiring process draws our attention to three important points. First is the argument that by analyzing how culture/education and quality are normative concepts that shape professional subjectivity, we may better understand the various forms of regulation and governing in late-socialist China. Incorporation of these norms into the hiring process is another site in the microphysics of power that shaped professional subjectivity and the shift from assignee to employee. In addition, focusing on new middle-class consumption practices without considering productive processes (labor)—and the way people have been pulled into these processes by employers—diverts our attention from significant sites of power and regulation.

Second, this discussion helps us understand the complexity of new social-class formations emerging in the global city. How employers integrated ideas of culture, competence, and background into the hiring process raises important questions about the reproduction of social hierarchies. Contemporary practices of self-cultivation coincided with wider global trends in a shift away from traditional urban industrial economies to knowledge economies and a belief in the value of human innovation, creativity, and technological expertise as critical "assets" for future growth in the city. Palpable tension has developed between distinctions based on the home environment (*jiating huanjing*) and governmental technologies that incited people to make investments in the self. Across the social spectrum, people have absorbed the idea that market demands for workers of a certain quality and level were legitimate, logical, and reasonable. Arbitrary distinctions thus became part of society's commonsense, fitting into a logic of social organization naturally. The social logic that has associated status with culture and ability-based accomplishments as a more natural form of social organization has given such accomplishments a new and powerful currency in urban social relations. In the process, discourses that referenced embodied characteristics, the home environment, and rational social structures raised the possibility of naturalizing class distinctions.

Third, the discussion draws our attention to the prominence of and tensions around self-cultivation, self-care, and self-enterprise practices in the reform era. Although practices of self-cultivation are not new in China, the part of the self being worked on, cultivated, regulated, and "improved" in contemporary times is not the same as that within the Confucian tradition. For instance, the cultured individual in the Confucian tradition was the "gentleman," so self-cultivation and high *wenhua* levels corresponded directly to one's gender (see Chapter 6). Also, in the contemporary moment, a different kind of "knowledge" has been required for status and social mobility that does not necessarily come from studying and imitating the past but rather fosters an outward-looking, entrepreneurial self also situated in processes of class formation. Revaluations of *wenhua* and *suzhi* are central to this process and have been linked with market as well as historical/cultural practices. After years of severe degradation during the Maoist years, culture—*wenhua*—has taken on a profoundly significant role in these young people's lives and in official political discourses. The post-Mao reevaluation of professionals' behavior is, in essence, the reason discourses and practices around *wenhua* have become so important in establishing ideas of competence and credentials.

By examining the historical specificity of these discourses and their connection with particular kinds of governmental problematizations, this chapter also questions the idea that markets "naturally" reformed "irrational" social, labor, and economic systems and problematizes the natural-ness of new class formations emerging in the city. As college graduates actively participated in their own subjectivation, they also were subject to disciplinary mechanisms and normalizing processes that potentially impacted their opportunities to turn *wenhua* into profit. In Chapter 6, I further the discussion of the contested nature of subject formation by considering the cross-section of gender regimes, self-enterprise, and the legacy of the socialist urban welfare package.

6

Gendering Security and the State in Urban China

When I met Liu Lihua soon before her graduation from Dalian University of Technology (DUT), she was facing a job choice between a foreign company where she was working in a temporary position and the municipal tax bureau where her father had used connections to find her a job (*ta tuole hen duo renqing*). Each had its advantages: The foreign company offered her the chance to "use her knowledge" and the "potential to develop herself," while the government office provided security and stability "for a young woman." Liu explained:

> Everyone says it [the taxation bureau] is a good job for me, including my sister, they say it is better than the foreign employer. *The government is more stable,* and the taxation bureau is profitable. It is a *good job for a girl.*[1] In a foreign office, there is more risk, and you face many challenges, and they don't believe I can face such difficulties. I really hesitate about which job to choose. At the time I started working, I didn't know if I could do the work in the foreign office, but you know, the government offices are not very busy. (emphasis added)

Liu's employment decision exemplifies a dilemma felt by many young female professionals, torn between dreams of developing themselves as *rencai* (talent)—paralleling reform-era narratives of growth and development—and conforming to ideals of femininity embedded in the virtuous wife and good mother role (*xianqi liangmu*). As a young woman, Liu faced pressure to take a "stable" job in a "safe" place, "in" an office, and, significantly, "inside" the state sector. For years, urban families had received benefits through their state work units (*danwei*) as part of the "iron rice bowl" welfare package, including housing, steady salaries, medical care, and schooling for their children. The material and symbolic legacy of this system meant that urban families associated security and stability with the state. Therefore, for women like Liu, the state was often seen as a safe employer in terms of the moral security it provided as a paternalistic and protected sphere, and in terms of the potential for household security in light of new structural instabilities generated by reforms in the welfare system. Decision making about employment intersected gendered regimes that had spatial components (e.g., distinctions between "inside" and "outside" spaces) as well as the legacy of, and reforms in, the socialist urban welfare package. By examining the ways gender was incorporated into employment choices, we understand not only that the production of professional subjectivity was not a predetermined process but also that the state was implicated in subject formation in gendered ways. A critical component of professional subject formation was the intersection of gendered experiences of security and gendered relationships with the state.

Building on arguments about the wedding of patriotism with self-enterprise and the place of *wenhua* and *suzhi* in the hiring process, in this chapter I advance the perspective that multiple technologies of governing in a variety of domains shaped norms of professionalism. Practices of mutual choice were informed by cultural discourses of inside and outside, middle-class femininity and masculinity, security and risk, and the state and private sectors, all influencing who occupied the sought-after domain of the talented and "necessary" employee. The young people discussed in the following ethnographic stories actively engaged these various norms and in the process helped rework and reinforce what was considered appropriate (*heshi*) for a professional woman or man to do. Examining the struggles over identity and security these young people faced—and the transgressions across gendered boundaries that they made—also reminds us that "in power relations there is necessarily the possibility of resistance" (Foucault 1997b: 292).

Careers, Families, Security: Conflicts over Middle-Class Femininity

Considering personal deliberations about which job to take, how to manage family and work, and the best way to face new risks in the reform era is a helpful way to understand how multiple technologies of governing were integrated into professional subjectivity. Liu's story also allows us to explore how appropriate employment for women was symbolically aligned with the state. Her parents, sister, and boyfriend all pressured her to pursue stability and security over "opportunity" and "risk" in the foreign company. She explained that in China, parents did not expect a daughter to be "a very successful woman. She doesn't need to take such pains to do that." She continued:

> If you do spend that much energy on your job, then your household is not very satisfied, because you don't have a lot of time to take care of the family. . . . I know I am lucky to have two choices, but I really want to work in the Danish company. It is full of risk, but it is also full of challenges, and I can use my specialty fully. The chemical company is worldwide, and it wants to expand here. It is a good chance for me if I can catch it. I don't want to be limited [*youxian*].

Liu was graduating from the five-year combined chemical engineering–English major, one of the most demanding at DUT and that accepted only students with the best scores, and imagining what she could accomplish had much to do with her social position as an educated woman in a global city. But she also felt compelled to perform and continuously reference her femininity.

The reaction of Hu Yangren, a thirty-year-old professional who had been listening to Liu explain her situation, is exemplary of the critique women faced as they developed their careers. After hearing about Liu's employment dilemma, he said, "In a Chinese corporation, a female secretary, and I think at present that is her position, she must be beautiful and must have public relations ability, and I don't think this girl has that ability. She just graduated and doesn't have a lot of social relationships in this city, and she doesn't know how to arrange some daily affairs because she has no experience." Although appearance was important for men and women in the job search, beauty was an explicit criterion for women, as this man proclaimed. Educated professional women were expected to dress in a simultaneously fashionable and conservative manner, to speak in particular ways, and to have certain skills.

Foreign-language ability, verbal persuasion, and natural beauty were typical. Hu also said as a manager, he would likely use this young woman only for the trial period of three months and then dismiss her. He thought she would need to change positions several times to be experienced and successful, concluding that "in spite of having a family, she would be successful":

> She doesn't care about her family [bu guan jiating], she only cares about her job. My own classmates, especially the women, they want stable jobs more than high salaries, because they will be a husband or wife in a family, and they must be responsible to their families [bixu dui tamen jiating kai fuze]. Right? Especially the women, my classmates hope they can stay in a stable job and have a lower salary. They think that is enough. It is not very good if a girl wants to go to a foreign corporation. That is just a foreign corporation with a higher salary. She must not be a good wife or good mother, but she will be a successful woman.

In another interview, a man, speaking of his wife's situation, reinforced the idea that women did not need to make money (zhuan qian). "I want my wife to have an 'iron rice bowl' and to support my career," he said. "I don't care if her salary is only 200 to 300 RMB a month."

Liu's boyfriend, a local Dalian man who did not have any household registration (hukou) problems if he stayed in the city, found a position at a profitable state-run import and export company that provided good benefits, retirement insurance, and housing options after he got married. The Danish company, on the other hand, did not have such benefits (fuli daiyu), but, Liu explained, in the tax bureau, "I would be a public official [gongwuyuan], and I would have even better benefits than his corporation gets. . . . My boyfriend wants me to work in the government, because he works in a foreign-trade corporation. Even though his corporation is a good one, foreign trade has not been very good in recent years, so he wants me to find more stable work." Another critique Hu made of Liu's situation pointed directly to this issue of workplace benefits. In explaining why he thought she would not be a good wife or mother, he said, "Because her job is not stable. She said she must have some risk, because in this company she has no benefits or welfare or medical insurance. If she were dismissed, she would have nothing."

Multiple disciplinary mechanisms, such as these comments from Hu, framed women "inside" (the state, the office, or the home) and men "outside" (the state, the home, in the world of business), infusing calculative decisions about where to work with a gendered spatial component. The gendered ideal of the virtuous wife and good mother was central to this spatialization, creating conflicts for women like Liu as they confronted the celebration of their "talented" selves as well as the regulation of where they went and what they did as women. The division between working "inside the walls of the family house or compound" and working outside is symbolically powerful, as it draws on historical and cultural images of traditional courtyard homes in China (Jacka 1997: 3–4; see also Bourdieu 1990; Moore 1986). In this case, however, the safe boundaries of the home have been extended to the walls surrounding state work units. Walls thus may be understood as a "positive technology" (Bray 2005: 125) that produced middle-class, gendered social forms.[2] The inside/outside dichotomy encompasses "a division between family and non-family" as well as a distinction between productive work and reproductive family activities (Jacka 1997: 4). In contrast to the turbulent sea of business, state employment and even physical presence inside the walls of a traditional work unit offered security and a sense of protection. These spatial distinctions produced arenas within which "forms of social life" could "operate" (Bray 2005: 145), influencing decisions young couples like Liu and her boyfriend made about how to establish some security in a time of constant reform and great flux.

Like Liu and her boyfriend, many young families decided to manage risks generated by the commodification of employment, housing, and overall reforms in the urban welfare system by deliberately deploying their human capital assets in more than one sector of the economy. This strategic management of risks across the urban economy led to a new family formation known as "one household, two systems" (*yi jia, liang zhi*). The term "*yi jia, liang zhi*" is a take-off on the phrase "*yi guo, liang zhi*" (one country, two systems) that describes the Hong Kong–China relationship after the British returned the colony to Beijing's authority in 1997. Although Hong Kong was once again a part of China, it also had its own legal and financial systems—hence, one country with two systems. "One household, two systems" refers to one person (usually the wife) staying in the state system while the spouse (usually the husband) ventured into private business. A number of families I met opted for this strategy, such as a young professor turned entrepreneur and his wife, who stayed at the university as an accountant while he "went out."[3] When I told him I was hearing from a number of people that young mothers had state-affiliated employment, he explained that "women stay [in state units] because they like the insurance, the secure feeling [*baozhang*]." When speaking about hiring practices with another young man who had started his own company and then found a foreign partner, making it a joint venture, I learned that his wife also remained in the state system. This man explained that even though he made more in one day than what she earned in a month at her job in the state-run international travel office, they thought she should work, because they were young and should learn about the world. "Her job is stable, and going out to work means you can understand more," he explained. "If you just stay at home, you are backwards. You can't meet different people or situations." The one household, two systems family formation was a way young couples maneuvered within China's socialist (and) market economy(ies) and a way gender and security were constituted and reiterated (see DeHart 2010).

Ideologies about safety, protection, and stability in an environment emphasizing change effectively promoted the idea that women were better off in positions that did not require them to travel regularly or to go out at night.[4] Men and women alike considered libraries, schools, and banks good places for women to work, because the environment (huanjing) was good, which meant, as one woman said of the bank where she would work, "the building is nice, there is air conditioning, and I won't go outside, so I won't be very tired. I will do something with the computer," although she later lamented that the work in a bank was simple and boring, "work that a trained dog would do if you just gave it some bread." I asked a DUT graduate what she said to a company that refused to hire her for a position involving travel because of worry over her safety. "I don't worry," she said, "I tell these companies I am very independent and can work alone and travel by myself, but they don't agree with me. It does not make me angry; it is the most common thing to happen to girls."

For the Communist Party, getting women out of the home and into the public patriotic workforce was an important revolutionary accomplishment that defined equality between the sexes. Yet in the post-Mao era, spatially organized narratives associated women with spaces "inside" the home, the state, and the office and with the assumed security of such spaces, in the name of protecting the reputation of the xianqi liangmu. Lu Jiulong, the manager of the forwarding office mentioned in Chapter 5, for instance, thought it was appropriate for women to stay inside the office for their safety. "Men and women each have their own advantages and weaknesses," he said. "In sales, they have to travel a lot to Heilongjiang province in the northeast, and the women have difficulties. The parents worry, and the husband is not satisfied. There also is the problem of personal security, and they have to drink and entertain the customers." To explain, he recited a poem about the drinking requirement for salespeople. "*Yao ni he, he bu he, ni bu he bu heshi* [I need them to drink, do they drink? And if they don't drink, then it is not suitable]. So, I need a man to do this work," he concluded. "They know how to drink [*hui he jiu*], and they can cope with it." He also argued that parents, boy-friends, and husbands "worried" (*bu fangxin*) if their daughters, girlfriends, or wives traveled for business. Enterprises understood their roles to be protec-tors of these young women and hence confined them to in-office work. If a woman worked in a pretty office with air-conditioning and food brought in for lunch, her reputation was safe. A man in his mid-twenties doing the hiring for a collective enterprise said he was looking for four people, including one woman to do office work (*neiqin*). The term "*neiqin*," with "*nei*" literally mean-ing "inside," referred to work done inside the office rather than outside. Concomitantly, it was understood that men were not suited to such sedentary work, because they would become restless and bored.

Emphasis on *guanxi* (relationship) building in business deals of all sorts also extended the working day late into the evening as groups of men went to dinner, drank, danced, and sang karaoke in practices of "making friends" (*jiao pengyou*) and establishing trust between partners, blurring the separation between work and leisure.[5] Women, however, were expected to "have time" (*you shijian*) to take care of family matters, buy meat, chop vegetables, pick up the child at school, and clean. Coupling these expectations with serious misgivings about the movement of women through urban spaces after dark (particularly when unaccompanied by family) often meant women were pre-cluded from participating in male business/leisure pursuits and thus from accumulating the same types and amounts of capital as men. Attempts to limit women's career potential in an atmosphere where long hours and travels could mean monetary success and social mobility denied them equal access to the cultural and economic capital-producing arena of talent. Gendered "daily paths" not only shaped subjectivity but also "enable[ed] and constrain[ed] the build-up of a somewhat different body of discursive knowledge" and material reality (Pred 1990a: 41). During my research, academics, employers, and friends all told me they thought it was suitable that I wanted to be a teacher and that my husband was in business. Being married was important as well and made my meetings with young professionals "safer." In fact, the knowledge that I aspired to what was an appropriately female profession in their estimation often made our relationships stronger. Masculine capital, on the other hand, had direct ties to economic wealth, which made young men who were "stuck" in universities and other unprofitable units undesirable husbands. Such spatialized forms of social control, "whether enforced through the power of convention or symbolism, or through the straightforward threat of violence," Doreen Massey argues, "can be a fundamental element in the constitution of gender in its (highly varied) forms" (1994: 180). Associations between women and inside work extended from office jobs to state employment in general, helping shape the one household, two systems formation. Moreover, work habits associated with some state sectors (e.g., schools, universities, libraries, banks), such as flexible working hours, unoccupied time due to overstaffing, and an early end to the workday, became feminized.

When Yang Yumei, a woman with whom I spent a good deal of time and first met in the mid-1990s, was still engaged, her future husband, Wang Xiaolong, explained to me that he had certain expectations for his future wife: "I want Yang Yumei to sacrifice [xisheng] her career to take care of family things. If I didn't have a good job and if she did, then I would sacrifice my career, but one of us must sacrifice." Yang looked over at him and raised her eyebrows, making a questioning sound before laughing. She looked at me and said, "He is conservative, but he really is very kind to me."[6] At that time, Yang was working as a teacher in a school attached to a central level ministry, but she was unhappy with the level of her students and wanted to find something else to do for her own stimulation and for some extra money. She had applied for a managerial position at Kentucky Fried Chicken downtown, and they had offered her the job. The only problem was she would have to be a waitress for the first six months, eight hours a day. The thought of being on her feet for that many hours convinced her she would be too tired, so she said no. Her future mother-in-law then got her an offer at her unit as an interpreter. "I am still thinking about it," she said. "It would mean less free time than now." Wang, however, had made it clear he did not want her to work in a foreign company or a joint venture where she would have to "work too much and too hard." Yang needed "to sacrifice" her career goals for the sake of the family, which meant staying within the state system where she had extra time and flexible working hours.

Despite proclamations that women "held up half of the sky," the "double burden" of career and family responsibilities remained a serious issue for women.[7] The restrictions Yang faced meant she could not accumulate the money and social capital she had hoped for as talent in a global city, but she could accumulate symbolic capital as a virtuous wife and good mother. It was difficult for her to watch people become rich and have "interesting" jobs while she waited to get married and pregnant, which she did. However, she also valued her future roles as a mother and wife. Her flexibility as a teacher and the proximity of family meant they would not need to worry about child care, and she could fulfill her womanhood at the same time. Yet this fulfillment was a contested and contradictory process that produced a fragmented subjecthood for professional women. Her husband changed jobs several times in the following years, regularly working in private, entrepreneurial high-tech businesses and doing very well financially. In the early 2000s, they had a new, spacious home in a convenient location, they learned how to drive and bought a car, and they invested in after-school activities for their son. By 2007, they had upgraded to a larger apartment that was beautifully decorated and located next to a highly ranked primary school. Yang remained at the state unit, but she spent much of her time taking care of her son and learning how to cook different cuisines.

One afternoon when I was talking with Li Guilan, a young woman who worked at Finance University, about how graduating seniors were finding work, she noted how important gender was. She explained that just over half the students at Finance University were female and that their college-entrance exam scores were in fact higher than those of their male counterparts,[8] but when they graduated, it was harder for the young women to find work. When I asked why, she said that "at twenty-four she gets married, has a child and then maybe won't work for one to two years. If she is from outside of Dalian, she must stay at home with the baby, because there is no family support to look after the child. Being male is a condition in the labor market, just like one's language ability."

The "limited market" in child care and domestic services (jiating fuwu) was cited by many new parents as a reason they needed flexibility in at least one parent's job, even as young rural women who saw no future in the countryside migrated to cities for these jobs (e.g., H. Yan 2003b). A professor who had gone into business said, for instance, "Domestic services are not good here in the north, and we have a small child to look after. If we both are out of the school working, then we are not sure of the time we can come to pick up our child. Anyway, women mostly look after the child." He finished by noting that, in general, "men, in terms of ability, are stronger. There are many women who are talented, but men are still stronger." This young man, like others, switched easily from a logic of the sexual division of labor to that of class-specific considerations for his small family to that of gendered ability. Such logics reinforced the spatial separations that made it morally acceptable for husbands to move into uncertain economic and social spaces beyond the confines of stable but "limiting" state positions. They were encouraged by knowledge that their wife was at home and by the legacy of a system of state-based subsidies that produced feelings of stability for urban college graduates.

Although this young man said women liked the secure feeling, one must consider how men transferred their own anxieties about security and stability onto women and the state. If women maintained the hearth in a time of flux, then perhaps one's family could be secure, even without developed social services.

In addition to forming the one household, two systems family, another risk-management strategy for young families was to move in with parents. Frequently, newborn babies were shipped off to live with grandparents so their mothers and fathers could work at their studies or jobs. Perhaps the parents wanted to get ahead in an environment of deal making and increasing salaries, or perhaps they just wanted to stay afloat in an environment of laid-off workers and shrinking pay. If the young couple had no relatives in the city in which they lived, this could mean the baby was far away from his or her parents, and visits were restricted to a few times a year, as was the case for a recent master's graduate and mother who chose to work outside the university in the convention industry. It could also mean the couple moved in with one set of grandparents to ensure they had child care.

Thus, even as narratives and disciplinary mechanisms framed women in particular spaces, stories of the every day illustrate that women regularly crossed these boundaries. Recent research by Laurie Duthie (2005) shows, for instance, that women did comparatively well in multinational companies. Because men entered the companies to do sales—jobs on the "outside"— women were hired for positions in the office, which also required stronger foreign-language ability; "a common stereotype [is] that women are better at learning a foreign language" (Duthie 2005: 5). In these jobs, the women had "greater access to corporate decision makers," had the opportunity to build trusting relationships with the expatriate managers, and thus often were chosen for promotions over males in their cohort (Duthie 2005: 6). Gendered ideas about the appropriateness of women in those positions were produced by the women applying, local personnel managers, and expatriate managers who assumed men would be good at some jobs and women at others (Duthie 2005: 6). The success of young women in these companies and their promotions to positions with greater authority illustrate that despite appeals to morality, family responsibility, and appropriate femininity, women found ways to live with and to resist potentially conflicting narratives of what was desired in post-Mao times—being a xianqi liangmu and being a high-quality worker. In discussions with one young woman, who was secretary to the president of a large Sino-U.S. joint venture, about her future plans, she forcefully said, "A Chinese man considers his wife his accessory [fushupin]." While she hoped to marry, she acknowledged it would be difficult for someone like her. She was a college graduate, was proud of her professional accomplishments, and had a very high salary for someone her age. She considered that only a businessman who made more than she did would probably be willing to accept her salary, but she noted that most had little education, creating a real dilemma for her as successful talent in the city.

Zhang Xue is another good example of someone who negotiated her often-conflicting identities as a mother, a woman, and a well-educated, ambitious career-oriented professional. We met for the first time at a municipal job fair in the fall of 1995, when a young woman who spotted me came over to practice what she was going to say to a Taiwanese man who was testing everyone's English as part of the interview process. Upon speaking English, I was immediately surrounded and was asked what company I was representing, what I was doing there, and where I was from. Zhang, who was at the far end of the hall helping her husband find employees for his company, saw me, a foreign woman, being surrounded. She quickly came over, knowing that her English was very good and certain she could help me out of the situation.

When she appeared at my side, having easily maneuvered through the growing crowd, she began chatting in English and asked what I was doing there. I explained I was doing research about the new talent market and about how people were making employment decisions. Never wanting to miss an opportunity to interview someone, just as those surrounding me never wanted to miss an opportunity to practice their English, I asked Zhang what she did and how many jobs she had had. Her current position selling industrial equipment was in the second company for which she had worked. I asked why she had switched jobs, and Zhang responded, "Because I got pregnant, and they did not want a pregnant employee. And," she added with emphasis, "I have self-respect, so I left that company." She and her husband struggled with the decision to keep the baby, ultimately deciding to go ahead and to move in with her parents for help with child care. Like Liu, who was deciding between the foreign firm and the tax bureau, Zhang negotiated between often-conflicting norms and forms of regulation.

Several days after meeting Zhang at the job fair, I called her at her office and suggested we get together. She seemed quite excited. "What shall we do?" she asked "Go shopping?" Shopping was not what I had in mind for someone who had blurted out issues of self-respect in the middle of a crowded scene.[9] Zhang and her husband had met at university. He was studying for his doctorate in civil engineering while she was getting her master's degree in mechanical engineering. "When I went to school in 1985, it was what all the best students studied. The ones with the highest entrance scores went into these areas, and the ones with the lower scores studied literature, accounting, trade, and foreign language. But when I graduated, it wasn't fair—all the good jobs were for the humanities students. Engineers went to factories and to state-run units, while the others got to go to better jobs where they could make more money. But now that has changed around, so that the best students go into foreign trade, law, and foreign language and then find good jobs when they leave." This explained why her brother, who was number one in his provincial college entrance exam, was in Beijing, studying foreign trade and preparing for the GMAT so he could apply to U.S. MBA programs. Zhang herself opted for graduate school to better her chances.

After finishing her thesis, she had nothing to do before graduation, so she found a job through a friend. Zhang sold technical products at this company and often went out of town to make sales calls, but she had recently married and was pregnant before she knew it, with morning sickness making her feel awful on these trips. Her boss told her she could not do the work, and it was not going to work out with her being pregnant. Yet having the child was not an easy decision for her. "It was too early for us. If I hadn't had my child then, I probably still wouldn't have a child now" [about three years later]. Zhang and her husband were tormented with the decision but decided to keep the baby. Much later, the following spring, she told me that this boss called her home several times, trying to get her to come back to work for the company. She would put him off and not really say no until one day her mother answered the phone and got very angry with him about the way he had treated her daughter. The boss never called back again.

Zhang and her husband decided to move in with her parents so they could watch their son and she could go back to her career selling imported machinery in the oil industry. Zhang readily admitted that Chinese women had to work and take care of the home, but her reasoning was that they dealt with it because otherwise the families had no money. Zhang did not present it as a case of nature but rather as one of reason, a reason that allowed people to be consumers and to fulfill their desires to acquire goods. "There is no choice if they want money. If both of them are at home, and they spend more time together and share in the duties more equally, then they have no money. They would not have nice furniture, decorations in the home, clothes and toys for the child. This way they have material satisfaction." When I asked her what she did about the housework, since she and her husband worked long hours, she made a fairly forceful hand motion of pushing away and said with emphasis, "We push it onto our parents. If my parents weren't willing to raise my son, then we would go to his parents' home. But my parents are not only willing, they spoil my son. Anyway," she continued, "the service sector, day care, and things like that are not very developed in China."

New insecurities generated by the phasing out of state distributions to urban families and the commodification of such necessities as housing meant that making money was fundamental for families. The material reality of little trustworthy nonstate day care and home help conflicted directly with modernization strategies that called for educated people to be out in the public working world and for the development of a middle class, but coincided with the free labor of women and the desire by many young women to locate their identities in such "natural" child-bearing activities.[10] These conditions did not stop Zhang and her husband, however. Zhang learned of a five-day school for children age five years and older, and they sent their son to this boarding school for several years. They moved into their own, newly built apartment and devoted themselves to developing their real estate company. Several years later, when I visited Zhang, she took me to their office building, where her son was playing on the computer, and then she showed me the new upscale housing community they had constructed next door. Her role was to take care of things in the office, while her husband went out to negotiate contracts and to find new business opportunities. She justifiably was proud of their economic and business success, but Zhang also positioned herself as an educated professional. She regularly met with a group of female classmates—all with graduate degrees and successful in their own careers—to read books and have discussions. They began with the Chinese classic *Journey to the West* and at that time were reading Adam Smith's *Wealth of Nations*.

Constant iterations of these gender regimes did not mean transgressions did not occur, nor did it mean the uncontested production of ideal middle-class masculinity and femininity. Ambitious professional women learned how to meet their own needs, whether by finding the right mates for their futures or by managing to have children and careers at the same time. And women who chose not to marry, were lesbians, or did not or could not have children struggled with the post-Mao norms of sexuality that normalized heterosexual reproduction (see Evans 1995; Rofel 2007). These young women transgressed boundaries of morality, renegotiating what was acceptable at the same time that these discourses produced "commonsense" distinctions of gender and nature.

These stories also illustrate how labor could be a site of self-reflection and meaning for educated workers at a time when, as Lisa Rofel argues, "the category 'labor' as a foundation for liberation or identity" had waned (1999: 19).

In her work on different generations of silk workers in Hangzhou, Rofel states that although the older generation of workers narrated stories that pointed to labor in a socialist job as a site of social meaning and identity, what Margery Wolf calls "a symbol of their personal liberation from the tyranny of domestic labor" (1985: 60) in their bid to "figur[e] out how to 'become' women," the younger cohort of workers had turned more exclusively to naturalized ideas of motherhood, heterosexual monogamy, and hyperfemininity to determine their identities (Rofel 1999: 19). Liu and Zhang certainly felt tension between the category "woman" and the category "*rencai*" (talent), but their difficulties suggested that in post-Mao times employment could be an important source of identity for young professional women.

At times, the goals and dreams of these young people contradicted what was expected of them as gendered individuals; at others, these distinctions and prohibitions were said to express unproblematic "natural" differences between the sexes. Under Mao Zedong, and particularly during the Cultural Revolution, the Party considered self-adornment bourgeois and politically dangerous, stifling sexual expression for many. A masculinized working class norm became the Party's ideal. Women were expected to do the same jobs as men and even look like them. When the reform era began and official policies allowed increased social differentiation and expressions of femininity, cultural struggles over the meaning of femaleness and maleness ensued, producing a situation in which "gender became visible, audible, and full of controversy" (Gilmartin et al. 1994: 10; see also Anagnost 1989a).[11] As gender relations were reworked, men and women turned away from class struggle and from ideals of "androgynous" laboring bodies (that took the male body as the norm) to "celebrat[e] the 'recovery' of the *natural genders* buried beneath a supposedly asexual socialism" (Rofel 1999: 19; emphasis added). Even in intellectual communities, women discarded the Maoist state category of woman (*funu*), because it had "de-sexed" women, and instead opted for terms that focused on differences from men, such as *nuren* (woman) and *nuxing* (female; Barlow 1991a, 1994),[12] and differences rooted in biological and scientific discourses.[13] Similar to the "naturalization" of new social class distinctions discussed in Chapter 5, people contrasted these post-Mao distinctions between men and women to what were termed the "unnatural attempt[s] to change innate femininity" during Mao's rule (Rofel 1999: 218; see also Evans 1995; Jacka 1997).

Yet these naturalized sex differences were not just an expression of a person's "'animal' behavior," which one finds in Western evolutionary theories

(Yanagisako and Delaney 1995: 6), for they were heavily infused with a class-specific sense of morality that referred to what was appropriate (*heshi*) for a professional male or female. Along with this resurgence of natural femininity was the popularization of the virtuous wife and good mother (*xianqi liangmu*) ideal that was imbued with moral meaning, making deviations not only potentially unnatural but also possible acts of moral transgression. The experiences of Liu, Yang, and Zhang resonate with class-formation processes in other parts of Asia, where cultural struggles over femininity, masculinity, the home, professional credentials, and respected career success were "key aspects of the cultural production" of professionalism and middle class–ness (Stivens 1998: 116; see also Ong 1991, 1995; PuruShotam 1998).

Refiguring the State and Masculinity with Reforms in Urban Welfare

In addition to employment in the state sector and distinctions between inside and outside, reforms in the socialist urban welfare package itself have been central to production of gender norms and professionalism in post-Mao China. The legacy of state distributions of jobs, housing, ration coupons, and other necessities for living in the city meant that even as people had employment opportunities outside the state sector, they associated the state with stability, particularly in terms of housing provisions. Young families acknowledged the rapid change in their lifetimes and wondered how they could partake in the promise of prosperity while establishing some stability in their lives. Although commodification of labor, housing, and medical care offered the opportunity for men and women not to rely on the state, the reality was that many families in Dalian, especially in the late 1990s, not only remained tied to the state sector but also wanted to keep these ties. Acquiring a certain standard of housing was particularly important for this growing urban middle class and was intimately linked with constructions of masculinity for many of the young professionals, echoing cultural traditions of living with the husband's family and socialist practices of distributing housing through the husband's work unit. Private purchase was beyond the reach of most young people starting their careers, but finding a way to secure home ownership reflected on a man's sense of self and masculinity.

Wu Kaizhuang, who I originally met at a municipal job fair and discussed in Chapter 4, was convinced that his lack of housing or a high salary that would enable him to purchase an apartment on his own was why he was not yet engaged. We had numerous conversations about his love-life troubles. He pined for younger women even as he moved well into his thirties, which he felt was an old age not to be married. The women he found attractive often told him their families objected to their relationship because his job was not stable, as he was in a private company. These feelings of instability were confounded by his lack of housing. I would try to reassure him he was still young and had time to find other work and to meet the right woman, but he responded by reminding me that things were "different in China." Several years later, Wu purchased an apartment, but it was far from the city center, so he continued to live with his parents. Thus, although the state reduced its guarantee of housing and employment, ideas about stability, security, and the state intermingled, reproducing cultural ideologies of masculinity and femininity.

Under high socialism, a job assignment to an urban work unit gave college graduates access to the socialist welfare package of guaranteed salaries, ration coupons, medical care, pensions, and housing, known as cradle-to-grave security or the iron rice bowl. Although city governments also built some housing,[14] most college graduates, as members of state-sector units, received housing from the state through their workplaces. Reproducing earlier cultural patterns of brides moving to their grooms' homes and an emphasis on patrilineality, units generally distributed housing to its married male members and expected its married female members to live in apartments at their husbands' units.[15] Also, the legacy of socialist welfare meant that many families still lived in and relied upon subsidized housing from the work unit in the late 1990s (Whyte 2005),[16] leading to tensions around welfare reforms, as people assumed that the government had a "matching obligation" to provide security and services (Croll 1999: 685).

Worries about security and stability were common topics in interviews, but associating the state (and its material reality in the form of housing) with such feelings in a time of continuing layoffs and economic uncertainty is noteworthy. In particular, it was the central state (*guojia*) that people "trusted" and thought would care for (*baohu*) them, while they often critiqued "the local state" (*zhengfu*) for "poor administration and corruption" (Cheek 2006: 30).[17] As challenges to subsidized and state-distributed housing progressed and families realized they would have to pay more of their own income for housing, a number of couples said that they looked to the husbands' units for help with housing (e.g., through low-interest loans) and to the wifes' for what they called a decoration fee (*zhuangxiu fei*). In the first years of the reform era, households generally paid very little rent for their living space (1 percent of cash income in the 1980s [J. Zhu 2000: 508]), although that

FIGURE 6.1 New housing community. *(Courtesy of Lisa Hoffman.)*

has increased dramatically with the phasing out of distribution mechanisms and subsidized units.

When I was in Dalian in 2003, I was struck by the number of new housing projects that had been built in the city (Figure 6.1). Discussions of price per square meter permeated everyday conversations, as did comments on home decoration. Families invited me to their homes to show off their shiny, new spaces. Not all the families I visited had purchased their homes from commercial developers, however, for two processes of housing commodification have developed in China, creating what some have called a "dual-housing market" (J. Zhu 2000; see also Bian et al. 1997; P. Lee 1995). First, work units (*danwei*) have been privatizing their housing stock by selling flats to their occupants. Prices in these exchanges have been highly subsidized and based on a person's number of years at the unit, rank, and salary. Professors I knew, for instance, acquired "ownership" of their existing apartments this way and then used their own funds to upgrade what for many were poor living conditions. Other state-owned units invested in new buildings (sometimes with private developers) and "sold" them to long-time unit members at similarly discounted prices. A few people told me in the late 1990s, however, that their units were resisting directives to privatize *danwei* housing and that unit leaders were finding ways to continue subsidizing this high-socialist-era benefit.

Second, the central government had been pushing for diversification of housing providers and a greater commercial presence in the housing market. Most of the colorful and even flashy housing compounds have been developed by private companies. The housing compound developed by Zhang and her husband's company is a good example of the new residential developments appearing throughout the city. These compounds, often termed "gardens" (*huayuan*) and "communities" (*shequ*), targeted a variety of population segments, leading Li Zhang to argue that class identity in contemporary urban China has a distinct spatial quality (2008).[18]

Although more people were buying private homes in the early 2000s with loans from employers and banks, the majority of young professional families I interviewed, particularly in the late 1990s, could not afford the risks of leaving the state system all together, even as their confidence in the long-term stability of the state was tested and they willingly acknowledged that no job was safe forever. So although it was increasingly possible for a husband and wife to work in "unstable" locations and secure housing on their own and without any subsidy, it was not the norm. Even in 2000, according to government statistics, more than 55 percent of Dalian's workforce was in the state sector, compared to 32.2 percent in nonstate and noncollective ("other ownership") workplaces.[19]

As argued above, families managed these new economic (versus political) risks in several ways, such as spreading their human capital across sectors of the economy. Others, such as Pan Deren, simply lived with his parents in the apartment they received from the state many years earlier. Pan, however, resisted the pressure from his parents to get married precisely because he did not have his own home. "My parents are not satisfied. They don't like that I don't have a girlfriend. There is no daughter-in-law, they say. They want me to find a housewife [*jiating funu*] who will support my work. You know, if I had my own separate house, a lot of things could be solved." In addition to freedom from his parents, housing symbolized married life and family life for Pan. Yet for someone who worked outside the state system—and who changed jobs frequently—the likelihood of getting an apartment or at least a subsidized one was low. Unlike earlier socialist state policies of apartment distribution that led to early marriages so people could get on the waiting list for an apartment, Pan resisted finding a *jiating funu* to live with him and his parents. In fact, he found numerous ways to resist the pressure he felt from his parents.

When he lost his job, for instance, he avoided telling his parents by leaving the house every morning, playing tennis with friends during the day, and returning in the evening. By the time he found another position, his parents had never realized he had been unemployed.

Managing Risks for Middle-Class Families

Similar to reforms in employment allocation that adopted market mechanisms and practices of choice, challenges to the urban welfare system presented new kinds of "intersecting risks" (Mole 2008) for families, suggesting it is important that we not "conceptually compartmentalize" risk-management strategies "into separate realms of employment, family life, and so on" (Ekinsmyth 1999: 354). Management of and engagement with these risks occurred through decisions and choices neither necessary nor available under high socialism. The strategic gendered deployment of the family's "assets" in the one household, two systems family formation highlights how choice in the contemporary moment has a calculative and economic quality. It also underlines the manner in which risk was not necessarily something to be avoided but was also "productive" of "risk-taking" subjects and their spatial positionings, as Liu's desire to work in the foreign company illustrates (see Zaloom 2004). In fact, many new graduates complained that their parents wanted them to work in stable and traditional jobs in the state sector, while they longed for ways to develop their careers and fulfill their potential in more risky positions. Song Yan's father, mentioned in Chapter 3, commented that his daughter's generation "liked a lot more adventure and risk [maoxian]" and that they had "less sense of responsibility to the government for training them." Later, Song told me that "when the country was closed, people had old ideas. For example, my parents thought they should work their whole life for the country, but our ideas have changed a lot in ten years."

Yet as Liu's story also reminds us, risk was experienced in gendered ways in the city; discourses of femininity and masculinity were central to professional self-understanding and subject formation. Companies, job applicants, and parents regularly commented that some jobs were better for women or men, more suitable for one or the other, and even naturally better for one or the other to do, setting up boundaries in an environment of shifting identities and increasing risks. As I argue throughout this book, choices are not simply experiences of freedom, nor are they a naturally occurring human characteristic. Rather, choice is a vital technology in the making of professional subjectivity. Calculative choices by young couples to adopt the one house-hold, two systems formation, to "jump into the sea" (*xia hai*) of private busi-ness, or to postpone marriage until they had secured their own home worked through a calculative process of decision making that incorporated market rationalities and their attendant risks, embodying what Fabian Muniesa, Yuval Millo, and Michel Callon term "economic agencement" (2007; see also Rose 1996b). They propose the notion of agencement to help understand how "market devices" are a part of subject formation. The subject then "is not external to the device," for "subjectivity is enacted in a device" (Muniesa, Millo, and Callon 2007: 2).[20] The Maoist era also certainly exhibited calculat-ing choices, but those decisions were about managing quotas from the state, hoarding what resources the work unit had, and making trades with other unit leaders—a different form of economics than the market device being incorporated into subject forms today. Mayfair Yang's work has shown, for instance, that strategies to acquire goods and resources in the Maoist and early reform eras relied on personal relations, so a "gift economy" essentially func-tioned alongside the formal state redistributive system (M. Yang 1994).

This historically specific understanding of how particular economic devices are a part of subject formation also differs from Pierre Bourdieu's more generalized discussion of "economism" and the "balance sheets" people use to make decisions, whether about economic or symbolic capital. My analysis takes "balance sheet" calculations, what Nikolas Rose describes as "calculative choice," as a technique that is a part of the subject-formation process and as being specifically framed around acts of autonomous self-enterprise. In addi-tion, although I find Bourdieu's analysis of how symbolic capital is accrued (and the economic rationality of these processes) very helpful, I do not want to analyze the young professionals' decisions as "disguising" or "concealing" some real material forms of capital (see Bourdieu 1972: 171–183). DUT graduates explained how they "calculated" the number of years they would have to work in a foreign firm at a higher wage to afford a home in the private commercial market. They then compared this to benefits from state work-places, especially higher-level ministries that offered subsidized housing, interest-free loans, and even direct distribution of apartments as long as they stayed with the unit for a certain amount of time (e.g., five or ten years). After going through the numbers, they often concluded it made more sense to stay with the state system to secure housing—echoing the decisions Liu and her boyfriend faced. Decisions by the young families I met were clearly not only market-based calculative decisions, for they intersected with the symbolic and material legacy of the state welfare system as well as gendered distinctions between "inside" and "outside." Yet they also did not conceal some other reality from these young people. Rather, such choices and calculations helped shape the norm of professionalism itself.

In each chapter of this book, I take a different look at the emerging professional subject and emphasize the multiple governmental technologies, norms, and regulatory regimes at play in a variety of domains. In this chapter, I focus on how gender norms and links made between the state sector and feelings of security are a part of the subject-formation process. Not only was the state associated with security because of the legacy of the welfare package that came with a job assignment in an urban work unit, but the state also came to represent a safe, "inside" space, particularly for women—even as guarantees associated with state employment continued to diminish. In addition, because work units under high socialism typically distributed housing— a key benefit of this welfare package—to its married male members, this legacy of state security and challenges inherent to reforms were linked with the production of masculinity as well.

Yet, as evidenced by the one household, two systems family formation, challenges to the socialist urban welfare package and new insecurities in urban life did not mean that the state had retreated and disappeared. Reforms in housing, for instance, certainly have shifted the responsibility for acquiring it from the state to the work unit, and increasingly to the individual employee.[21] Rather than state planners being the authorities in this process, new practices of calculation in families and new sites of decision making have emerged. The responsibilization of the self and the local (as in procurement of housing) and the regulation of individuals through their calculative choices (as in decisions about where to work) are neoliberal technologies of governing. Yet this discussion has also emphasized that neoliberal governmentality in late-socialist China is not separated from the state—that is, *de-statized*— in the same way that it is in other advanced liberal regimes. The redeployment of housing subsidies, whether through workplace-based home loans, distribution of housing as long as a person stays at a unit, or offers of decoration fees are some examples. The late-socialist governmentality I describe in this book includes a strong state presence, albeit now in conjunction with a diversity of forms and sites of governing. This governmentality-informed analysis of talent in the global Chinese city not only elucidates late-socialist neoliberalism but also offers tools to study unexpected social formations in other sites as well.

7

Going Forward

China, Neoliberalism, and Economic Crises

> The world is undergoing a knowledge revolution, unique in the speed and pervasiveness of change. The codification of our scientific understanding of nature and the rapid dissemination and exploitation of all knowledge are driving this revolution. China cannot afford to miss this. It must seize the 21st century—exploiting knowledge to regain its place in the world economy. (Dahlman and Aubert 2001: 3)

I begin with this quote from the World Bank Report *China and the Knowledge Economy: Seizing the 21st Century,* published just prior to China's accession to the World Trade Organization, for a reason. The logic in the report clearly supports China's post-Mao emphasis on developing the nation's human resources and raising the quality of the population. The report provides numerous recommendations to China about how to develop its "human capital" and the kinds of governmental changes that are needed for success in the twenty-first century, such as less governmental "control" of labor markets, decentralization of decision making, and utilization of the country's "entrepreneurial people" (Dahlman and Aubert 2001: 5). Such recommendations are based on a governmental rationality that takes the market as a marker of "good" government, especially in contrast to high-socialist central planning and population-control measures. It also marks the contemporary moment as one that needs particular kinds of talented human capital and human-capital investments—even in times of economic crisis.

Similarly, a recent white paper on employment in China issued by the Chinese Information Office of the State Council underlines the role of the market in the distribution of workers and the importance of self-employment and entrepreneurship:

> It is necessary to give more play to the fundamental role of the market mechanism in the allocation of labor resources, and form, in particular, a new employment pattern characterized by free choice of jobs by laborers. In view of the trend of diversification of employment demands, it is necessary to introduce flexible and different forms of employment according to circumstances; to improve the environment for starting businesses, and to encourage individuals to start their own businesses, so as to promote employment. (China's Employment Situation and Policies 2004)

Together, we may understand these two quotes as underscoring neoliberal governmental technologies in China, such as the marketization of labor distribution, the fostering of a self-enterprising ethic, and an emphasis on individual choice and autonomy rather than state distribution. And yet this white paper further explains that China has a "proactive employment policy" that aims to develop the economy, diverse job opportunities, and employment services.

These policies include, for instance, the government's role in promoting industries that offered competitiveness in the knowledge economy and policies that subsidized certain career paths in response to a slowing global economy and crises in credit markets, the financial industry, real estate, and employment. The information technology industry (IT), a "pillar" of Dalian's current economy, was slated to be "boosted" by the government, for example, "to create more than 1.5 million jobs in three years," including almost 1 million positions for college graduates (*China Daily* 2009a). As factories producing lower-tech consumer goods for export closed across southern China in late 2008 and 2009, forcing the return migration to rural areas for many Chinese workers, investments in industries in the "knowledge economy" continued. In another case, because of the tight employment market in 2009, a college graduate who had promised his parents he would find a job in Beijing had taken advantage of policies that encouraged graduates to go to smaller cities—without being assigned to such a city. The report on this young man notes that those who remain in jobs in such places "for at least three years will receive financial subsidies or preferential treatment in graduate school entrance exams and public service tests later. . . . Students are now encouraged to work in less developed areas, in small or private companies, to join the army or start their own businesses" (*China Daily* 2009b). In light of the tight market, the central government also asked universities "to expand their job placement services" and local governments to begin "recruitment campaigns" that encouraged graduates to take certain positions and help maintain social stability. Preferential admissions, subsidies, and tax breaks for small businesses, as well as the state's investment in the IT industry, are all examples of proactive policies. These quotes thus also speak to ongoing global debates about the state's role in the marketplace.

In this book, I have examined the intersection of more and less "distanced" (Rose 1996b) modes of governing, illustrated most explicitly in patriotic professionalism. Graduates and young professionals in China have grown accustomed to mutual choice and the market-based allocation of workers. In pursuing their careers, they actively engaged in self-focused development while also keeping the nation in mind. The Director of Dalian University of Technology's (DUT) career guidance office explained in 2003, "The graduates want the country to be powerful [*qiangda*]. . . . In the past, they just had to wait for a job assignment. Now they have individual aspirations. Society also has needs though. Only by fulfilling all kinds of needs can there be development. If the country does become powerful, they will not necessarily have their own development. So, we encourage our students to consider the country." In explaining the work of their office, the director wanted me to understand that an individual's desires, society's needs, and an enterprise's requirements all needed to coincide for development to occur. Guidance (*zhidao*) by her and her colleagues required thinking about this combination and how they could explain to students not only that they should find jobs where they could develop themselves and their skills but also that they had a social responsibility and should consider the country if they wanted to make it strong. The logic embedded in her comments combined a rationality found in the World Bank Report with official and popular discourses of caring for the nation. These quotes also illustrate the blending of neoliberal technologies of governing and socialist politics of nation building and ethics of self-formation in contemporary governmental rationalities in China.

One could take a number of analytical perspectives to study the cultivation of talent in the global city and China's turn to science, technology, and higher education as productive forces. The analysis here has been informed by what Michel Foucault calls an "analytic" of truth and government that asks questions about "how" governing occurs, particularly when one "way of doing things" (e.g., central state planning) was problematized (see Foucault 1991, 1997a; Gordon 1991). It is this analytical stance that helps us understand that job choice was a different way of doing things and thus could be analyzed as a technique of governing that also specified how the governed—cities and professionals—conducted themselves. As such, making choices is not taken as a naturally occurring human attribute but rather as a cultivated form of personhood; willful subjects who make choices do not exist a priori but are enabled through force relations. By arguing that choice is a technique of governing, I do not mean to suggest that no change has taken place in China or that the state controls who does what, when, and where. Rather, this analysis emphasizes that neoliberalism is about the refiguring of the state rather than the retreat of the state and the end of governance.

It is important when analyzing professional subjectivity and late-socialist neoliberalism to have conceptual flexibility for making sense of unexpected and undocumented governmental forms. In this book, I offer an approach with that flexibility by analytically disaggregating the various elements that constitute late-socialist governmentality and by examining norms and mechanisms of governing across social domains. Specifically, I argue that a governmentality approach is a productive way to make sense of governmental forms that combine devices, mechanisms, modes of self-care, and political projects with diverse historical trajectories and genealogies. This approach allows one to recognize the presence of neoliberal techniques in China but also to understand that they did not necessarily predetermine the political or social formations that emerged. The neoliberal governmentality we see in China, moreover, is not a duplication, imitation, or corruption of some original or pure Western form of neoliberalism, nor has it simply deceived the young professionals to support capitalist political projects. In addition, the combination of autonomous choice, the marketization of labor, proactive employment policies by the Chinese state, and the linking of national strength and individual career development did not necessarily produce fundamental incompatibilities for the individuals. Instead the wedding of self-focused career development with a socialist duty to the nation—enacted through labor—produced patriotic professionalism. This is not to say that it has been an uncontested and seamless process, for much of my discussion in this book highlights the difficulties and contradictions the young people faced as well. Opportunity and insecurity went hand in hand for them as they negotiated sometimes-conflicting norms; embraced new alignments of status, wealth, and education as rational; and faced the naturalization of class distinctions in the city.

Although the analysis of China generally and of new employment markets more specifically provides an opportunity to recognize generative forms of neoliberalism in non-Western sites, it also offers a moment to reflect on the contingent, diverse, and yet interrelated nature of neoliberal governmental forms themselves. In this sense, neoliberalism may be described as a global form, where global refers not to an all-encompassing universal but rather to "a distinctive capacity for decontextualization and recontextualization, abstractability and movement, across diverse social and cultural situations and spheres of life" (Collier and Ong 2005: 11). This capacity also means we should not be surprised to find different forms of neoliberalism and change in the constitution of such forms over time, a perspective that may be helpful in making sense of the 2008–2009 global financial crisis. For example, within Western neoliberalism, we can see changes since the height of Frederick Hayek's and Milton Friedman's influence at the University of Chicago and the Ronald Reagan and Margaret Thatcher free-market ideologies. A "Beijing Consensus" was identified (Ramo 2004), for instance, that offered a different combination of markets, international development, and definitions of global citizenship than the Washington Consensus did (see also Hoffman, DeHart, and Collier 2006). More recently, Gordon Brown's "nationalization" of British banks with the credit crisis has shifted the way governments think about how global capitalism may work. French President Nicolas Sarkozy was quoted as saying in September 2008 that "self-regulation, to fix all problems, is over. Laissez-faire is over." And in a recent column, Nobel Prize for Economics winner Paul Krugman writes that Wall Street is essentially "a ward of the state, every bit as dependent on government aid as recipients of Temporary Aid to Needy Families, aka 'welfare'" (2009).

Identification of a Beijing Consensus, London's leadership, and the partial nationalization of major financial institutions in the United States and Europe do not portend the end, however, of markets as a test of "good" governing or the emphasis on entrepreneurship and innovation. As this crisis leads to critical reflections on the system—perhaps reflections that will be sustained over time—the possibility exists that new understandings of how best to govern may emerge. Therefore, it is particularly urgent that we have the tools to reflect on the regimes of governing that emerge to fix new problems. Thus, the approach in this book may contribute to current discussions about the appropriate mix of state regulation and free-market activities generated by the crisis and seen in debates about government bailouts for specific industries, Barack Obama's fiscal stimulus plan, and Congress's role in regulating the financial industry. Moreover, by taking a governmentality perspective, and more specifically by disaggregating the various elements that constitute neoliberalism, we may better understand not only how governing occurs but also what is at stake in these governmental forms.

In this book, I also speak to the current global moment, and the analysis of capitalist crises more generally, through my focus on employment and production. Although many studies of the new professional middle classes have centered on people's consumption practices and lifestyle choices, the current economic slowdown and dissolution of private wealth reminds us that labor is a critical lens to understand self- and class formation as well as what matters in these processes. In addition, the current crisis in overconsumption and focus on sustainability remind us we must keep questions of production on the research agenda. In this book, I also focus on the formation of talented human capital and professionalism at a time of great change in China, specifically the decade following the acceleration of reforms after Deng Xiaoping's 1992 southern tour. Human resources and the enterprising capacity of workers have been touted by politicians and pundits alike as a fundamental strength in such shifts, whether in China or the United States. In this book, therefore, I speak to this governmental concern and offer a way to analyze the fostering, training, and production of talented personnel.

Anthropological fieldwork—and a focus on subject formation—lends itself well to such inquiries. Subjectivity does not necessarily follow ideological lines of political projects, allowing us to understand how neoliberalism and socialism, for instance, may intersect. In China, multiple techniques and norms across a variety of domains, including global city building, rationalities of enterprise, job choice, discourses of *wenhua* and *suzhi,* remnants of the welfare package, and gender regimes, have shaped the emergence of professionalism. This process has necessarily been about the government of others, such as household registration restrictions, and about the government of the self, as in projects of self-improvement and self-enterprise. Thus, this study has not concentrated on the relationship between the state and its subjects but has considered further regulatory regimes and normative concepts that shape how people act upon themselves and upon others. As we concern ourselves with new forms of governing, we must remember that the production of subjects and spaces occurs in a variety of domains and through various forms of social ordering and technologies. Recognizing the diversity of sites and norms shaping subjectivity and the tensions between points of truth in these practices also illustrates how becoming a professional, and subject formation broadly, is a heterogeneous and contested experience.

Notes

CHAPTER 1

1. This was a common refrain from Senator John McCain and Senator Barack Obama during the 2008 presidential campaign season.

2. The "socialist market economy" was formally adopted at the 14th Party Congress in 1992, after the "planned commodity economy" that had been adopted in 1984 and the "socialist planned commodity economy" in 1987 (Wong and Zheng 2001).

3. The entrepreneurialization of city management and the related processes of inter-urban competition, the commodification of place, and the appearance of new geographies of city-regions and strategic hubs have been noted by many urban scholars. See Broudehoux 2004; Dirlik 1999; Friedman 2002; Harvey 1989b; Jessop 1998, 1999; Jessop and Sum 2000; Liu, Ji, and Chang 1994; Scott 2001; Sum 1999; Wu 2003.

4. By far, the greatest number of students in 1980, almost 74 percent, was at teaching colleges. See China Statistical Yearbook 1981: 445.

5. China Statistical Yearbook 2001: 652. These numbers are for graduates of all Regular Institutions of Higher Education. The number of enrollments jumped to more than twenty million in 2008.

6. Following Michel Foucault's writings on governmentality, this concern with the health and wealth of the population is called "bio-politics."

7. In 1990, there were 9,313 graduates (Liaoning Economic Statistical Yearbook 1990: 269), and in 2000, there were 13,971 graduates (Dalian Statistical Yearbook 2000: 414), an increase of 50 percent.

8. The announcement was made in March 2007. See www.liaoning-gateway.com/74593067851579392/20070330/2188970.shtml. In a separate interview, the CEO noted that "what the Dalian government plans for its development in the next few years is in correspondence to the self-innovation China's central government has been calling for." See http://www.runsky.com/2007-03/27/content_939556.htm.

9. It also is important to ask whether "neoliberal" should be modifying "subject" in any situation.

10. Policies adopted after *nanxun,* Deng's southern tour, have led to significant changes in the country, leading *nanxun* to be described as "a political landmark," marking "a new era" (Wong and Zheng 2001: 3, 7), and "a watershed" in China's reforms (Ding 2001: 51). Although I use this political event as an important marker in this discussion, see also Wang Hui's identification of 1989 rather than 1992 as key to phases of intellectual debates about neoliberalism (2004).

11. Prior to his 1992 tour, foreign direct investment during 1979–1991 totaled US$23.3 billion, and after *nanxun,* it jumped dramatically to US$287 billion for the period 1991–1999 (J. Wong 2001: 44). In Dalian, foreign investments also increased after 1992. For example, up to the end of 1990, Japan led Hong Kong in investments with US$551 million, but by the spring of 1993, investments attributed to Hong Kong totaled US$1.1 billion, Japan US$900 million, the United States US$270 million, Taiwan US$170 million, and Korea US$100 million (Jacobs and Hong 1994: 244, 252).

12. Urban population increases are due to natural population growth, rural-to-urban migration, and the regular reclassification of administrative areas in China. This helps to explain the jump from 193 cities in 1978 to 663 registered cities in 2000 (K. Zhang 2004: 35). On the rural-to-urban migration and factory production that has been fueling this growth, see Anagnost 2004; Pun 2005; Solinger 1999; H. Yan 2003a, 2003b; L. Zhang 2001.

13. By problematization, I mean "the ensemble of discursive and non-discursive practices that make something enter into the play of true and false and constitute it as an object of thought (whether in the form of moral reflection, scientific knowledge, political analysis, etc.)" (Foucault, *Dits et ecrits,* 4:670; quoted in Rabinow and Rose 1994: xviii). See also Foucault 1997d.

14. Here, I build on the work of Li Zhang (2001), who makes a clear distinction between late and high socialism in China.

15. A rich literature is available on the self-fashioning of middle-class identity through consumption and individual choices. See, for example, Chua 2000; Davis 2000a; Farrer 2002; Fong 2004; Liechty 2003; Pinches 1999; Robison and Goodman 1996; L. Zhang 2008. See also Mei Zhan's argument about how the discursive and visceral aspects of consumption actually produce "unruly subjectivities and identities" (2005: 32). In this book, I argue that choice (e.g., as used in discussions of consumption) is precisely the kind of practice that we should analyze as a technique of governing.

16. The literature embedded more directly in debates about the relationship among economic liberalization, the rise of a public sphere, democratic political movements, and the constitution of class in and of itself is vast. See Embong 2001; Fernandes 2006; Goldman 1995, 1999; Madsen 1993; Pearson 1997; Pun 2005; Saich 1994; Wakeman 1993. See also Wang Hui's discussion of intellectual debates on these topics and what he

argues was a post-1989 "alliance that had been struck between the state and special interest groups in their common desire to combat social movements" (2004: 42). A number of recent studies have questioned the direct link between economic liberalization and political opposition (e.g., Wang 2004), although they still frame their analyses around this process, the chances for political evolution, and the search for the political "will to act" (Pearson 1997: 27; see also D. Goodman 1996, 1999; Robison and Goodman 1996; Rocca 1994). New cultural expressions in music, art, television, and radio talk shows have also been presented as evidence of a middle class (although not currently politicized), and religious associations, clubs, and women's groups are offered as evidence of voluntary associations. See Davis et al. 1995; Goldman 1999; Hertz 1998; Whyte 1992; M. Yang 1989a, 1999. These associations denote the possibility of the development of a civil society and thus a sphere separate from and independent of the state. Nevertheless, debates about the applicability of civil society and public sphere to China, historically and in contemporary times, also are well established. See Calhoun 1993; Chamberlain 1993; B. Goodman 1992; P. Huang 1993; Madsen 1993; Rankin 1993; Rowe 1989, 1990, 1993; Schein 2000; Strand 1989; Wakeman 1993; Whyte 1992.

17. See also Foucault 1978: 81–102, 1991; Rabinow 1984; Rose 1996b: 41–43.

18. For other interventions that aim to disrupt "narratives of transition," see Rofel 2007; H. Wang 2004; Zhan 2005.

19. See Barry, Osborne, and Rose 1996; Burchell 1996; Ong 2003, 2006; Rose 1992, 1993, 1996b, 1999. By choosing to write about subject formation rather than about political interests and agency of the professionals per se, I avoid the assumption that unified and unitary subjects exist outside power relations, regulatory norms, and discursive and nondiscursive practices. On this point, see also Mahmood 2005; Sigley 2004.

20. Although this book's aim of unpacking and denaturalizing the choosing subject is similar to Rofel's project of understanding the desiring subject, I am particularly interested in examining how critical reflections on the planned economy have led to new rationalities of governing that cultivate the proper professional subject.

21. Rose (1996b) notes three changes from welfare regimes with advanced liberalism: (1) a responsibilization of expertise to individual citizens, creating a more "formal" character to mechanisms of governing; (2) the turn toward self-governing communities and away from the relationship "between social citizens and their common society" (56); and (3) the specification of subjects who embrace their choices, freedom, and liberty but also are regulated through these practices.

22. Markets, of course, should not, as Yan reminds us, be "taken to be a natural formation but [are] both a system and a subjectivity that has to be actively produced and facilitated" (2003a: 510). See also Rofel 2007.

23. Kipnis takes Jean Comaroff and John Comaroff's issue of *Public Culture* (2000) on "millennial capitalism" as emblematic of the Marxist cultural and ideological approach. For a similar critique, see Hsu 2007.

24. See also Greenhalgh and Winckler 2005, and see Hubbert 2006a on the ambiguity of value.

25. On this point, see Barnett 2005; Larner 2003. It is also why I do not believe that late-socialist neoliberalism needs to be placed within a historical trajectory and story. Rather, I take a genealogical approach to this form of governance.

26. Wang notes that after 1997, intellectual debates in China examined "egalitarian trends within liberal theory," creating a "liberal left wing" and, he argues, offering new ways to critique the market radicalism of "neoliberals" (2004: 50). The liberal tradition, the basis of neoliberalism, thus does not necessarily lead to a neoconservative political position. See also Collier forthcoming.

27. This 2007 chapter by Jamie Peck and Adam Tickell allows for much more variance and combinations of elements forming neoliberalism. The discussion, however, identifies these forms of neoliberalism as "messy," positing a clean, nonmessy neoliberal standard.

28. See, for example, Brenner and Theodore 2002; Brin-Hyatt 1997. Also, in distinguishing between governing in state welfare and in advanced liberal regimes, Nikolas Rose argues the "subject of welfare was a subject of needs, attitudes and relationships, a subject who was to be embraced within, and governed through, a nexus of collective solidarities and dependencies" (1996b: 40). In contrast, advanced liberal rule is a "new formula" that governs individuals not as "citizens of society, but as members of heterogeneous communities of allegiance" (1996a: 41).

29. In China studies specifically, see also the work of Louisa Schein, who discusses China's "curious hybrid of command and market" (2004: 9), and of Gary Sigley, who uses the term "hybrid Chinese socialism-cum-neoliberalism" (2004: 566).

30. Thus, although I find Clive Barnett's critique of theories of neoliberalism to be quite powerful, I disagree with him that "neoliberalism-as-governmentality" takes "subject-formation as a process of 'getting-at' ordinary people in order to make them believe in things against their best interests" (2005: 11). It is precisely this point that I think may be avoided with such an approach, for any process of subject-formation requires active participation (self-governance) from the subject.

31. Wang argues that this integration ended up accommodating corruption and special interests, conservatism, and even authoritarianism rather than democracy and social equality (2004).

32. This point emerged in workshops with Collier and Monica DeHart. I thank them for these discussions.

33. Even in 1997, statistics indicate that 92 percent of all college graduates lived in urban areas, suggesting an urban concentration of the educated elite, and that students from rural areas stayed in urban areas upon graduation (China Statistical Yearbook on Population 1997).

34. The term "vocabulary of enterprise" is from Rose 1998: 154. See also Heelas and Morris 1992.

35. These studies rarely provide a detailed account of who these workers are, however, as I do in this book. Saskia Sassen (1998) addresses the question of identities that emerge with these global processes, but her focus is more on making immigrants and transnational migration visible.

36. The ideal was a combination of the two, but the emphasis remained on politically acceptable behavior and thought until the 1980s. One of the reasons Deng was purged (along with Liu Shaoqi) during the Cultural Revolution was that he had suggested promoting experts and those with technical training rather than those who were ideologically committed. For more on redness versus expertise, see H. Chen 1981; Cleverley

1991; H. Lee 1978; Meisner 1986, 1989; Misra 1998; Pepper 1996; Perry 1993, 1997; Price 1970; Rosen 1984; Shirk 1982; Unger 1982; L. White 1978; Wei-Wei Zhang 1996.

37. An important part of the technocratic movement was elimination of class status from all personnel and educational decisions. These kinds of reforms led Martin Whyte (1993) to argue that significant political changes occurred during the Deng era, even though researchers commonly focused only on economic reforms. For more on political implications of the technocratic movement, see Hughes 2006, Li and White 1991; on reforms generally, see Naughton 1996, Pepper 1984, Solinger 1993; on management reforms specifically, see Chamberlain 1987, Chevrier 1990, Child 1994, Naughton 1996; on contract labor, see Pun 2005, Sensenbrenner 1996, G. White 1987.

38. See also "Respect Knowledge, Respect Talent," *FBIS Daily Report* 1 (132): K12–13. See also Deng 1994b for the interview when he called management "scientific," thus making it a legitimate career within late-socialist politics.

39. In 1985, Wan Li, a member of the Central Committee, said at a conference, "although China needed people like Marx, it also needed its Newtons, Watts, Edisons and Einsteins" (Hughes 2006: 31).

40. Hughes draws on the work of Adam Segal (2003) for his use of the term "techno-nationalism"; it is important to remember that a focus on science for national development in the Deng era also referenced "the heyday of scientistic ideologies" during the May Fourth period (1919–1928) as well as Marxist "scientific" methods (Miller 1996: 5).

41. Even as they were privileged in this process, college graduates did struggle with residency restrictions and tried to temper their own dreams of living in major metropolitan centers as they drew on family connections and wealth to get around residency rules. Their urban aspirations focused on living in Beijing and Shanghai and included the assumption that they would be able to get permanent legal residencies somehow, someday. On these migration issues, see Chan and Zhang 1999; Clark 1999; Solinger 1999; L. Zhang 2001; Daping Zhou 1998.

42. On the powerful symbolic associations made between modernity and urbanity that affect subjectivity, see Chen et al. 2001; Fong 2007; H. Yan 2003a, 2003b; Zheng 2007.

43. Dorothy Solinger makes a compelling argument not only that the urban poverty that emerged in the late 1990s was created by state policies but also that "those same reforms . . . have offered the authorities the means to forestall, dull or quell the associated disaffection among the urban populace" (2006: 185). See also Croll 1999.

44. On several other days, I also passed out surveys to the general population at the talent market (e.g., on November 19, 1995, sixty-four men and forty-one women filled out a questionnaire). The surveys provided a broad picture of the situation to help me place my more in-depth interviews in context. Thus, they were more useful as background checks than as any scientific evidence of particular trends. In conjunction with Professor Liu Zhongquan, I passed out a general "new generation of talent" (*xinyidai ren-cai*) questionnaire in the late spring and summer of 1996 as well. Thirty-six of the forty-seven to whom I distributed surveys returned it (twenty-one men and fifteen women).

45. A total of seventy-two students filled out the questionnaires (thirty-one men and forty-one women). Follow-up interviews were conducted in May and June 1996 with a total of forty students from these classes (twenty-two men and eighteen women).

Eighteen of the students in DUT's chemical-engineering class agreed to and made themselves available for the interviews (sixteen men and two women; this breakdown unfortunately had a greater percentage of males than those who filled out the first questionnaire—eighteen men and nine women); thirteen of the English for science and technology students agreed to be interviewed (one man and twelve women; again, of those who filled out the questionnaire, ten were men and nineteen were women); and nine of the international finance majors agreed to be interviewed (five men and four women; only three men and thirteen women filled out the first questionnaire). Twenty-four of the forty students I interviewed had filled out the original questionnaire (eleven men and thirteen women).

46. The situation at the secondary school was slightly different. Forty-seven students filled out the same initial survey and then, because these students were assigned positions by the ministry of which they were a part, I had time only for a second questionnaire and not for interviews before they left town. Thirty-three students filled it out. The timing was urgent that year, because officials in the school were concerned that the students would resort to vandalism and other forms of destruction to express their anger over placements in unprofitable or remote units. Their concern was not without precedence, as almost all street and path lights on the campus had been smashed by the students.

CHAPTER 2

1. The environmental awards Dalian has accumulated include the United Nations Global 500 Environment Programme Award in May 2001, a state award for "Sanitary City, the Model City in Environmental Protection, the Advanced City in Green-Making, the Garden-Like City, the Advanced City in Water Saving, the Excellent Tourist City, and the Model City for Environment Improvement in the Asian-Pacific Region." Mayor Bo Xilai was awarded the UN Habitat Scroll of Honor Award in 1999. Dalian's urban environmental construction project was awarded the Best Practice Award in Dubai International Human Settlements Development of the Year 2000. Dalian was elected as one of the Ten Best Habitable Cities in China at the National Advanced Forum for Real Estate on July 1, 2000 (see C. Liu 2000). On the role of environmentalism in urban governance in China, see Boland 2003; Hoffman 2009, forthcoming.

2. Vladivostok, Russia's other Pacific Rim option, had a concentration of military forces and was blocked by icebergs during the winter. Japan was also interested in possible control of Korea, which was considered the ultimate prize. See Buck 1978; L. Young 1998.

3. See JPRS 1962: 127; M. Li 2003: 37; Murphey 1974. In 1895, the Russians gained a leasehold on the Liaodong Peninsula after Western powers objected to Japanese control of the peninsula following their victory in the Sino-Japanese war. After the Japanese defeated the Russians in 1905, they inherited the Russian leasehold on the peninsula, the railway links, and the "so-called railway zone" that ran alongside the tracks (L. Young 1998: 25; see also Clausen and Thogersen 1995). With this defeat, people in Russia began calling Dalian "Lish'nii," meaning "superfluous," instead of "Dal'nii," the original Russian term for the city, which meant "far away" (Perrins 1999).

4. Adachi Kinnosuke, Manchuria, 1925 (quoted in Schinz 1989: 424–425).

5. An English traveler and writer noted in 1935 that "Dairen is a sort of Japanese Hong Kong, very orderly and hygienic and up to date. . . . The general atmosphere of the place is suggestive of a garden suburb" (quoted in Perrins 1999).

6. See the work of Saskia Sassen (1991, 1994, 2002) for the argument that nations and national economies are not the most important framework for understanding cities and global processes.

7. In 1945, when the Japanese surrendered, the Yalta Agreement and Sino-Soviet friendship pact were signed. At that time, 175,000 Japanese, a full quarter of the total population of 700,000 residents, returned to Japan. The Yalta Agreement granted rights in Manchuria to the Soviet Union in exchange for entering the war against the Japanese. Soviet rights included use of Port Arthur's naval base (Lushunkou) and joint management by the Chinese and Soviets of the Chinese Eastern Railroad and the South Manchurian Railway (Gillin and Myers 1989: 3). Soon after the Nationalists were notified of the agreement, they signed a Sino-Soviet Treaty of Friendship and Alliance, which confirmed the Yalta Agreement. Soviet advisors remained in the area until they gave full control of the region to China in 1955. A friend living in Dalian in the mid-1990s said he talked to an old woman in the Heishijiao neighborhood who confirmed she had Russian neighbors until the mid-1950s. I thank Chris Cosgrove for sharing this story and Chi Yang for confirming the distribution of housing to Russians.

8. For more on the building of cities under Mao and socialist cities more generally, see Fei 1986; Lewis 1971; Smith 1996; Szelenyi 1996; Tang 2000, 2006; Whyte and Parish 1984. Ivan Szelenyi clearly articulates the impact of central economic planning and public ownership of property on spatial organization in the city. He also argues that the low population growth found in socialist cities (as opposed to capitalist cities during industrialization), what he calls "under-urbanization," was "a spatial expression of distinctively socialist economic growth" (1996: 296). It also is important to remember that the limited urban population growth of the Maoist era was accomplished through strict control of rural-to-urban migration and policies that sent rightists, counter-revolutionaries, and young educated urbanites to work in the countryside. In addition, despite a commitment to egalitarianism, inequalities emerged in the socialist city between workplaces and highly politicized class-status categories, creating hierarchical social relations across the city in the differential distribution of housing, health care, schooling for children, and even daily food. For more on the inequalities between work units, see Lin and Bian 1991; Zhou, Tuma, and Moen 1996, 1997.

9. See X. Lu 1997. For more on the origins of the work unit (danwei), a microcosm and hallmark of the socialist city in China, see Bray 2005; Gaubatz 1995; Lu and Perry 1997; Naughton 1997.

10. On new urban forms, see X. Chen 2005; Dirlik 1999; Forbes 1999; Friedman 2002; Jessop 1999.

11. David R. Phillipps and Anthony G. O. Yeh argue that the Coastal City designation was an extension of the initial successes of the SEZs while also trying to "redres[s] the southerly bias of the SEZs" (1989: 116; see also Chung 1999; Su 1985, 1986). Kwan-Yiu Wong notes that the SEZs were originally located in the south because they were "experimenting with a 'foreign' economic system and it is undesirable to locate

such zones near major population centres" (1987: 35). Three SEZs—Shenzhen, Zhuhai, and Shantou—were approved in 1979. Xiamen was added in 1980. The other Coastal Cities are Qinhuangdao, Tianjin, Yantai, Qingdao, Lianyungang, Nantong, Shanghai, Ningbo, Wenzhou, Fuzhou, Guangzhou, Zhanjiang, and Beihai. The 1984 push for more open areas came on the heels of Deng Xiaoping's visit to the SEZs in that year, but by 1985 "doubts were being expressed by some about the SEZ experiment" (e.g., costs were too high, they attracted the wrong kind of investments, exports and production received little focus), which led to the further central government concentration on development in only four cities—Dalian, Shanghai, Tianjin, and Guangzhou (Phillipps and Yeh 1989: 116, 121–127; K. Wong 1987). By the 1990s, there was a distinct "fever" for development zones (Cartier 2001).

12. See Chung 1999; Gu and Tang 2002; Phillipps and Yeh 1989; Sassen 2002; Sum 1999; K. Wong 1987; Yeung and Hu 1992.

13. Aihwa Ong uses the term "baroque or complex ecology" to refer to reterritorial-izations that construct hubs "in an ecosystem created from the mobilization of diverse global elements—knowledge, practices, and actors—interacting at a high level of perfor-mance," as in Singapore (2006: 180).

14. Michael Yahuda suggests that the term "NET" was coined by Robert Scalapino to discuss the relations between Hong Kong, Taiwan, and mainland China (1994: 269). For more on the urban belt of the Bohai region, see Hoffman and Liu 1997; Liu, Ji, and Chang 1994; Z. Liu n.d.; Rozman 1998; Walcott 2003; Yahuda 1994.

15. Although Zones should be established and legitimized by the central govern-ment, many local places have opened their own spaces of "special policies and privileges" to attract investors and employment. Higher levels of government have retroactively vali-dated many of them. See Shukai Zhao 2007 on how rural cadres are evaluated ("audited") in terms of how much money they attract to their locality, fueling the preapproved open-ing of such zones.

16. Dalian's FTZ was the only state-level FTZ in the northeast. On Shanghai's Pudong development, see Marshall 2003.

17. The city proper (versus the administrative reach) is divided into several districts—Zhongshan, Xigang, Ganjingzi, and Shahekou—and covers almost 2,500 square kilo-meters, a significant expansion from the original Russian development of 4.25 square kilometers. The administrative jurisdiction of Dalian was extended beyond the original city limits in the 1960s to help control urbanization and migration flows and to imple-ment more comprehensive development strategies. It was not until the 1990 plan, how-ever, that a comprehensive strategy including all administrative districts (Zhongshan, Xigang, Shahekou, Ganjingzi, Lushunkou, Jinzhou, Wafangdian, Pulandian, Zhuanghe, and Changhai) was developed (see M. Li 2003: 42).

18. Victor Sit thus calls this kind of investment and development, such as export processing zones, in areas of former colonial rule "pseudo urbanization": "Such uses of land reflect the subordinate relationship that still exists between these cities and their ex-colonial rule or dominant outside power" (1985: 3).

19. The decentralization of economic decision making was extended to cities across the country beginning in the 1980s, such as Shenyang, Xian, Chongqing, and Ningbo (D. Goodman 1989). See also Chung 1999; Schueller 1997.

20. This comes from a statement written by Jiang Zemin in 1999 that after one hundred years of difficulties, "the pearl of Northern China looks even brighter." See also Y. Wang 2007.

21. The Grand Dalian (or Greater Dalian) plan (Da Dalian) was promoted in 2002 by Sun Chunlan, secretary of the Communist Party Committee in Dalian, and reversed some of Mayor Bo's population-control measures. On the Greater Dalian plan and its emphasis on the port, financial sector, innovative industries education, strategic urban planning, and expansion of the urban development area, see Pang, Chen, and Yang 2003; W. Wang 2003; Wang and Zhao 2004; and Daxin Zhou 2003. For caution about excessive urbanization, see Yan 2006.

22. See Xiao 2007 for more on urban tourism in Dalian.

23. See Anagnost 1992; Parris 1993, 1994; L. Zhang 2001.

24. See Bo 1993; Liu, Ji, and Chang 1994: 4; Yahuda 1994: 262.

25. See also Dirlik 1999; Harvey 1989b; Jessop 1999; Short and Kim 1999.

26. The renovation of squares has "been used as a major element to regenerate the central city" in Dalian since 1993 (M. Li 2003: 103). This policy resonates with the aestheticization of the city and emergence of the symbolic economy in many urban centers (Broudehoux 2004; Zukin 1991).

27. In the mid-1990s, a directive from the State Council declared that no streets or buildings could be named after individuals, which meant that Stalin Square became People's Square, and Stalin Road was renamed People's Road.

28. Mimi Li argues that much money was "wasted" with these beautification campaigns, creating cities that were "more and more indistinct and featureless" (2003: 22).

29. During the Maoist era, Liaoning Province had the largest economy in China and was well supported by the socialist state. By 2001, however, the three northeast provinces of Liaoning, Heilongjiang, and Jilin together approximated the economy of Guangdong Province in southeast China alone (C. Chow 2003).

30. Dalian's use of the feminine subverts the more typical representation of the north as industrial and masculine, which people often oppose to feminine images of southern China, its commercial success, and its minority populations. See also Gladney 1994; Schein 2000.

31. Traditionally, a registration booklet had a red cover and was kept either in a home or workplace, with college students being a part of a "collective registration" (jiti hukou) kept by the school (Whyte and Parish 1984: 19; L. White 1978: 154). Today, many young professionals keep their registrations at the talent service centers as part of a collective registration.

32. Yu Zhu makes the important point that nonagricultural (feinongye) did not necessarily mean urban status, for one could be living in a rural area but be on the state's payroll (e.g., a rural cadre) and thus be "non-agricultural by household registration status, but enjoy the benefits provided by the State for urban non-agricultural residents" (1999: 103). Thus, Zhu argues that a "main purpose" of limiting the number of nonagricultural households "is to avoid the burden on the State budget" (1999: 103). These restrictions and distinctions had a gender dimension as well. Since fathers were considered "more likely to get a nonagricultural job in town" and thus to acquire a nonagricultural registration, another way to control population growth in cities was to make the child's legal

registration dependent on the mother's (Whyte and Parish 1984: 18). Although such a rule would separate families, it also meant that the male laborer was incentivized to return "home" rather than move his entire family to his new urban workplace. Recent rural-to-urban migration trends by what is called the "floating population" certainly challenge this assumption. For more on the question of urban citizenship for migrants, see Chan 1995; Solinger 1999; L. Zhang 2001.

33. See L. White 1978: 148–175; Dutton 1992, 1998; Goldstein 1990; Gui and Liu 1992; Tang and Parish 2000; Whyte and Parish 1984; K. Zhou 1996.

34. For studies in Seoul, see Song 2006a, 2006b.

35. See also Ma 2002 for a slightly different argument about the "central role that the Party-state has played in affecting the processes and outcomes of urbanization and urbanism" (1563) and Tang 2006 for a governmentality perspective on how the state still matters in urban planning.

36. For an interesting argument that denaturalizes capital mobility that fuels much of these urban politics, see Pendras 2009.

37. For critiques of the generalizability of Florida's argument and policy prescriptions to multiple sites, see Boyle 2006; Houston et al. 2008; Peck 2005; Stam, deJong, and Marlet 2008; Vorley, Mould, and Smith 2008. See also Sassen's (1998) critique of theorizations of globalization that ignore those who clean the toilets, make the take-out food, and make deliveries.

CHAPTER 3

1. Although work units had little say in the individuals they received from school distributions, female workers were discriminated against for some positions after the Cultural Revolution. Factories in particular wanted only men in certain technical positions, which were deemed "difficult" or "dirty."

2. Both of Song Yan's parents were loyal Party members and had been active Red Guards during the Cultural Revolution.

3. See Whyte and Parish 1984: 359; Tang and Parish 2000: 27. Wenfang Tang and William Parish note that "lifetime job security" had been "the rule" in the majority of all urban jobs in the state sector (80 percent), but by 1997 only 25 percent of the urban population was "entitled to full urban benefits" (2000: 35, 31).

4. In addition to intellectuals, skilled workers were identified as important to the cause. For instance, in 1949, Chen Yun referred to skilled workers as "a 'national treasure' (guobao)" in a speech titled "Skilled Personnel Are an Indispensable Force in Implementing National Industrialization" (Perry 1997: 46). This emphasis also is similar to the growth of a technocratic intelligentsia in the Soviet Union and early on in China is "reflected in party recruitment policies, which favored intellectuals, technicians, and skilled workers" (Meisner 1989: 99). See also Davis 2000b: 255–256 on the importance of skilled workers in the labor movement as well as how skill was "as much a socially and culturally constructed attribute as it was an embodiment of objective production abilities" (Perry 1993: 37).

5. Meisner points in particular to Mao's 1927 "Hunan Report" for early writings on his dislike of intellectuals. Mao's call for new citizens who were "red and expert" and

"jacks of all trades" parallels Karl Marx's ideas about the importance of free, voluntary, and nonspecialized productive labor. For more on the amateur ideal historically, see Levenson 1957.

6. Entrance exams were reinstituted in 1977. What happened during the Cultural Revolution and the general "contraction of advanced education and denigration of specialists" under Mao are often noted as a striking contrast to the Soviet Union, even as China pursued a Soviet-style five-year model for industrialization (Rozman 1985: 137). On the intelligentsia in Soviet socialist states, see Eyal, Szelenyi, and Townsley 1998; Gazso 1992; Konrad and Szelenyi 1979; Rozman 1985; Verdery 1991.

7. Meisner castigates Deng for his "astonishing ignorance of Marxism" and for his declaration that intellectuals were part of the working class, which disregarded "the conflicting social class interests inevitably produced by that distinction" (1989: 107).

8. Christopher Hughes argues that based on the reform-era correlation of "revolution" (*geming*) "with 'liberation of productive forces' . . . the status of the rising professional classes could be established as 'revolutionary'" (2006: 64).

9. Michael Agelasto notes that public criticism of the assignment system appeared in the later 1980s (1998: 263).

10. Although many people made the distinction between the way older state units "wasted" talent and how more "modern" and foreign enterprises made "wise" human resource decisions, some individuals criticized all Chinese companies. An example is an aspiring young professional, originally from the countryside, who had taught himself Japanese and was working for a Japanese company. "Chinese companies may know to write it on the advertisement that they want a particular major," he said, "but they don't understand how to test and evaluate people. When they hire them, they think many specialties are the same. They don't know how to listen to what *rencai* [talent] can do." In contrast, to get the job at the Japanese company, he had to take multiple tests that assessed his skills and personality, proving to him that he would be placed effectively and rationally in the company.

11. Demand-meet-supply reforms (see below) began in 1985 in Dalian, according to a city personnel bureau report. This publication was not dated, and statistics end in 1995, as do the three stages of reform identified in the report: 1985–1989, 1989–1991, and 1991–1995 (DRJ n.d.). Most likely, it was distributed to officials at the end of 1995 or early 1996.

12. This was less than one year after the influential CPC Central Committee's Decision on Economic Structural Reform was adopted, which "defined the essence of the socialist economy as a 'planned commodity economy'" (Wei-Wei Zhang 1996: 112). For information on the 1985 education directive as well as the 1986 Compulsory Education Act when education for quality (*suzhi jiaoyu*) was adopted, see Murphy 2004 and Chapter 5 in this book. For more on education reforms, see Agelasto 1998; Agelasto and Adamson 1998; Hayhoe 1989, 1993, 1996; Hughes 2006; C. Li 1999; Pepper 1984, 1990, 1995; Rai 1991; X. Wang 2003; World Bank 1997; L. Zhou 2006.

13. In an interview with the director of a large, successful state-owned enterprise in Dalian, he told me that his work unit continued to receive "assignments." In 1993, they received ten; in 1994, six; in 1995, six; and even in 1996, they received three graduates. "This is left over from the planned system," he explained, "and starting next year everyone

will have to go through mutual choice. There will be no more assignments." This company also relied on one-year contracts to test out their new employees. If they did well, they would rehire them typically on a three-year contract. If they continued to do well, they would increase the time to five years and then again for three years. The director of the company explained that being in the company for three years made an employee eligible for certain benefits, such as housing. In other words, loyalty paid.

14. Professor Liu and I went through this history with administrators at a number of universities, but one time he chuckled and commented that it was like reforms in marriage choice as well.

15. The publications were *Guanyu gaige gaodeng xuexiao biyesheng fenpei zhidu de baogao* and *Gaodeng xuexiao biyesheng fenpei zhidu gaige fangan* (C. Li 1999: 19).

16. College seniors often used the Spring Festival holiday to look for work in their hometowns while they visited their parents.

17. The Mandarin for "5" and "1" is wu3 yao1. This sounds like wo3 yao4, which means "I want," so the Web site's name reads as "I want a job." I thank my research assistant, Wang Xiuping, for originally leading me to this site.

18. There has been a concerted effort to "raise the quality" of Party members and government officials by hiring more people with college and graduate degrees. See also Rosen 2004; Li and Walder 2001; and Chapter 5.

19. See below for more on the distinction between those for whom the school was responsible (sponsored students [*gongfei*]) and those for whom they were not (self-paying [*zifei*]). All students became fee paying in 1997.

20. Statistics for graduates in 2003 indicated that 25.5 percent went to state-owned enterprises, 13.9 percent went to government and civil offices, 36.3 percent went to foreign-invested companies, and 15.8 percent went to private companies (DUT 2003). In 1996, more than 80 percent of the graduates went into state-affiliated units, and in 1997 about 70 percent did. In 1996, 23 percent went to units in the civil service, research institutes, and educational units; and 61 percent went to factories or enterprises (*qiye*)—thus not a significant change in the early 2000s, although more were continuing on to graduate school (28 percent of DUT graduates in 2003). Nationally, of the 1,759,691 new graduates from universities, colleges, and technical schools in 1996, 879,268 (or almost 50 percent) received formal employment in state-owned enterprises (*qiye*), and 706,219 (or 40 percent) went into state institutions (*shiye danwei*). Only 160,164 new graduates (or 9 percent) went to "other ownership" units (see China Statistical Yearbook on Labor 1997: 283, 284, 286, 393). The numbers of students from DUT going into the state sector broadly reflect the national statistics. Typical of a technical university, the number of students from DUT who went to enterprises (*qiye*; 61 percent in 1996) was higher than the national average for all graduates entering the labor force (almost 50 percent). National statistics from 1998 indicate 16.1 percent went to government institutions, 35.5 percent to state-owned enterprises, 14.5 percent to educational institutions, 5.2 percent to research institutes, 9.5 percent to foreign and joint venture companies, 5.8 percent to urban collectives, 1.3 percent to rural enterprise, 5.6 percent to private enterprises, and 6.6 percent to other kinds of organizations (in X. Wang 2003).

21. This quote is from Zhou Ji's description of the New-Century Teaching Reform Project in Higher Education Institutions launched in 2000. Zhou Ji has been minister of education since 2003.

22. The *zifei* option was available before 1952 for students who were just below the admissions cutoff (Seeberg 1998: 214). On these reforms, see Agelasto 1998; K. Cheng 1995, 1998; Hayhoe 1996; Kurlander 1998; M. Zhang 1998; Paine 1994; Seeberg 1998; Yin and White 1994.

23. At Finance University, for example, only 10 students were self paying in 1986, but by 1988 there were almost 200, and by 1992 the number had jumped to close to 500, out of approximately 1,300 students. National statistics indicate a jump in self-paying students from 3 percent of enrollment in 1986 to 25 percent in 1993 (Rosen 1997: 254). Just after the Tiananmen Square incident in 1989, however, the number of self-paying students allowed was cut back. The central government promoted this category of students so that universities could find their own sources of funding, but they did worry about their influence on campuses.

24. For example, DUT graduates in 1995 included 2,027 state-sponsored and 107 self-paying students, for a total of 2,134 graduates. Within the state-sponsored category, 459 were unit sponsored, and 59 were locally committed students (DUT 1995b).

25. Tuition payments began in Guangdong province in 1988 and extended to thirty-six other institutions under the SEC in 1989 (Pepper 1990: 155–156). Pilot schemes for students to pay fees extended further in 1993, blurring the distinction between self-paying and state-sponsored students (K. Cheng 1998: 22; M. Zhang 1998: 245). The costs have skyrocketed in recent years.

26. Students at DUT were offered reductions in loan payments and scholarship awards from 2,000–5,000 RMB if they agreed to go to remote areas that needed their talent. Dalian also loosened residency restrictions to fill difficult (*jianku*) posts (DRJ n.d.: 5).

27. Agelasto describes this process as "manpower planning," which refers to "macro-economic planning at the national level where the objective is to change employment patterns towards desired goals" so that education is linked to employment "for the sake of efficiency" (1998: 259–260). For more on curriculum reforms, see Hayhoe 1987, 1993; Pepper 1990; Yin and White 1994.

28. Official urban unemployment rates were 2.6 percent in 1993, 3 percent in 1996, and 4 percent in 2002 (Warner and Lee 2007: 4). Estimates in 2004 stated that 70 percent of those who were unemployed in urban areas were under age thirty-five (China's Employment Situation and Policies 2004). China has what Michael Webber and Zhu Ying term a "highly distinctive" definition of unemployment, for it includes only the urban registered unemployed, of a specific age, and those who "have registered with the local labor bureau for employment" (2007: 30). See also Hu and Sheng 2007; Gu 2001. For an interesting analysis of what it means for educated youth to be unemployed, see Jeffrey 2009.

29. See, for example, the journal *Zhongguo qingnian yanjiu* (China Youth Study) and Goodall and Burgers 1998.

30. See also Borge Bakken's discussion, for instance, of contemporary projects of "fostering" and ideas of "self-rule" as including Confucian notions of self-cultivation and Mencius's ideas of "self-examination (*fanshen*) or introspection (*fanxing*)" (2000: 92). See also Judd 2002; Chapter 5.

CHAPTER 4

1. "*Youhua peizhi rencai ziyuan, gouzhu beifang rencai gaodi,*" translated on the wall as, "To dispose perfectly the intellects resources; to construct the intellect highland of the North."

2. See, for example, Davis 2000a; Farrer 2002; Fong 2004; Liechty 2003; Pinches 1999; L. Zhang 2008. See also Chapter 1.

3. This literature is dominated by Florida 2002a, 2002b, 2005. See also Chapter 2.

4. My argument complements the perspective in Muniesa, Millo, and Callon; using their language, I would argue that making choices "is neither a universally homogeneous attribute of humankind, nor an anthropological fiction. It is the concrete result of social and technical arrangements" (2007: 5).

5. Cf. Hanser 2002a.

6. In late-imperial and early-Republican times, China's government engaged in state-strengthening and modernization projects. Although it is critical to recognize these genea-logical links, my focus here is on the integration of Maoist-era ideas about the nation-building power of labor with neoliberal mechanisms for labor distribution—that is, the intersection of neoliberalism and socialism.

7. "Style of reasoning" comes from Rose 1996b: 42.

8. Amy Hanser refers to the focus on the individual position as "job specificity" and the shift away from the importance of "the job unit and its location in the bureaucratic hierarchy" (2002a: 152; see also Bray 2005: 94–122).

9. In 1993, Dalian's Personnel Bureau assigned 180 people; in 1994, 250 people; and in 1995, 300 people. According to its statistics, 80 percent of these students "happily" (*yukuai*) took the positions (DRJ n.d.: 8). See also Jefferson and Rawski 1992: 46.

10. The use of scholarships in place of subsidies began at the end of 1987 either as "an award for excellence, as incentives into hardship areas (teaching, mining, agriculture), or to attract students to work in difficult regions after graduation" (K. Cheng 1998: 22; see also Pepper 1990: 156; M. Zhang 1998: 242, 246–247).

11. See Chapter 3 for more on the distinctions between self-paying students and state-sponsored students. In 1997, DUT went to a full fee-based enrollment system, although fee-paying students were grouped in differing categories. If the state paid for the student's entire education, he or she was required to work, in some form, for the state after graduation.

12. Tang and Wang 1992 is based on an American book. Related books I found later in the campus bookstore include *The New Employment Era* (*Xin jiuye shidai*; Yu 1999) and, for prospective students, *How to Choose a Major* (*Xue shenme zhuanye hao*; Xin Zhang 1999). See also Jiao 1995.

13. At job fairs, for instance, graduates knew the school might not approve an urban position for someone with a rural household registration, or perhaps it would veto a mediocre student going to a coveted unit in Beijing, because it feared the appointment was *guanxi* based (connection based) and ultimately would reflect poorly on DUT if the graduate did not do well.

14. Compare this to Fengshu Liu's emphasis on the "conflicting enjoinments for the subject" when participating in "two subjectification regimes" (2008: 203).

15. With the recent economic slowdown, graduates have again been turning to state-owned workplaces (*China Daily* 2009c).

CHAPTER 5

1. Because of this ambiguity in English, I either use the Chinese term "*wenhua*" or the combination of "education/culture" in the following discussion.

2. Andrew Kipnis notes the phrase "*suzhi jiaoyu*" (education for quality) "first appears in print in 1988" (2006: 298), and Vanessa Fong reports that interviewees said they became aware of the term "*suzhi*" starting in the early 1990s (2007). Susan Greenhalgh and Edwin Winckler argue that during 1979–1993, what they term "the long 1980s," "the dominant norm promoted by the state was one of quantity: one child for all" (2005: 215). Following this was an increased emphasis on quality in population-control programs in the post-Deng era, a norm they describe as "highly seductive" (2005: 217). See also Anagnost 1997a, 1997b, 2004; Fong 2002, 2004; Murphy 2004.

3. More recently, Chinese culture, familialism, and even patriarchal authoritarianism have been celebrated as foundations for the success of "Chinese capitalism," the development of such places as Singapore, and most recently for China's place in Olympic Games history and on the world stage (see Hubbert 2006b; Tu 1994).

4. For extended discussions of contemporary self-improvement practices, see Greenhalgh and Winckler 2005; Murphy 2004; H. Yan 2003a.

5. For more on the one-child policy and the investment in the next generation, see Anagnost 1997a, 1997b, 2004; Fong 2004; Greenhalgh and Winckler 2005; Kipnis 2006; Murphy 2004; Sigley 2004; Woronov 2002.

6. Here, I draw on Michel Foucault's notion of ethics as "the kind of relationship you ought to have with yourself, *rapport a soi* . . . and which determines how the individual is supposed to constitute himself as a moral subject of his own actions" (1997d: 263). See also Collier and Lakoff 2005; Lakoff and Collier 2004.

7. "Capital" in this usage draws on the work of Pierre Bourdieu (1972, 1984, 1987) in terms of different forms of capital (e.g., symbolic, economic) that can be converted into other forms. How valuable one form of capital, such as educational or cultural capital, is at a given moment is related to particular historical and social conditions (on this point, cf. Hsu 2007).

8. Compare this to Vanessa Fong's focus on the individual's interpretation of what "*suzhi*" means (2007).

9. Like *wenhua*, "*suzhi*" was used to refer to one's schooling, corrupt practices, ability to attract foreign capital, exposure to things foreign, and so forth.

10. On generations of intellectuals, see Hubbert 1999; Miller 1996.

11. In fact, Kipnis argues that the "use of *suzhi* in education circles has completely negated the term's earlier connotations of innateness" (2006: 300), although he has made more subtle claims in later writings (2007).

12. The work of such scholars as Ann Anagnost (1997a, 1997b, 2004), Susan Greenhalgh and Edwin Winckler (2005), Ngai Pun (2003), and Hairong Yan (2003a, 2003b) have been particularly helpful in understanding how market valuations of the self infuse subject-formation processes.

13. H. Yan quotes the *Anhui Daily* on this issue: "Without a high-*suzhi* human subject, capital cannot increase in value" (2003a: 511).

14. The original law was promulgated on July 7, 1981, and "allowed individual businessman to engage up to two 'assistants' and five 'apprentices,' thus diluting the ideologically sensitive issue of hiring outside labour. The notion of seven people was said to come from one of Marx's articles which mentioned the free association of workers up to seven people" (Wei-Wei Zhang 1996: 102). By the early 1980s, reforms in rural-land management had fueled several years of significant economic growth in the countryside, but urban areas felt the pressure of unemployment and growing inflation. Educated youth who had been sent to the countryside during the Cultural Revolution had returned to their urban homes and were looking for work. At the same time, more students were graduating from high schools and waiting for job assignments, known as *daiye qingnian* (youth waiting for work). Urban administrators worried about the possible social unrest that idle youth could cause as well as the lost production value of their labor. It was not until 1988 that private (*siying*) companies received "legal status for the first time since the 1950s." Private companies were allowed to have more than eight employees (Parris 1999: 265–266). See also Gold 1989, 1990; D. Goodman 1999.

CHAPTER 6

1. I have translated the term "*nuhaizi*," which she used, as "girl" rather than "woman."

2. David Bray is interested in how walls were a "positive technology for the production and bolstering of collective forms of social relationships" (2005: 125).

3. It is interesting to compare this with the experiences of many "working girls" (*dagongmei*) who traveled to large cities to work in factories, emphasizing the class-specific nature of these associations (see Pun 2005). In their new urban homes, however, the inside/outside distinction and social control of women was reproduced for these migrant women (see L. Zhang 2001).

4. Similar situations have been reported for factory workers where certain jobs were considered more or less morally appropriate, what Ching Kwan Lee refers to as "gendered substructures" (Lee 1998a). Families, for instance, considered factory jobs morally safe, although work in the service industry was not, prompting one rural father to tell his migrant daughter never to come home if she worked in a restaurant (Lee 1998a: 83; see also Pun 2005).

5. On blurring the line between work and leisure, see de Certeau 1984. For an interesting study of karaoke bars and sex work in Dalian, see Zheng 2009.

6. Yang was subject to moralistic language about where she should and should not go and what she should and should not do in a number of arenas, including bodily adornment and self-presentation. For instance, after she married and was settling into her new life as a wife and daughter-in-law, she cut her hair quite short. Her hair had been an issue for a while, as her new mother-in-law had insisted she get it permed after she married. It was the only proper thing to do in her mother-in-law's mind. Yang resisted her pressure and finally was able to get her father-in-law on her side, allowing her to keep it long and straight. Eventually, she decided to get it cut. When she did, men in the extended family critiqued what she had done and said that only "bad" girls had haircuts like that. No, it was not pretty, they protested. Yang was visibly upset during this exchange and shot back at them that if only they could see the fashion magazines, they would know it was all the rage in Shanghai.

7. See Hooper 1998 and X. Li 1994; this also raises questions about what has been termed the "postponed revolution" for women in China. See, for example, Andors 1983; Bauer et al. 1992; Croll 1983; Davin 1976; Hooper 1984; Rai 1992; Stacey 1983; Wolf 1985; M. Young 1989.

8. Fifty-two percent of the graduating seniors at Finance University in 1996 were women, compared to only 22 percent at DUT. In 1949, 20 percent of the students in universities and colleges were women, which increased to about one-third after universities reopened in the mid-1970s. When the examination system was reinstated in 1977, the number dropped to below one-quarter before rising again (Bauer et al. 1992: 338). In 1995, 35.4 percent of all university students were females, and by 2001 that number had increased to 42 percent (China Statistical Yearbook 2002).

9. Later, she confided she thought I would want to go shopping because of the way I looked. Apparently what I considered a professional look for the job fair (a skirt and blazer) indicated a concern with pretty clothes and bodily adornment to Zhang.

10. For anthropological work on the growing "domestic help" industry with the growth of middle classes, see also Constable 1997; Ong 2006; H. Yan 2003a, 2003b.

11. See Hooper 1998 and Notar 1994 for interesting discussions of how various representations of women have been incorporated into advertising in post-Mao China.

12. These representations of gender and sexuality were in tension with ideals of "iron girls" (*tie guniang*) and "imitation young men" (*jia xiaozi*) that circulated in political and educational campaigns during the Maoist years. See Honig and Hershatter 1988; Hooper 1998; Rosen 1994; M. Young 1989.

13. After the Marriage Law of 1950, the state used scientific discourses of sexuality to regulate sexual behavior and to support monogamous marriage while also suggesting procreation was for the benefit of socialist society rather than for patriarchal family lines. See also Evans 1995; Greenhalgh and Winckler 2005; Sigley 1998.

14. In addition to housing being distributed through work units, local governments invested in housing units and distributed apartments to those in need and to those working for municipal organizations. In older cities, such as Beijing or Shanghai, which kept much of their pre-Revolution housing, families continued to live in family-"owned" homes, although they often shared them with other new occupants.

15. Housing regulations such as these, as well as directives that called for women to "go back to the wok" (*huigui guotai*; Jacka 1990) or pressured mothers to retire so their

children could be employed in their places, institutionally reproduced gender hierarchies even under high socialism. See X. Huang 1999; Woo 1994.

16. Interestingly, Martin Whyte (2005) shows that in the mid-1990s, the legacy of this system also meant that aging parents were not likely to be living with their grown children; it was not necessary, as they had their own state-distributed apartments and because the job assignment and household-registration systems kept children in their hometowns and thus close enough to help support the parents.

17. Timothy Cheek describes this well by drawing on the work of Guo Xiaolin. Articles about the devastating 2008 earthquake in Sichuan, as well as the infant milk scandal just following the Beijing Olympic Games, reinforced the distinction between the local, corrupt officials and the hope that "the nation" (*guojia*) was there to help (see Yardley 2008).

18. Housing purchases have been studied as a way people mark class status in a number of settings (e.g., Fleischer 2007; Pinches 1999; Stivens 1998). On Beijing, the urban middle class, and community building, see Bray 2006; Tomba 2004; F. Xu 2008.

19. Compare this to 70 percent of the workforce in state units across the country in 2000 (China Statistical Yearbook on Labor 2001: 21). In Dalian, 55.3 percent was in state units, and collective ownership accounted for 12.5 percent of the workforce. The 32.2 percent for "other ownership" units includes foreign-funded, private, limited, and joint venture ownership structures and the like. The foreign-funded numbers account for a total of 16 percent of the workforce, with 81 percent of that sector in non–Hong Kong–, Macau-, and Taiwan-owned enterprises (Dalian Statistical Yearbook 2000: 35). See also Table 1.1.

20. They are building on the work of Gilles Deleuze here.

21. With the decentralization of housing provisions, there has been a shift from state investment to *danwei* (work unit) "responsibilities for the provision of housing to their employees using retained revenues" (J. Zhu 2000: 504) and then to individuals themselves. Citing World Bank sources, Jieming Zhu notes that before reforms began, the state paid for more than 90 percent of urban housing, but that "by 1988, the state contributed only 16%, and *danwei* financed 52% of annual housing investment on average" (2000: 511–512).

Glossary of Chinese Terms

baohu (保护): Care for
binggui (并轨): Merging tracks
biyesheng jiuye bangongshi (毕业生就业): Graduate employment offices
bu fangxin (不放心): Worried
bu heli (不合理): Irrational

chanpin (产品): Product
chuangxin (创新): Innovation

dagongmei (打工妹): "Working girls"
dangan (档案): Dossier
danwei (单位): State work units
dingxiang (定向): Committed, predetermined program
dongbeiya jingjiquan (东北亚 经济圈): Northeast Asian Economic Circle
duanlian ziji (锻炼自己): To get experience, to get practice
duikou (对口): Jobs that appropriately match majors
dushu de ren (读书的人): People who have studied

fahui nengli (发挥): To enhance one's abilities
fangquan rangli (放权让利): Decentralization of power and interests
fenpei (分配): Assignment system
fudi (腹地): Hinterland
fushupin (附属品): Accessory

ganbu (干部): Cadres
geming (革命): Revolution
getihu (个体户): Entrepreneurs
gongfei (工费): State-sponsored students
guanjian yinsu (关键因素): Key factor
guanxi (关系): Connections, relationships
guihua (规划): Macrolevel supervision
guobao (国宝): National treasure
guojia (国家): Nation, state, country; also refers to central government

heli (合理): Rational, reasonable
heli liyong (合理利用): Rational use
heshi (合适): Appropriate
hexie shehui (和谐社会): Harmonious society
hongguan diaokong (宏观调控): Macro-adjustment
huanjing (环境): Environment
huayuan (花园): Garden
hukou (户口): Household registration

jianku (艰苦): Difficult
jiao pengyou (交朋友): To make friends
jiating beijing (家庭背景): Family background
jiating funu (家庭妇女): Housewife
jiating fuwu (家庭服务): Domestic services
jihua (计划): Plan
jihui (机会): Opportunity
jingji jishu kaifa qu (经济技术开发区): Economic and Technical Development Zone
jishu renyuan (技术人员): Technical personnel
jiuye zhidao (就业指导): Career guidance

kuisun (亏损): Unprofitable

laodongju (劳动局): Labor bureau
luan (乱): Chaos

maoxian (冒险): To take a risk

nanxun (南巡): Southern tour by Deng Xiaoping, 1992
neiqin (内勤): Office work

pinzhi (品质): Character

qiangda (强大): Powerful
qiye (企业): Enterprises

rencai (人才): Talent
rencai dasha (人才大厦): (Talented) human resources building
rencai shichang (人才市场): Talent market
rencai ziyuan (人才资源): (Talented) human resources
renli ziyuan guanli (人力资源管理): Human resource management
renmin minzu zhuyi (人民民族主义): Popular nationalism
renpin (人品): Moral character
renshiju (人事局): Personnel bureau

shangren (商人): Businesspeople
shehui beijing (社会背景): Applicant's background/accomplishments
shequ (社区): Community
shihe (适合): Suitable
shiye danwei (事业单位): State-owned institutions
shoufei (收费): Pay a fee
shuangxiang xuanze (双向选择): Mutual choice
siying (私营): Private
suzhi (素质): Quality
suzhi jiaoyu (素质教育): Education for quality

tigao renminde suzhi (提高人民的素质): To raise the quality of the people

weituo peiyang (委托培养): Sponsored training
wenhua (文化): Culture/education
wenhua shuiping (文化水平): Cultural/educational level
wenming (文明): Civilization

xianqi liangmu (贤妻良母): Virtuous wife and good mother
xinyidai rencai (新一代人才): New generation of talent
xisheng (牺牲): Sacrifice
xiuyang (修养): Accomplishment in self-cultivation
xuanze (选择): Choices

yi jia, liang zhi (一家两制): One household, two systems
you shijian (有时间): To have time
yukuai (愉快): Happy

zhaopin (招聘): Advertise (for employees)
zhaopin huiyi (招聘会议): Job fairs
zhengfu (政府): Government (local)
zhengfu jiguan (政府机关): Government agency
zhidao (指导): Guide, guidance
zhidaoxing (指导性): Guidance system
zhiliang (质量): Quality, for objects

zhilingxing (指令性): Mandatory (plan)

zhishifenzi (知识分子): Intellectuals

zhishi jingji (知识经济): Knowledge economy

zhongdeng zhuanke xuexiao (中等专科学校): Secondary specialized school

zhongxiao cheng zhen (中小城镇): Smaller towns

zhuangxiu fei (装修费): Decoration fee

zhuanye renyuan (专业人员): Experts

zifei (自费): At one's own expense, self-paying (students)

ziwo fazhan (自我发展): Self-development

zunzhong rencai (尊重人才): To respect talent

zunzhong zhishi (尊重知识): To respect knowledge

References

Abramson, Larry. 2008a. Auto school wants to extend reach to China. NPR, *Morning Edition,* May 28, 2008. Available at www.npr.org/templates/story/story.php?storyId=90412952&ps=rs.

———. 2008b. Chinese city partners with New York school. NPR, *Morning Edition,* May 27, 2008. Available at www.npr.org/templates/story/story.php?storyId=90328077 &ps=rs.

Agelasto, Michael. 1998. Graduate employment: From manpower planning to the market economy. In *Higher education in post-Mao China.* Ed. Michael Agelasto and Bob Adamson, 259–280. Hong Kong: Hong Kong University Press.

Agelasto, Michael, and Bob Adamson, eds. 1998. *Higher education in post-Mao China.* Hong Kong: Hong Kong University Press.

Anagnost, Ann. 1989a. Prosperity and counterprosperity: The moral discourse on wealth in post-Mao China. In *Marxism and the Chinese experience.* Ed. Arif Dirlik and Maurice Meisner, 210–234. Armonk, NY: M. E. Sharpe.

———. 1989b. Transformations of gender in modern China. In *Gender and anthropology: Critical reviews for teaching and research.* Ed. Sandra Morgen, 313–342. Washington, DC: American Anthropological Association.

———. 1992. Socialist ethics and the legal system. In *Popular protest and political culture in modern China: Learning from 1989.* Ed. Jeffery Wasserstrom and Elizabeth Perry, 177–205. Boulder, CO: Westview Press.

———. 1997a. Children and national transcendence in China. In *Constructing China: The interaction of culture and economics.* Ed. Kenneth G. Lieberthal, Shuen-fu Lin, and

Ernest P. Young, 195–222. Ann Arbor: University of Michigan, Center for Chinese Studies.

———. 1997b. *National past-times: Narrative, representation, and power in modern China.* Durham, NC: Duke University Press.

———. 2004. The corporeal politics of quality (suzhi). *Public Culture* 16 (2): 89–208.

———. 2008. From "class" to "social strata": Grasping the social totality in reform-era China. *Third World Quarterly* 29 (3): 497–519.

Andors, Phyllis. 1983. *The unfinished liberation of Chinese women, 1949–1980.* Bloomington: Indiana University Press.

Bakken, Borge. 2000. *The exemplary society: Human improvement, social control, and the dangers of modernity in China.* New York: Oxford University Press.

Barlow, Tani. 1991a. Theorizing woman: *Funu, guojia, jiating* [Chinese women, Chinese state, Chinese family]. *Genders* 10:132–160.

———. 1991b. Zhishifenzi [Chinese intellectuals] and power. *Dialectical Anthropology* 16:209–232.

———. 1994. Politics and protocols of funu: (Un)making national woman. In *Engendering China: Women, culture, and the state.* Ed. Christina Gilmartin, Gail Hershatter, Lisa Rofel, and Tyrene White, 339–359. Cambridge, MA: Harvard University Press.

Barnett, Clive. 2005. The consolations of "neoliberalism." *Geoforum* 36:7–12.

Barry, Andrew, Thomas Osborne, and Nikolas Rose, eds. 1996. Introduction to *Foucault and political reason: Liberalism, neo-liberalism and rationalities of government.* 1–18. Chicago: University of Chicago Press.

Bauer, John, Wang Feng, Nancy E. Riley, and Zhao Xiaohua. 1992. Gender inequality in urban China: Education and employment. *Modern China* 18 (3): 333–370.

Becker, Gary. 1994. *Human capital: A theoretical and empirical analysis with special reference to education.* 3rd ed. Chicago: University of Chicago Press.

Beech, Hannah. 2005. Changing the game. *Time Magazine* (June 27): 40–44.

Bian, Yanjie. 1994. *Work and inequality in urban China.* Albany: State University of New York Press.

———. 1997. Bringing strong ties back in: Indirect ties, network bridges, and job searches in China. *American Sociological Review* 62:366–385.

Bian, Yanjie, and John R. Logan. 1996. Market transition and the persistence of power: The changing stratification system in urban China. *American Sociological Review* 61:739–758.

Bian, Yanjie, John R. Logan, Hanlong Lu, Yunkang Pan, and Ying Guan. 1997. Work units and housing reform in two Chinese cities. In *Danwei: The changing Chinese workplace in historical and comparative perspective.* Ed. Xiaobo Lu and Elizabeth J. Perry, 223–250. Armonk, NY: M. E. Sharpe.

Bo, Xilai. 1993. *Dalianshi shizhang Bo Xilai zai yantaohui shang de jianghua.* Reprint of seminar speech, May 5, in Beijing.

Boland, Alana. 2003. Environmental governance in urban China: Natural competition and the rescaling of the local. Paper presented at the international conference on globalization, the state, and urban transformation, December 12–15, at Hong Kong Baptist University.

Bourdieu, Pierre. 1972. *Outline of a theory of practice.* Trans. Richard Nice. Cambridge, UK: Cambridge University Press.

———. 1984. *Distinction: A social critique of the judgment of taste.* Cambridge, MA: Harvard University Press.

———. 1987. What makes a social class? On the theoretical and practical existence of groups. *Berkeley Journal of Sociology* 32:1–18.

———. 1990. *The logic of practice.* Trans. Richard Nice. Stanford, CA: Stanford University Press.

Boyle, Mark. 2006. Culture in the rise of tiger economies: Scottish expatriates in Dublin and the "creative class" thesis. *International Journal of Urban and Regional Research* 30, no. 2 (June): 403–426.

Bray, David. 2005. *Social space and governance in urban China: The danwei system from origins to reform.* Stanford, CA: Stanford University Press.

———. 2006. Building "community": New strategies of governance in urban China. *Economy and Society* 35 (4): 530–549.

Brenner, Neil, and Nik Theodore. 2002. Cities and geographies of "actually existing neoliberalism." *Antipode* 34 (3): 349–379.

Brin-Hyatt, Susan. 1997. Poverty in a "post-welfare" landscape: Tenant management policies, self-governance, and the democratization of knowledge in Great Britain. In *Anthropology of policy: Critical perspectives on governance and power.* Ed. Cris Shore and Susan Wright, 217–238. London: Routledge.

Broudehoux, Anne-Marie. 2004. *The making and selling of post-Mao Beijing.* New York: Routledge.

Buck, David D. 1978. *Urban change in China: Politics and development in Tsinan, Shantung, 1890–1949.* Madison: University of Wisconsin Press.

Burchell, Graham. 1996. Liberal government and techniques of the self. In *Foucault and political reason: Liberalism, neo-liberalism and rationalities of government.* Ed. Andrew Barry, Thomas Osborne, and Nikolas Rose, 19–36. Chicago: University of Chicago Press.

Cai, Yanwei. 1997. Residence suburbanization in Dalian. *China City Planning Review* 13 (2): 58–63.

Caldeira, Teresa, and James Holston. 2005. State and urban space in Brazil: From modernist planning to democratic interventions. In *Global assemblages: Technology, politics, and ethics as anthropological problems.* Ed. Aihwa Ong and Stephen J. Collier, 393–416. Malden, MA: Blackwell.

Calhoun, Craig. 1993. Civil society and the public sphere. *Public Culture* 5:267–280.

Cartier, Carolyn. 2001. *Globalizing south China.* Oxford, UK: Blackwell.

Castells, Manuel.1989. *The informational city: Information technology, economic restructuring, and the urban-regional process.* Oxford, UK: Blackwell.

Chamberlain, Heath B. 1987. Party-management relations in Chinese industries: Some political dimensions of economic reform. *China Quarterly* 112:631–661.

———. 1993. On the search for civil society in China. *Modern China* 19 (2): 199–215.

Chan, Kam Wing, and Will Buckingham. 2008. Is China abolishing the *hukou* system? *China Quarterly* 195:582–606.

Chan, Kam Wing, and Li Zhang. 1999. The hukou system and rural-urban migration in China: Processes and changes. *China Quarterly* 160:818–855.

Chan, Roger C. K. 1995. The urban migrants—the challenge to public policy. In *Social change and social policy in contemporary China*. Ed. Linda Wong and Stewart MacPherson, 166–187. Aldershot, UK: Avebury, Ashgate Publishing.

Cheek, Timothy. 2006. *Living with reform: China since 1989.* London: Zed Books.

Chen, His-en Theodore. 1981. *Chinese education since 1949: Academic and revolutionary models.* New York: Pergamon Press.

Chen, Nancy, Connie Clark, Susan Gottschang, and Lyn Jeffries, eds. 2001. *Ethnographies of the urban in contemporary China.* Durham, NC: Duke University Press.

Chen, Xiangming. 2005. *As borders bend: Transnational spaces on the Pacific Rim.* Lanham, MD: Rowman and Littlefield.

Cheng, Allen T. 2003. Dalian is shining like no other city. *South China Morning Post,* July 29, 2003. Reprinted in China Study Group News Archives. Available at www.china studygroup.org.

Cheng, Kai-ming. 1995. Education—decentralization and the market. In *Social change and social policy in contemporary China*. Ed. Linda Wong and Stewart MacPherson, 70–87. Aldershot, UK: Avebury, Ashgate Publishing.

———. 1998. Reforms in the administration and financing of higher education. In *Higher education in post-Mao China*. Ed. Michael Agelasto and Bob Adamson, 11–27. Hong Kong: Hong Kong University Press.

Chevrier, Yves. 1990. Micropolitics and the factory director responsibility system, 1984–1987. In *Chinese society on the eve of Tiananmen: The impact of reform*. Ed. Deborah Davis and Ezra Vogel, 109–134. Cambridge, MA: Council on East Asian Studies, Harvard University.

Child, John. 1994. *Management in China during the age of reform.* Cambridge, UK: Cambridge University Press.

China Daily. 1997. Farewell to free college education. May 2.

———. 2009a. China aims to create 1.5M IT jobs in 3 years. *China Daily Online,* April 15, 2009. Available at www.chinadaily.com.cn/china/2009-04/15/content_7681354 .htm.

———. 2009b. Graduates looking beyond city. *China Daily Online,* May 7, 2009. Available at www.chinadaily.com.cn/cndy/2009-05/07/content_7751264.htm.

———. 2009c. Graduates prefer state-owned to foreign companies. *China Daily Online,* August 31, 2009. Available at www.chinadaily.com.cn/china/2009-08/31/content _8635367.htm.

China Data Center Online [*Zhongguo shu ju zai xian*]. N.d. Ann Arbor: University of Michigan and All China Market Research. Available at http://chinadataonline.org.

China's Employment Situation and Policies. 2004. Information Office of the State Council. Available at www.china.org.cn/english/2004/Apr/93983.htm#2.

China Statistical Yearbook. 1981. Beijing: State Statistical Bureau of the People's Republic of China.

———. 1999. Beijing: State Statistical Bureau of the People's Republic of China.

———. 2000. Beijing: State Statistical Bureau of the People's Republic of China.

————. 2001. Beijing: State Statistical Bureau of the People's Republic of China.

————. 2002. Beijing: State Statistical Bureau of the People's Republic of China.

————. 2004. Beijing: State Statistical Bureau of the People's Republic of China.

China Statistical Yearbook on Labor. 1997. Beijing: China Statistical Publishing House.

————. 2001. Beijing: State Statistical Bureau of the People's Republic of China.

China Statistical Yearbook on Population. 1997. Beijing: China Statistics Press.

Chiu, Catherine C. H. 1999. The changing occupations and their prestige structure in urban China. In *China Review 1999*. Ed. Chong Chor Lau and Geng Xiao, 309–328. Hong Kong: Chinese University Press.

Chow, Chung-yan. 2003. Rust-belt giants striving for a future. *South China Morning Post,* October 19, 2003. Reprinted by China Study Group. Available at www.chinastudy group.org.

Chow, Gregory C. 2007. *China's economic transformation.* 2nd ed. Malden, MA: Blackwell.

Chowdhury, Anis, and Iyanatul Islam. 1993. *The newly industrializing economies of East Asia.* London: Routledge.

Chua, Beng-Huat, ed. 2000. *Consumption in Asia: Lifestyles and identities.* London: Routledge.

Chung, Jae Ho. 1999. A sub-provincial recipe of coastal development in China: The case of Qingdao. *China Quarterly* 160:919–952.

Clark, Connie. 1999. Big city, big dreams: In search of work and marriage in China's new urban paradise. Ph.D. diss., University of California at Berkeley.

Clausen, Soren, and Stig Thogersen. 1995. *The making of a Chinese city: History and historiography in Harbin.* Armonk, NY: M. E. Sharpe.

Cleverley, John. 1991. *The schooling of China: Tradition and modernity in Chinese education.* 2nd ed. Sydney: Allen and Unwin.

Cody, Edward. 2006. Students grow desperate over China's tight job market. *Washington Post,* November 24, p. A11.

Collier, Stephen J. 2005a. Budgets and biopolitics. In *Global assemblages: Technology, politics, and ethics as anthropological problems.* Ed. Aihwa Ong and Stephen J. Collier, 373–390. Malden, MA: Blackwell.

————. 2005b. *The spatial forms and social norms of "actually existing neoliberalism": Toward a substantive analysis.* New York: New School University.

————. Forthcoming. *Post Soviet social: Neoliberalism, biopolitics, and social modernity.* Princeton, NJ: Princeton University Press.

Collier, Stephen J., and Andrew Lakoff. 2005. On regimes of living. In *Global assemblages: Technology, politics, and ethics as anthropological problems.* Ed. Aihwa Ong and Stephen J. Collier, 22–39. Malden, MA: Blackwell.

Collier, Stephen J., and Aihwa Ong, eds. 2005. Global assemblages, anthropological problems. In *Global assemblages: Technology, politics, and ethics as anthropological problems.* 3–21. Malden, MA: Blackwell.

Comaroff, Jean, and John Comaroff. 2000. Millennial capitalism and the culture of neoliberalism. Special issue, *Public Culture* 12 (2): 291–343.

Constable, Nicole. 1997. *Maid to order in Hong Kong: Stories of Filipina workers.* Ithaca, NY: Cornell University Press.

CPC CC (Communist Party of China, Central Committee). 1985. *Reform of China's education structure: Decision of the Communist Party of China (CPC) central committee (May 1985).* Beijing: Foreign Languages Press.

———. [1994] 1999. Opinions of the central committee of the Chinese Communist Party regarding the further strengthening and improvement of moral education work in schools. *Chinese Education and Society* 32 (3): 88–102.

Croll, Elisabeth. 1983. *Chinese women since Mao.* London: Zed Books.

———. 1999. Social welfare reform: Trends and tensions. *China Quarterly* 159:684–699.

Dahlman, Carl J., and Jean-Eric Aubert. 2001. *China and the knowledge economy: Seizing the 21st century.* Washington, DC: World Bank.

Dai, Jinhua. 2002. Invisible writing: The politics of mass culture in the 1990s. In *Cinema and desire: Feminist Marxism and cultural politics in the work of Dai Jinhua.* Trans. Jingyuan Zhang. Ed. Jing Wang and Tani E. Barlow, 213–234. London: Verso.

Dai, Xuezhang, and Chuangnian Bai. 2006. Building an innovative city in Dalian [*Dalian jianshe chuangxin xing chengshi de sikao*]. *Journal of Dalian University* 27 (3): 93–96.

Dalian City Government Press Office. *Zhongguo beifang mingzhu: Dalian* [The Northern Pearl, Dalian, China]. 2001. Beijing: People's Fine Arts Publishing House.

Dalian Statistical Bureau. 2000. *Dalian Statistical Yearbook.* Dalian: Dalian Statistical Bureau.

Dalsimer, Marlyn, and Laurie Nisonoff. 1984. The new economic readjustment policies: Implications for Chinese urban working women. *Review of Radical Political Economics* 16 (1): 17–43.

Davin, Delia. 1976. *Woman work: Women and the Party in revolutionary China.* Oxford, UK: Clarendon.

Davis, Deborah. 1988. Unequal chances, unequal outcomes: Pension reform and urban inequality. *China Quarterly* 114:223–242.

———. 1990. Urban job mobility. In *Chinese society on the eve of Tiananmen: The impact of reform.* Ed. Deborah Davis and Ezra Vogel. 85–108. Cambridge, MA: Council on East Asian Studies, Harvard University.

———. 1992. "Skidding": Downward mobility among children of the Maoist middle class. *Modern China* 18 (4): 410–437.

———, ed. 2000a. *The consumer revolution in Urban China.* Berkeley: University of California Press.

———. 2000b. Social class transformation in urban China: Training, hiring, and promoting urban professionals and managers after 1949. *Modern China* 26 (3): 251–275.

Davis, Deborah S., Richard Kraus, Barry Naughton, and Elizabeth J. Perry, eds. 1995. *Urban spaces in contemporary China: The potential for autonomy and community in post-Mao China.* New York: Woodrow Wilson Center Press.

Dean, Mitchell. 1999. *Governmentality: Power and rule in modern society.* London: Sage.

de Certeau, Michel. 1984. *The practice of everyday life.* Trans. Steven Rendall. Berkeley: University of California Press.

DeHart, Monica. 2009. Fried chicken or pop? Redefining development and ethnicity in Totonicapan. *Bulletin of Latin American Research* 28 (1): 64–83.

———. 2010. *Ethnic entrepreneurs: Identity and development politics in Latin America.* Stanford, CA: Stanford University Press.

Deng, Xiaoping. 1985. Decide on major construction projects, make proper use of the talents of scientists and technicians, October 14, 1982. In *Build socialism with Chinese characteristics*. Trans. Bureau for the Compilation and Translation of Works of Marx, Engles, Lenin and Stalin under the Central Committee of the Communist Part of China. Ed. Department for the Research of Party Literature, Central Committee of the Communist Party of China, 6–9. Beijing: Foreign Languages Press.

———. 1994a. China cannot advance without science. In *Selected works of Deng Xiaoping*. Vol. 3. Trans. Bureau for the Compilation and Translation of Works of Marx, Engles, Lenin and Stalin under the Central Committee of the Communist Party of China. Ed. Editorial Committee for Party Literature, Central Committee of the Communist Party of China, 184. Bejing: Foreign Languages Press.

———. 1994b. *Da yidali jizhe aolingaina-falaqi wen* [Responding to Italian Reporter Oriana Fallaci], August 21, 23, 1980. In *Deng Xiaoping wenxuan* [Deng Xiaoping's selected works]. Vol. 2. Ed. Editorial Committee for Party Literature, Central Committee of the Communist Party of China, 344–353. Shenyang, China: People's Publishing.

———. 1994c. *Deng Xiaoping sixiang lilun dacidian* [Encyclopedia of Deng Xiaoping theory]. Shanghai: Shanghai Encyclopedia Publisher.

———. 1994d. We shall concentrate on economic development. In *Selected works of Deng Xiaoping*. Vol. 3. Trans. Bureau for the Compilation and Translation of Works of Marx, Engles, Lenin and Stalin under the Central Committee of the Communist Party of China, 20–22. Bejing: Foreign Languages Press.

———. 1994e. Zunzhong zhishi, zunzhong rencai [Respect knowledge and talent], May 24, 1977. In *Deng Xiaoping wenxuan* [Deng Xiaoping's selected works]. Vol. 2. Ed. Editorial Committee for Party Literature, Central Committee of the Communist Party of China, 40–41. Shenyang, China: People's Publishing.

Ding, Lu. 2001. China's institution development for a market economy since Deng Xiaoping's 1992 *nanxun*. In *The nanxun legacy and China's development in the post-Deng era*. Ed. John Wong and Zheng Yongnian, 51–73. Singapore: Singapore University Press.

Dirlik, Arif. 1999. Globalism and the politics of space. In *Globalisation and the Asia-Pacific: Contested Territories*. Ed. Kris Olds, Peter Dicken, Philip F. Kelly, Lily Kong, and Henry Wai-chung Yeung, 39–56. London: Routledge.

DRJ (Dalian renshiju [Dalian Personnel Bureau]). N.d. *Jiji tansuo, ba biyesheng jiuye zhidu gaige wenbu tuixiang qianjin* [Positive exploration, take the reform of the graduates' career system and push it steadily forward]. Dalian: Dalian Personnel Bureau.

DTSC (Dalian rencai fuwu zhongxin [Dalian Talent Service Center]). 1995. *Dalianshi rencai gongzuo fuwu zhinan* [Guide to the work of Dalian City's Talent Service]. Dalian: Dalian Talent Service Center.

Dunn, Elizabeth Cullen. 2008. Postsocialist spores: Disease, bodies, and the state in the republic of Georgia. *American Ethnologist* 35 (2): 243–258.

DUT (Dalian University of Technology). 1995a. *Dalian ligong daxue jiuliu jie beyesheng (ben, zhuanke) jiuye gongzuo shishi xize* [Rules for the implementation of 1996 graduates of DUT (3- and 4-year) career work]. *Daxuesheng jiuye* [University students' employment] 55 (November): 1–2. Dalian: Dalian University of Technology Admissions and Graduate Employment Office.

———. 1995b. *Jiuwu jie 1995 biyesheng jiuye qingkuang jianjie* [Brief introduction to the situation of 1995 graduates' jobs]. *Daxuesheng jiuye* [University students' employment] 54 (October): 1. Dalian: Dalian University of Technology Admissions and Graduate Employment Office.

———. 1997. *Dalian ligong daxue jiuqi jie biyesheng (ben, zhuanke) jiuye gongzuo zongjie* [Summary of employment work for 1997 graduates of DUT (3- and 4-year)]. Dalian: Dalian University of Technology.

———. 2003. *2003 ju biyesheng jiuye diaocha baogao* [Employment report for 2003 graduates]. *Daxuesheng jiuye* [University students' employment] 93 (July): 2. *Xuesheng jiuye zhongxin* [Dalian University of Technology Student Employment Center].

———. 2004. *Dalian ligong daxue nianjian* [Dalian University of technology yearbook]. Dalian: Dalian University of Technology.

Duthie, Laurie. 2005. White collars with Chinese characteristics: Global capitalism and the formulation of a social identity. *Anthropology of Work Review* 26 (3): 1–12.

———. 2006. White collar China: Global capitalism and the formation of a new social identity in urban China. Paper presented at China Colloquium, Jackson School of International Studies, University of Washington, January 5, in Seattle.

Dutton, Michael. 1988. Policing the Chinese household: A comparison of modern and ancient forms. *Economy and Society* 17 (2): 195–224.

———. 1992. *Policing and punishment in China: From patriarchy to "the people."* London: Cambridge University Press.

———, ed. 1998. *Streetlife China.* Cambridge, UK: Cambridge University Press.

Ekinsmyth, Carol. 1999. Professional workers in a risk society. *Transactions of the Institute of British Geographers* 24:353–366.

Embong, Abdul Rahman, ed. 2001. *Southeast Asian middle classes: Prospects for social change and democratisation.* Bangi, Malaysia: Penerbit Universiti Kebangsaan Malaysia.

Evans, Harriet. 1995. Defining difference: The "scientific" construction of sexuality and gender in the People's Republic of China. *Signs: Journal of Women in Culture and Society* 20 (2): 357.

Eyal, Gil, Ivan Szelenyi, and Eleanor Townsley. 1998. *Making capitalism without capitalists: The new ruling elites in Eastern Europe.* London: Verso.

Farrer, James. 2002. *Opening up: Youth sex culture and market reform in Shanghai.* Chicago: University of Chicago Press.

Fei, Hsiaotung. 1986. *Small towns in China: Functions, problems and prospects.* Beijing: New World Press.

Ferguson, James, and Akhil Gupta. 2002. Spatializing states: Toward an ethnography of neoliberal governmentality. *American Ethnologist* 4 (29): 981–1002.

Fernandes, Leela. 2006. *India's new middle class: Democratic politics in an era of economic reform.* Minneapolis: University of Minnesota Press.

Fincher, John. 1990. Rural bias and the renaissance of coastal cities. In *China's spatial economy: Recent developments and reforms.* Ed. G.J.R. Linge and D. K. Forbes, 35–58. Hong Kong: Oxford University Press.

Fleischer, Friederike. 2007. "To choose a house means to choose a lifestyle." The consumption of housing and class-structuration in urban China. *City and Society* 19 (2): 287–311.

Florida, Richard. 2002a. The economic geography of talent. *Annals of the Association of American Geographers* 92 (4): 743–755.

———. 2002b. *The rise of the creative class: And how it's transforming work, leisure, community and everyday life*. New York: Basic Books.

———. 2005. *Cities and the creative class*. New York: Routledge.

Fodor, Eva. 1997. Gender in transition: Unemployment in Hungary, Poland, and Slovakia. *East European Politics and Societies* 11 (1): 470–500.

Fong, Vanessa. 2002. China's one-child policy and the empowerment of urban daughters. *American Anthropologist* 104 (4): 1098–1109.

———. 2004. *Only hope: Coming of age under China's one-child policy*. Stanford, CA: Stanford University Press.

———. 2007. Morality, cosmopolitanism, or academic attainment? Discourses on "quality" and urban Chinese-only-children's claims to ideal personhood. *City and Society* 19 (1): 86–113.

Forbes, Dean. 1999. Globalisation, postcolonialism and new representations of the Pacific Asian metropolis. In *Globalisation and the Asia-Pacific*. Eds. Kris Olds, Peter Dicken, Philip F. Kelly, Lily Kong, and Henry Wai-chung Yeung, 238–254. London: Routledge.

Foti, Klara. 1994. The labour market in transition: Unemployment in Hungary. *Journal of Communist Studies and Transition Politics* 10 (4): 37–54.

Foucault, Michel. 1978. *The history of sexuality: An introduction*. Vol. 1. New York: Vintage Books.

———. 1979. *Discipline and punish: The birth of the prison*. New York: Vintage Books.

———. 1988. The political technology of individuals. In *Technologies of the self: A seminar with Michel Foucault*. Ed. Luther H. Martin, Huck Gutman, and Patrick H. Hutton, 145–162. Amherst: University of Massachusetts Press.

———. 1991. Governmentality. In *The Foucault effect: Studies in governmentality*. Ed. Graham Burchell, Colin Gordon, and Peter Miller, 87–104. Chicago: University of Chicago Press.

———. 1997a. The birth of biopolitics. In *Michel Foucault ethics: Subjectivity and truth, essential works of Foucault 1954–1984*. Vol. 1. Ed. Paul Rabinow, 73–80. New York: New Press.

———. 1997b. The ethics of the concern for self as a practice of freedom. In *Michel Foucault ethics: Subjectivity and truth, essential works of Foucault 1954–1984*. Vol. 1. Ed. P. Rabinow, 281–301. New York: New Press.

———. 1997c. On the geneaology of ethics: An overview of work in progress. In *Michel Foucault ethics: Subjectivity and truth, essential works of Foucault 1954–1984*. Vol. 1. Ed. P. Rabinow, 253–280. New York: New Press.

———. 1997d. Polemics, politics, and problematizations: An interview with Michel Foucault [1984]. In *Michel Foucault ethics: Subjectivity and truth, essential works of Foucault 1954–1984*. Vol. 1. Ed. P. Rabinow, 111–119. New York: New Press.

Freeman, Richard B. 1994. What direction for labor market institutions in Eastern and Central Europe? In *The transition in Eastern Europe: Restructuring.* Vol. 2. Ed. Olivier Jean Blanchard, Kenneth A. Froot, and Jeffrey D. Sachs, 1–35. Chicago: University of Chicago Press.

Friedman, John. 2002. *The prospect of cities.* Minneapolis: University of Minnesota Press.

Fu, Jing. 2006. Beijing drops out of top 10 "best city" list. China Daily.com.cn, January 1, 2006. Available at www.chinadaily.com.cn.

Gaubatz, Piper Rae. 1995. Urban transformation in post-Mao China: Impacts of the reform era on China's urban form. In *Urban spaces in contemporary China: The potential for autonomy and community in post-Mao China.* Ed. Deborah S. Davis, Richard Kraus, Barry Naughton, and Elizabeth J. Perry, 28–60. New York: Woodrow Wilson Center Press.

Gazso, Ferenc. 1992. Cadre bureaucracy and the intelligentsia. *Journal of Communist Studies* 8 (3): 76–90.

Gillin, Donald G., and Ramon H. Myers, eds. 1989. *Last chance in Manchuria: The diary of Chang Kia-ngau.* Trans. Dolores Zen and Donald Gillin. Stanford, CA: Hoover Institution Press.

Gilmartin, Christina, Gail Hershatter, Lisa Rofel, and Tyrene White, eds. 1994. Introduction. In *Engendering China: Women, culture, and the state.* Ed.Christina Gilmartin, Gail Hershatter, Lisa Rofel, and Tyrene White, 1–26. Cambridge, MA: Harvard University Press.

Gladney, Dru. 1994. Representing nationality in China: Refiguring majority/minority identities. *Journal of Asian Studies* 53 (1): 92–123.

Glaeser, Edward L. 2005. Review of Richard Florida's *The rise of the creative class. Regional Science and Urban Economics* 35:593–596.

Gold, Thomas B. 1989. Guerilla interviewing among the *Getihu.* In *Unofficial China: Popular culture and thought in the PRC.* Ed. Perry Link, Richard Madsen, and Paul Pickowitz, 175–192. Boulder, CO: Westview Press.

———. 1990. Urban private business and social change. In *Chinese society on the eve of Tiananmen: The impact of reform.* Ed. Deborah Davis and Ezra F. Vogel, 157–178. Cambridge, MA: Council on East Asian Studies, Harvard University.

Goldman, Merle. 1981. *China's intellectuals: Advise and dissent.* Cambridge, MA: Harvard University Press.

———. 1992. The intellectuals in the Deng Xiaoping era. In *State and society in China: The consequences of reform.* Ed. Arthur Lewis Rosenbaum, 193–218. Boulder, CO: Westview Press.

———. 1995. Is democracy possible? *Current History* (September): 259–263.

———. 1999. The emergence of politically independent intellectuals. In *The paradox of China's post-Mao reforms.* Ed. Merle Goldman and Roderick MacFarquhar, 283–307. Cambridge, MA: Harvard University Press.

Goldstein, Sidney. 1990. Urbanization in China, 1982–87: Effects of migration and reclassification. *Population and Development Review* 16 (4): 673–701.

Goodall, Keith, and Willem Burgers. 1998. Frequent fliers? Chinese MBAs in a turbulent job market. *Am Chat Newsletter* (May): 1, 5–6. Shanghai: American Chamber of Commerce in Shanghai.

Goodman, Bryan. 1992. New culture, old habits: Native-place organization and the May fourth movement. In *Shanghai sojourners*. Ed. Frederic Wakeman, Jr., and Wen-hsin Yeh, 76–107. Berkeley: Institute of East Asian Studies and Center for Chinese Studies, University of California.

Goodman, David S. G., ed. 1989. Political perspectives. In *China's regional development*, 20–37. London: Routledge.

———. 1996. The People's Republic of China: The party-state, capitalist revolution and new entrepreneurs. In *The new rich in Asia: Mobile phones, McDonald's and middle-class revolution*. Ed. Richard Robison and David S. G. Goodman, 225–242. London: Routledge.

———. 1999. The new middle class. In *The paradox of China's post-Mao reforms*. Ed. Merle Goldman and Roderick MacFarquhar, 241–261. Cambridge, MA: Harvard University Press.

Gordon, Colin. 1991. Governmental rationality: An introduction. In *The Foucault effect: Studies in governmentality*. Ed. Graham Burchell, Colin Gordon, and Peter Miller, 1–52. Chicago: University of Chicago Press.

Gramsci, Antonio. [1971] 1989. *Selections from the prison notebooks*. Ed. and trans. Quintin Hoare and Geoffrey Nowell Smith. New York: International Publishers.

Greenhalgh, Susan. 2005. Globalization and population governance in China. In *Global assemblages: Technology, politics, and ethics as anthropological problems*. Ed. Aihwa Ong and Stephen J. Collier, 354–372. Malden, MA: Blackwell.

———. 2008. *Just one child: Science and policy in Deng's China*. Berkeley, CA: University of California Press.

Greenhalgh, Susan, and Edwin Winckler. 2005. *Governing China's population: From Leninist to neoliberal biopolitics*. Stanford, CA: Stanford University Press.

Gries, Peter Hays. 2004. *China's new nationalism: Pride, politics, and diplomacy*. Berkeley: University of California Press.

Gu, Felicity Rose, and Zilai Tang. 2002. Shanghai: Reconnecting to the global economy. In *Global networks, linked cities*. Ed. Saskia Sassen, 273–308. New York: Routledge.

Gu, Xin 2001. Employment service and unemployment insurance. In *The nanxun legacy and China's development in the post-Deng era*. Ed. John Wong and Zheng Yongnian, 143–169. Singapore: Singapore University Press.

Gui, Shixun, and Xian Liu. 1992. Urban migration in Shanghai, 1950–88: Trends and characteristics. *Population and Development Review* 18 (3): 533–548.

Gupta, Akhil, and James Ferguson. 1999. Culture, power, place: Ethnography at the end of an era. In *Culture, power, place: Explorations in critical anthropology*. Ed. Akhil Gupta and James Ferguson, 1–31. Durham, NC: Duke University Press.

Hackler, Darrene, and Heike Mayer. 2008. Diversity, entrepreneurship, and the urban environment. *Journal of Urban Affairs* 30 (3): 273–307.

Hanser, Amy. 2002a. The Chinese enterprising self: Young educated urbanites and the search for work. In *Unofficial China: Popular culture and thought in the People's Republic*. Ed. Perry Link, Richard Madsen, and Paul Pickowicz, 189–206. Boulder, CO: Westview Press.

———. 2002b. Youth job searches in urban China: The use of social connections in a changing labor market. In *Social connections in China: Institutions, culture, and the changing nature of guanxi.* Ed. Tom Gold, Doug Guthrie, David Wang, 137–161. Cambridge, UK: Cambridge University Press.

Harvey, David. 1989a. *The condition of postmodernity.* Cambridge, MA: Blackwell.

———. 1989b. From managerialism to entrepreneurialism: The transformation in urban governance in late capitalism. *Geografiska Annaler, Series B, Human Geography* 71 (1): 3–17.

———. 2005. *A brief history of neoliberalism.* New York: Oxford University Press.

Hayhoe, Ruth. 1987. China's higher curricular reform in historical perspective. *China Quarterly* 110:196–230.

———. 1989. *China's universities and the open door.* Armonk, NY: M. E. Sharpe.

———. 1993. China's universities since Tiananmen: A critical assessment. *China Quarterly* 134:291–309.

———. 1996. *China's universities, 1895–1995: A century of cultural conflict.* New York: Garland Press.

He, Ping. 2002. *China's search for modernity: Cultural discourse in the late 20th century.* New York: Palgrave Macmillan.

Heelas, Paul, and Paul Morris, eds. 1992. *The values of the enterprise culture: The moral debate.* London: Routledge.

Hertz, Ellen. 1998. *The trading crowd: An ethnography of the Shanghai stock market.* Cambridge, UK: Cambridge University Press.

Hindess, Barry. 1996. Liberalism, socialism and democracy: Variations on a governmental theme. In *Foucault and political reason: Liberalism, neo-liberalism and rationalities of government.* Ed. Andrew Barry, Thomas Osborne, and Nikolas Rose, 65–80. Chicago: University of Chicago Press.

———. 2004. Liberalism—what's in a name? In *Global governmentality: Governing international spaces.* Ed. Wendy Larner and William Walters, 23–39. London: Routledge.

Hoffman, Lisa. 2001. Guiding college graduates to work: Social constructions of labor markets in Dalian. In *China urban: Ethnographies of contemporary culture.* Ed. Nancy Chen, Constance Clark, Susan Gottschang, and Lyn Jeffery, 43–66. Durham, NC: Duke University Press.

———. 2003. Enterprising cities and citizens: The re-figuring of urban spaces and the re-making of post-Mao professionals. *Provincial China* 8 (1): 5–26.

———. 2005. Urban transformation and professionalization: Translocality and rationalities of enterprise in post-Mao China. In *Translocal China.* Ed. Tim Oakes and Louisa Schein, 109–135. London: Routledge.

———. 2006. Autonomous choices and patriotic professionalism: On governmentality in late-socialist China. *Economy and Society* 35 (4): 550–570.

———. 2009. Governmental rationalities of environmental city-building in contemporary China. In *China's governmentalities: Governing change, changing government.* Ed. Elaine Jeffreys, 107–124. London: Routledge.

———. Forthcoming. Contemporary technologies of city building in China: Urban "modeling" and regimes of green urbanism. In *Worlding cities: Asian experiments and the art of being global.* Ed. Ananya Roy and Aihwa Ong. Oxford: Blackwell.

Hoffman, Lisa, Monica DeHart, and Stephen J. Collier. 2006. Notes on the anthropology of neoliberalism. *Anthropology Newsletter* 47 (4): 9–10.

Hoffman, Lisa, and Zhongquan Liu. 1997. Rural urbanization on the Liaodong peninsula: A village, a town, and a nongmin cheng. In *Farewell to peasant China: Rural urbanization and social change in the late twentieth century.* Ed. Gregory Eliyu Guldin, 151–182. Armonk, NY: M. E. Sharpe.

Holmes, Stephen. 1995. *Passions and constraint: On the theory of liberal democracy.* Chicago: University of Chicago Press.

Holston, James. 1989. *The modernist city: An anthropological critique of Brasilia.* Chicago: University of Chicago Press.

Honig, Emily, and Gail Hershatter. 1988. *Personal voices: Chinese women in the 1980's.* Stanford, CA: Stanford University Press.

Hooper, Beverley. 1984. China's modernization: Are young women going to lose out? *Modern China* 10 (3): 317–343.

———. 1998. "Flower vase and housewife" women and consumerism in post-Mao China. In *Gender and power in affluent Asia.* Ed. Krishna Sen and Maila Stivens, 167–194. London: Routledge.

Houston, Donald, Allan Findlay, Richard Harrison, and Colin Mason. 2008. Will attracting the "creative class" boost economic growth in old industrial regions? A case study of Scotland. *Geografiska Annaler: Series B, Human Geography* 90 (2): 133–149.

Howard, Ebenezer. 1965. *Garden cities of to-morrow.* Ed. F. J. Osborn. Cambridge, MA: MIT Press.

Hsieh, David. 1999. The green revolution: In China's industrial north, Dalian shows cleaning up the environment is good for business. *Asiaweek.com.* Available at www.asiaweek.com.

Hsu, Carolyn L. 2007. *Creating market socialism: How ordinary people are shaping class and status in China.* Durham, NC: Duke University Press.

Hu, Angang, and Xin Sheng. 2007. Urban unemployment in China: A background analysis (1995–2003). In *Unemployment in China: Economy, human resources and labour markets.* Ed. Grace O. M. Lee and Malcolm Warner, 36–62. London: Routledge.

Hu, Yi. 2003. Permit reform offers "drifters" in Beijing first-class benefits. *South China Morning Post,* July 8, 2003. Reprinted in China Study News Archive. Available at www.chinastudygroup.org.

Huang, Philip C. C. 1993. "Public sphere"/"civil society" in China? The third realm between state and society. *Modern China* 19 (2): 216–240.

Huang, Xiyi. 1999. Divided gender, divided women: State policy and the labour market. In *Women of China: Economic and social transformation.* Ed. Jackie West, Zhao Minghua, Chang Xiangqun, and Cheng Yuan, 90–107. London: Macmillan Press.

Hubbert, Jennifer. 1999. The long march to modernity: Intellectuals, generations, and moral authority in post-Mao China. Ph.D. diss., Cornell University.

———. 2006a. (Re)collecting Mao: Memory and fetish in contemporary China. *American Ethnologist.* 33 (2): 145–161.

———. 2006b. Visualizing the nation: Counting down to China's Olympics in 2008. Paper presented at American Anthropological Association Annual Meetings, November 15–19, San Jose, California.

Hughes, Christopher R. 2006. *Chinese nationalism in the global era.* London: Routledge.

Ikels, Charlotte. 1996. *The return of the God of wealth: The transition to a market economy in urban China.* Stanford, CA: Stanford University Press.

Jacka, Tamara. 1990. Back to the wok: Women and employment in Chinese industry in the 1980s. *Australian Journal of Chinese Affairs* 24:1–23.

———. 1997. *Women's work in rural China: Change and continuity in an era of reform.* Cambridge, UK: Cambridge University Press.

———. 2007. Population governance in the PRC: Political, historical and anthropological perspectives. *China Journal* 58:111–126.

Jacobs, Bruce J., and Lijian Hong. 1994. Shanghai and the lower Yangzi valley. In *China deconstructs: Politics, trade, and regionalism.* Ed. David S. G. Goodman and Gerald Segal, 224–252. London: Routledge.

Jefferson, Gary H., and Thomas G. Rawski. 1992. Unemployment, underemployment, and employment policy in China's cities. *Modern China* 18 (1): 42–71.

Jeffrey, Craig. 2009. Fixing futures: Educated unemployment through a north Indian lens. *Comparative Studies in Society and History* 51 (1): 182–211.

Jessop, Bob. 1997. The entrepreneurial city: Re-imagining localities, re-designing economic governance, or re-structuring capital? In *Realising cities: New spatial divisions and social transformation.* Ed. Nick Jewson and Susanne MacGregor, 28–41. London: Routledge.

———. 1998. The narrative of enterprise and the enterprise of narrative: Place marketing and the entrepreneurial city. In *The entrepreneurial city: Geographies of politics, regime, and representation.* Ed. Tim Hall and Phil Hubbard, 77–99. Chichester, UK: Wiley.

———. 1999. Reflections on globalization and its (il)logic(s). In *Globalisation and the Asia-Pacific.* Ed. Kris Olds, Peter Dicken, Philip F. Kelly, Lily Kong, and Henry Wai-chung Yeung, 19–38. London: Routledge.

Jessop, Bob, and Ngai-ling Sum. 2000. An entrepreneurial city in action: Hong Kong's emerging strategies in and for (inter)urban competition. *Urban Studies* 37 (12): 2287–2313.

Jiao, Shuqing, ed. 1995. *Daxuesheng jiuye zhidao* [University Graduates Career guidance]. Beijing: Higher Education Press.

JLS (Jones Lang LaSalle). 2007. China 30: China's rising urban stars. In *World winning cities series, emerging city winners.* Jones Lang LaSalle company report.

JPRS (Joint Publications Research Service). [1959] 1962. *Economic geography of northeast China (Liaoning, Kirin, Heilungkiang).* Translation of *Tung-pei Ti-chu Ching-chi Ti-li.* Ed. Sun Ching-chih and K'o-Hsueh Ch'u-pan-she. Washington, DC: U.S. Department of Commerce, Joint Publications Research Service.

Judd, Ellen R. 2002. *The Chinese women's movement: Between state and market.* Stanford, CA: Stanford University Press.

Keeley, Brian. 2007. Human capital: How what you know shapes your life. Paris: Organization for Economic Co-operation and Development (OECD).

Kipnis, Andrew. 1997. *Producing guanxi: Sentiment, self, and subculture in a north China village.* Durham, NC: Duke University Press.

———. 2006. Suzhi: A keyword approach. *China Quarterly* 186:295–313.

———. 2007. Neoliberalism reified: *Suzhi* discourse and tropes of neoliberalism in the People's Republic of China. *Journal of the Royal Anthropological Institute* 13:383–400.

Konrad, George, and Ivan Szelenyi. 1979. *The intellectuals on the road to class power.* New York: Harcourt Brace Jovanovich.

Krugman, Paul. 2009. Money for nothing. *New York Times,* April 26, 2009. Available at www.nytimes.com/2009/04/27/opinion/27krugman.html.

Kurlander, Greg. 1998. Agricultural universities: Engines of rural development? In *Higher education in post-Mao China.* Ed. Michael Agelasto and Bob Adamson, 165–188. Hong Kong: Hong Kong University Press.

Lakoff, Andrew, and Stephen J. Collier. 2004. Ethics and the anthropology of modern reason. *Anthropological Theory* 4 (4): 419–434.

Larner, Wendy. 2003. Neoliberalism? *Environment and Planning D: Society and Space* 21:509–512.

Lee, Ching Kwan. 1998a. *Gender and the south China miracle: Two worlds of factory women.* Berkeley: University of California Press.

———. 1998b. The labor politics of market socialism: Collective inaction and class experiences among state workers in Guangzhou. *Modern China* 24 (1): 3–33.

Lee, Grace O. M., and Malcolm Warner. 2007. Developing labour market policies in China: The experience of Shanghai. In *Unemployment in China: Economy, human resources and labour markets.* Ed. Grace O. M. Lee and Malcolm Warner, 151–165. London: Routledge.

Lee, Hung Yung. 1978. *The politics of the Chinese cultural revolution.* Berkeley: University of California Press.

———. 1991a. From revolutionary cadres to bureaucratic technocrats. In *Contemporary Chinese politics in historical perspective.* Ed. Brantly Womack, 180–206. Cambridge: Cambridge University Press.

———. 1991b. *From revolutionary cadres to party technocrats in socialist China.* Berkeley: University of California Press.

Lee, Peter Nan-shong. 1995. Housing privatization with Chinese characteristics. In *Social change and social policy in contemporary China.* Ed. Linda Wong and Stewart MacPherson, 113–139. Aldershot, UK: Avebury, Ashgate Publishing.

Lee, W. O. 1997. Moral education policy in China: The struggle between liberal and traditional approaches. In *Education and political transition: Themes and experiences in east Asia.* Ed. Mark Bray and W. O. Lee, 201–219. Hong Kong: Comparative Education Research Centre, University of Hong Kong.

Lemke, Thomas. 2001. The birth of bio-politics: Michel Foucault's lecture at the College de France on neo-liberal governmentality. *Economy and Society* 30 (2): 190–207.

Levenson, Joseph. 1957. The amateur ideal in Ming and early Ch'ing society: Evidence from painting. In *Chinese thought and institutions.* Ed. John Fairbank, 320–341. Chicago: University of Chicago Press.

Lewis, John Wilson, ed. 1971. *The city in communist China.* Stanford, CA: Stanford University Press.

Li, Bobai, and Andrew G. Walder. 2001. Career advancement as party patronage: Sponsored mobility into the Chinese administrative elite, 1949–1996. *American Journal of Sociology* 106 (5): 1371–1408.

Li, Cheng, and Lynn T. White III. 1991. China's technocratic movement and the world economic herald. *Modern China* 17 (3): 342–388.

Li, Chengan. 1999. *Zhongguo gaodeng xuexiao biyesheng jiuye shichang jizhi yanjiu* [A study of the mechanism of employment markets for graduates of China's higher education institutes]. Master's thesis, Dalian University of Technology, Liaoning Province.

Li, Mimi. 2003. *Urban regeneration through public space: A case study of squares in Dalian, China.* Master's thesis, University of Waterloo.

Li, Tania Murray. 2007. Practices of assemblage and community forest management. *Economy and Society* 36 (2): 263–293.

Li, Xiaojiang. 1994. Economic reform and the awakening of Chinese women's collective consciousness. In *Engendering China: Women, culture, and the state.* Trans. S. Katherine Cambell. Ed. Christina Gilmartin, Gail Hershatter, Lisa Rofel, and Tyrene White, 360–384. Cambridge, MA: Harvard University Press.

Liaoning Economic Statistical Yearbook [*Liaoning jingji tongji nianjian*]. 1990. Shenyang, China: Liaoning People's Publisher.

Liechty, Mark. 2003. *Suitably modern: Making middle-class culture in a new consumer society.* Princeton, NJ: Princeton University Press.

Lin, Nan, and Yanjie Bian. 1991. Getting ahead in urban China. *American Journal of Sociology* 97 (3): 657–688.

Lin, Nan, and Wen Xie. 1988. Occupational prestige in urban China. *American Journal of Sociology* 93 (4): 793–832.

Linge, G.J.R., and D. K. Forbes, eds. 1990. The space economy of China. In *China's spatial economy: Recent developments and reforms.* 11–34. Hong Kong: Oxford University Press.

Litzinger, Ralph. 2000. *Other Chinas: The yao and the politics of national belonging.* Durham, NC: Duke University Press.

Liu, Changde. 2000. Urban environment construction and protection, Dalian, China. Paper presented at International Seminar on Best Practices: UN Local Leadership Programme on Sustainable Development, October 20–22, in Hangzhou.

Liu, Fengshu. 2008. Constructing the autonomous middle-class self in today's China: The case of young-adult only-children university students. *Journal of Youth Studies* 11 (2): 193–212.

Liu, Zhongquan. n.d. *2010 nian huan Bohai jingji quandaizhuang chengshiqun kaifa zhanlue yanjiu: Xiangmu jianyi shu* [Research on the strategy of opening and developing the Bohai economic ring's urban group for the year 2010: Recommendation piece]. Paper presented at a conference at the Dalian University of Technology, Shandong Province.

Liu, Zhongquan, Xiaolan Ji, and Baixin Chang. 1994. *Dalian xiandai chengzhen tixi yu jiasu quyu chengsihuade zhuanlue xuanze* [Dalian's strategic choices for city and town systematization and rapid urbanization]. Dalian: Dalian Urban Economy Working Group.

Liu, Zhongquan, and Qingxi Sui. n.d. *Guanyu Dalian weilai chengshi xingtai de yanjiu* [An inquiry into the study of Dalian's future urban pattern]. Dalian: Dalian University of Technology, Dalian Science and Technology Committee.

Liu, Zhongren, ed. 1999. *Daxuesheng xuanye zhinan* [College graduate guide for choosing a profession]. Beijing: China Materials Publisher.

Low, Setha. 2000. *On the plaza: The politics of public space and culture.* Austin: University of Texas Press.

Lu, Jianhua. 1997. Zuoxiang xin jiegou [Moving toward a new structure]. In *Guanjian shike: Dangdai zhongguo jidai jiejue de 27 ge wenti* [A critical moment: Twenty-seven problems of contemporary China needing urgent solutions]. Ed. Xu Ming, 436–451. Beijing: Jinri Zhongguo Chubanshe.

Lu, Xiaobo. 1997. Minor public economy: The revolutionary origins of the *danwei.* In *Danwei: The changing Chinese workplace in historical and comparative perspective.* Ed. Xiaobo Lu and Elizabeth J. Perry, 21–41. Armonk, NY: M. E. Sharpe.

Lu, Xiaobo, and Elizabeth J. Perry, eds. 1997. *Danwei: The changing Chinese workplace in historical and comparative perspective.* Armonk, NY: M. E. Sharpe.

Ma, Laurence J. C. 2002. Urban transformation in China, 1949–2000: A review and research agenda. *Environment and Planning A* 34 (9):1545–1569.

Madsen, Richard. 1993. The public sphere, civil society and moral community. *Modern China* 19 (2): 183–198.

Mahmood, Saba. 2005. *Politics of piety: The Islamic revival and the feminist subject.* Princeton, NJ: Princeton University Press.

Mao, Tsetung. 1971. *Selected readings from the works of Mao Tsetung.* Peking: Foreign Languages Press.

Markusen, Ann. 2006. Urban development and the politics of a creative class: Evidence from a study of artists. *Environment and Planning A* 38 (10):1921–1940.

Marshall, Richard. 2003. *Emerging urbanity: Global urban projects in the Asia Pacific Rim.* London: Spon Press.

Massey, Doreen. 1992. Politics and space/time. *New Left Review* 196:65–84.

———. 1993. Power-geometry and a progressive sense of place. In *Mapping the futures: Local cultures, global change.* Ed. Jon Bird, Barry Curtis, Tim Putman, George Robertson, and Lisa Tickner, 59–69. New York: Routledge.

———. 1994. *Space, place, and gender.* Minneapolis: University of Minnesota Press.

Massey, Doreen, and John Allen, eds., with John Anderson, Susan Cunningham, Christopher Hamnett, and Philip Sarre. 1984. *Geography matters! A reader.* Cambridge, UK: Cambridge University Press.

McDowell, Linda. 1983. Towards an understanding of the gender division of urban space. *Environment and Planning D: Society and Space* 1:59–72.

Meisner, Maurice. 1977. *Mao's China: A history of the People's Republic.* New York: Free Press.

———. 1986. *Mao's China and after: A history of the People's Republic.* New York: Free Press.

———. 1989. Marx, Mao, and Deng on the division of labor in history. In *Marxism and the Chinese experience: Issues in contemporary Chinese socialism.* Ed. Arif Dirlik and Maurice Meisner, 79–116. Armonk, NY: M. E. Sharpe.

Miller, H. Lyman. 1996. *Science and dissent in post-Mao China: The politics of knowledge.* Seattle: University of Washington Press.

Misra, Kalpana. 1998. *From post-Maoism to post-Marxism: The erosion of official ideology in Deng's China.* New York: Routledge.

Mitchell, Katharyne. 2004. *Crossing the neoliberal line: Pacific Rim migration and the metropolis.* Philadelphia: Temple University Press.

Mole, Noelle J. 2008. Living it on the skin: Italian states, working illness. *American Ethnologist* 35 (2): 189–210.

Moore, Henrietta. 1986. *Space, text and gender: An anthropological study of the Marakwet of Kenya.* New York: Guilford Press.

Muehlebach, Andrea K. 2007. *The moral neoliberal: Welfare state and ethical citizenship in contemporary Italy.* Ph.D. diss., University of Chicago.

Muniesa, Fabian, Yuval Millo, and Michel Callon. 2007. An introduction to market devices. *Sociological Review* 55 (2): 1–12.

Murphey, Rhoads. 1974. The treaty ports and China's modernization. In *The Chinese city between two worlds.* Ed. Mark Elvin and G. William Skinner, 17–72. Stanford, CA: Stanford University Press.

Murphy, Rachel. 2004. Turning peasants into modern Chinese citizens: "Population quality" discourse, demographic transition and primary education. *China Quarterly* 177:1–20.

Naughton, Barry. 1988. The third front: Defense industrialization in the Chinese interior. *China Quarterly* 115:351–386.

———. 1996. *Growing out of the plan: Chinese economic reform 1978–1993.* Cambridge, UK: Cambridge University Press.

———. 1997. *Danwei*: The economic foundations of a unique institution. In *Danwei: The changing Chinese workplace in historical and comparative perspective.* Ed. Xiaobo Lu and Elizabeth J. Perry, 169–194. Armonk, NY: M. E. Sharpe.

Newman, Richard J. 2005. The rise of a new power. *U.S. News and World Report* (June 20): 40–51.

Notar, Beth. 1994. Of labor and liberation: Images of women in current Chinese television advertising. *Visual Anthropology Review* 10 (2): 29–44.

Olds, Kris. 2001. *Globalization and urban change: Capital, culture and Pacific Rim megaprojects.* Oxford: Oxford University Press.

Olds, Kris, and Nigel Thrift. 2005. Cultures on the brink: Re-engineering the soul of capitalism—on a global scale. In *Global assemblages: Technology, politics and ethics as anthropological problems.* Ed. Aihwa Ong and Stephen Collier, 270–290. Boston: Blackwell.

Olds, Kris, and Henry Wai-Chung Yeung. 2004. Pathways to global city formation: A view from the developmental city-state of Singapore. *Review of International Political Economy* 11 (3): 489–521.

Olesen, Alexa. 2006. Chinese president issues list of virtues. *Associated Press, Yahoo News,* March 15.

Ong, Aihwa. 1991. The gender and labor politics of postmodernity. *Annual Review of Anthropology* 20:279–309.

———. 1995. State versus Islam: Malay families, women's bodies, and the body politic in Malaysia. In *Bewitching women, pious men: Gender and body politics in southeast Asia.* Ed. Aihwa Ong and Michael Peletz, 159–194. Berkeley: University of California Press.

———. 1996. Cultural citizenship as subject-making. *Current Anthropology* 37 (5): 737–762.

———. 1999. *Flexible citizenship: The cultural logics of transnationality.* Durham, NC: Duke University Press.

———. 2003. *Buddha is hiding: Refugees, citizenship, the New America.* Berkeley: University of California Press.

———. 2006. *Neoliberalism as exception: Mutations in citizenship and sovereignty.* Durham, NC: Duke University Press.

———. Forthcoming. Worlding cities, or the art of being global. In *Worlding cities: Asian experiments and the art of being global.* Ed. Ananya Roy and Aihwa Ong. Oxford, MA: Blackwell.

Ong, Aihwa, and Stephen J. Collier. 2005. *Global assemblages: Technology, politics, and ethics as anthropological problems.* Malden, MA: Blackwell.

Orleans, Leo. 1987. Graduates of Chinese universities: Adjusting the total. *China Quarterly* 111:444–449.

Paine, Lynn Webster. 1994. Progress and problems in China's educational reform. In *China Briefing 1994.* Ed. William A. Joseph, 113–131. Boulder, CO: Westview Press.

Pan, Zhongdan, Chin-chuan Lee, Joseph Man Chuan, and Clement K.Y. So. 2005. To cheer for the family-nation: The construction of Chinese nationalism during the Hong Kong handover. In *Cultural studies in China.* Ed. D. F. Tao and Y. P. Jin, 40–67. Singapore: Marshall Cavendish Academic Press.

Pang, Guobin, Jinggen Chen, and Yunxia Yang. 2003. Challenges and countermeasures of higher education in building "Greater Dalian" ["Da Dalian" jian she dui gao deng jiao yu de tiao zhan he dui ce]. *Journal of Dalian University of Technology (Social Sciences Edition)* 24 (2): 83–86.

Parris, Kristen. 1993. Local initiative and national reform: The Wenzhou model of development. *China Quarterly* 134:242–263.

———. 1994. Reinventing local identity in Wenzhou. Paper presented at the Symposium on "Chinese Identities," at the Center for Chinese Studies, University of California, February 25–26, in Berkeley.

———. 1999. The rise of private business interests. In *The paradox of China's post-Mao reforms.* Ed. Merle Goldman and Roderick MacFarquhar, 262–282. Cambridge, MA: Harvard University Press.

Pearson, Margaret M. 1997. *China's new business elite: The political consequences of economic reform.* Berkeley: University of California Press.

Peck, Jamie. 2005. Struggling with the creative class. *International Journal of Urban and Regional Research* 29, no. 4(December): 740–770.

Peck, Jamie, and Adam Tickell. 2002. Neoliberalizing space. In *Spaces of neoliberalism.* Ed. Neil Brenner and Nik Theodore, 33–57. Malden, MA: Blackwell.

———. 2007. Conceptualizing neoliberalism, thinking Thatcherism. In *Contesting neoliberalism: Urban frontiers.* Ed. Helga Leitner, Jamie Peck, and Erik S. Sheppard, 26–50. New York: Guilford Press.

Pendras, Mark. 2009. Urban politics and the production of capital mobility in the United States. *Environment and Planning A* 41 (7): 1691–1706.

People's Daily. 1999. Cultivating Innovative Talents, March 12, p. 2.

Pepper, Suzanne. 1984. *China's universities: Post-Mao enrollment policies and their impact on the structure of secondary education, a research report.* Ann Arbor, MI: Center for Chinese Studies.

———. 1990. *China's education reform in the 1980s: Policies, issues, and historical perspectives.* Berkeley: Institute of East Asian Studies and Center for Chinese Studies at UC Berkeley.

———. 1995. Regaining the initiative for education reform and development. In *China Review 1995.* Ed. Lo Chi Kin, Suzanne Pepper, and Tsui Kai Yuen, 18.2–18.49. Hong Kong: Chinese University Press.

———. 1996. *Radicalism and education reform in twentieth-century China: A search for an ideal development model.* New York: Cambridge University Press.

Perrins, Bob. 1999. Contractual formal empire in South Manchuria: Russian and Japanese efforts to build a northern Hong Kong in Dalian, 1898–1932. Paper presented at Center for Asian Studies, University of Hong Kong, June 29, in Hong Kong.

Perry, Elizabeth J. 1993. *Shanghai on strike: The politics of Chinese labor.* Stanford, CA: Stanford University Press.

———. 1997. From native place to workplace: Labor origins and outcomes of China's danwei system. In *Danwei: The changing Chinese workplace in historical and comparative perspective.* Ed. Xiaobo Lu and Elizabeth J. Perry, 42–59. Armonk, NY: M. E. Sharpe.

Phillipps, David R., and Anthony G. O. Yeh. 1989. Special economic zones. In *China's regional development.* Ed. David S. G. Goodman, 112–134. London: Routledge.

Pinches, Michael, ed. 1999. *Culture and privilege in capitalist Asia.* London: Routledge.

Pred, Allan. 1990a. "In other wor(l)ds": Fragmented and integrated observations on gendered languages, gendered spaces and local transformation. *Antipode* 22 (1): 33–52.

———. 1990b. *Lost words and lost worlds: Modernity and the language of everyday life in late nineteenth-century Stockholm.* Cambridge: Cambridge University Press.

———. 1990c. *Making histories and constructing human geographies: The local transformation of practice, power relations, and consciousness.* Boulder, CO: Westview Press.

Pred, Allan, and Michael John Watts. 1992. *Reworking modernity: Capitalisms and symbolic discontent,* New Brunswick, NJ: Rutgers University Press.

Price, Ronald. 1970. *Education in communist China.* New York: Praeger.

Pun, Ngai. 1999. Chinese labour at the end of the 20th century. In *China review 1999.* Ed. Chong Chor Lau and Geng Xiao, 329–344. Hong Kong: Chinese University Press.

———. 2003. Subsumption or consumption: The phantom of consumer revolution in "globalizing China." *Cultural Anthropology* 18 (4): 469–492.

———. 2005. *Made in China: Women factory workers in a global workplace.* Durham, NC: Duke University Press.

PuruShotam, Nirmala. 1998. Between compliance and resistance: Women and the middle-class way of life in Singapore. In *Gender and power in affluent Asia.* Ed. Krishna Sen and Maila Stivens, 127–166. London: Routledge.

Rabinow, Paul, ed. 1984. Introduction to *The Foucault reader,* 3–29. New York: Pantheon Books.

―――. 1989. *French modern: Norms and forms of the social environment.* Cambridge, MA: MIT Press.

―――. 2003. Ordonnance, discipline, regulation: Some reflections on urbanism. In *The anthropology of space and place: Locating culture.* Ed. Setha Low and Denise Lawrence-Zuniga, 353–362. Boston: Blackwell.

Rabinow, Paul, and Nikolas Rose, eds. 1994. Introduction: Foucault today. In *The essential Foucault: Selections from essential works of Foucault, 1954–1984.* vii–xxxv. New York: New Press.

Rai, Shirin M. 1991. *Resistance and reaction: University politics in post-Mao China.* New York: St. Martin's Press.

―――. 1992. "Watering another man's garden": Gender, employment and educational reforms in China. In *Women in the face of change: The Soviet Union, Eastern Europe and China.* Ed. Shirin Rai, Hilary Pilkington, and Annie Phizacklea, 20–40. London: Routledge.

Ramo, Joshua Cooper. 2004. *The Beijing consensus.* London: Foreign Policy Centre.

Rankin, Mary Backus. 1993. Some observations on a Chinese public sphere. *Modern China* 19 (2): 158–182.

Robinson, Jennifer. 2002. Global and world cities: A view from off the map. *International Journal of Urban and Regional Research* 26 (3): 531–554.

Robison, Richard, and David S. G. Goodman, eds. 1996. The new rich in Asia: Economic development, social status and political consciousness. In *The new rich in Asia: Mobile phones, McDonald's and middle-class revolution,* 1–18. London: Routledge.

Rocca, Jean-Louis. 1994. The new elites. In *China review 1994.* Ed. Maurice Brosseau and Lo Chi Kin, 16.1–16.21. Hong Kong: Chinese University Press.

Rofel, Lisa. 1994. Liberation nostalgia and a yearning for modernity. In *Engendering China: Women, culture, and the state.* Ed. Christina Gilmartin, Gail Hershatter, Lisa Rofel, and Tyrene White, 226–249. Cambridge, MA: Harvard University Press.

―――. 1999. *Other modernities: Gendered yearnings in China after socialism.* Berkeley: University of California Press.

―――. 2007. *Desiring China: Experiments in neoliberalism, sexuality, and public culture.* Durham, NC: Duke University Press.

Rose, Nikolas. 1992. Governing the enterprising self. In *The values of the enterprise culture: The moral debate.* Ed. Paul Heelas and Paul Morris, 141–164. London: Routledge.

―――. 1993. Government, authority and expertise in advanced liberalism. *Economy and Society* 22 (3): 283–299.

―――. 1996a. The death of the social: Refiguring the territory of government. *Economy and Society* 25 (3): 327–356.

―――. 1996b. Governing "advanced" liberal democracies. In *Foucault and political reason: Liberalism, neo-liberalism, and rationalities of government.* Ed. Andrew Barry, Thomas Osborne, and Nikolas Rose, 37–64. Chicago: University of Chicago Press.

―――. 1998. *Inventing our selves: Psychology, power, and personhood.* Cambridge: Cambridge University Press.

―――. 1999. *Powers of freedom: Reframing political thought.* Cambridge: Cambridge University Press.

Rose, Nikolas, and Peter Miller. 1992. Political power beyond the state: Problematics of government. *British Journal of Sociology* 43 (2): 172–205.

Rosen, Stanley. 1984. New directions in secondary education. In *Contemporary Chinese education*. Ed. Ruth Hayhoe, 65–91. London: Croom and Helm.

———. 1994. Chinese women in the 1990s: Images and roles in contention. In *China review 1994*. Ed. Maurice Brosseau and Lo Chi Kin, 17.1–17.28. Hong Kong: Chinese University Press.

———. 1997. Education and education reform. In *China handbook*. Ed. Christopher Hudson, advisers Marc Blecher and Judy Curry, 250–261. Chicago: Fitzroy Dearborn Publishers.

———. 2004. The victory of materialism: Aspirations to join China's urban moneyed classes and the commercialization of education. *China Journal* 51:27–51.

Rowe, William T. 1989. *Hankow: Conflict and community in a Chinese city, 1796–1895*. Stanford, CA: Stanford University Press.

———. 1990. The public sphere in modern China. *Modern China* 16 (3): 309–329.

———. 1993. The problem of "civil society" in late imperial China. *Modern China* 19 (2): 139–157.

———. 1998. Northeast China: Waiting for regionalism. *Problems of Post-Communism* 45 (4): 3–13.

Rozman, Gilbert. 1985. *A mirror for socialism: Soviet criticisms of China*. Princeton, NJ: Princeton University Press.

———. 1998. Northeast China: Waiting for regionalism. *Problems of Post-Communism* 45 (4): 3–13.

Saich, Tony. 1994. The search for civil society and democracy in China. *Current History* (September): 260–264.

Sassen, Saskia. 1991. *The global city: New York, London, Tokyo*. Princeton, NJ: Princeton University Press.

———. 1994. *Cities in a world economy*. Thousand Oaks, CA: Pine Forge Press.

———. 1998. *Globalization and its discontents: Essays on the new mobility of people and money*. New York: New Press.

———. 2002. Introduction: Locating cities on global circuits. In *Global networks, linked cities*. Ed. Saskia Sassen, 1–38. New York: Routledge.

Schein, Louisa. 2000. *Minority rules: The miao and the feminine in China's cultural politics*. Durham, NC: Duke University Press.

———. 2001. Urbanity, cosmopolitanism, consumption. In *China urban: Ethnographies of contemporary culture*. Ed. Nancy Chen, Constance Clark, Susan Gottschang, and Lyn Jeffery, 225–241. Durham, NC: Duke University Press.

———. 2004. Media, entrepreneurship, transnationality: Moments in production and reception. Paper presented at the Social, Cultural, and Political Implications of Privatization conference, June 27–29, in Shanghai.

Schinz, Alfred. 1989. *Cities in China*. Berlin: Gebruder Borntraeger.

Schueller, Marot. 1997. Liaoning: Struggling with the burdens of the past. In *China's provinces in reform: Class, community and political culture*. Ed. David S. G. Goodman, 93–121. London: Routledge.

Scott, Allen J. 2001. *Global city-regions: Trends, theory, policy.* Oxford: Oxford University Press.

SEC (State Education Commission [Guojia jiaoyu weiyuanhui]). 1992. *Putong gaodeng xuexiao zhaosheng gongzuo nianjian* [Yearbook of ordinary higher education enrollment work]. Beijing: People's Education Press.

————. 1993. *Putong gaodeng xuexiao zhaosheng gongzuo nianjian* [Yearbook of ordinary higher education enrollment work]. Beijing: People's Education Press.

Seeberg, Vilma. 1998. Stratification trends in technical-professional higher education. In *Higher education in post-Mao China.* Ed. Michael Agelasto and Bob Adamson, 211–236. Hong Kong: Hong Kong University Press.

Segal, Adam. 2003. *Digital dragon: High technology enterprises in China.* Ithaca, NY: Council on Foreign Relations.

Segal, Gerald. 1994. Deconstructing foreign relations. In *China deconstructs: Politics, trade, and regionalism.* Ed. David S. G. Goodman and Gerald Segal, 322–355. London: Routledge.

Sen, Krishna, and Maila Stivens, eds. 1998. *Gender and power in affluent Asia.* London: Routledge.

Sensenbrenner, Julia. 1996. *Rust in the iron rice bowl: Labor reforms in Shanghai's state enterprises, 1992–1993.* Ph.D. diss., Johns Hopkins University.

Shanghaishi gaoxiao biyesheng jiuye zhidao zhongxin [Shanghai Higher Education Graduates' Career Guidance Center]. 1998. *Recruit book Shanghai: Career information volume 2 (free).* Shanghai: *Shanghaishi gaoxiao biyesheng jiuye zhidao zhongxin.*

Shi, Jianhua. 2000. Zuojin guoji mingcheng [Becoming a famous international city]. *Dalian Daily,* May 19.

Shirk, Susan L. 1982. *Competitive comrades: Career incentives and student strategies in China.* Berkeley: University of California Press.

————. 1985. The politics of industrial reform. In *The political economy of reform in post-Mao China.* Ed. Elizabeth J. Perry and Christine Wong, 195–221. Cambridge, MA: Council on East Asian Studies, Harvard University.

Shore, Cris, and Susan Wright, ed. 1997. *Anthropology of policy: Critical perspectives on governance and power.* London: Routledge.

Short, John Rennie, and Yeong-Hyun Kim. 1999. *Globalization and the city.* Harlow, England: Pearson/Prentice Hall.

Sigley, Gary. 1996. Governing Chinese bodies: The significance of studies in the concept of governmentality for the analysis of government in China. *Economy and Society* 25 (4): 457–482.

————, ed. 1998. Getting it right: Marriage, sex, and pleasure. Special issue, *Chinese Sociology and Anthropology* 31 (1).

————. 2004. Liberal despotism: Population planning, subjectivity, and government in contemporary China. *Alternatives* 29 (5): 557–575.

————. 2006. Chinese governmentalities: Government, governance, and the socialist market economy. In *Economy and Society* 35 (4): 487–508.

Sit, Victor F. S. 1985. Introduction: Urbanization and city development in the People's Republic of China. In *Chinese cities: The growth of the metropolis since 1949.* Ed. Victor F. S. Sit, 1–66. Oxford: Oxford University Press.

Siu, Noel Y. M., and C. P. Lau. 1998. Training and development practices in the People's Republic of China. *China Report* 34 (1): 47–67.

Smart, Alan, and Li Zhang. 2006. From the mountains and the fields: The urban transition in the anthropology of China. *China Information* 20 (3): 481–518.

Smith, David M. 1996. The socialist city. In *Cities after socialism: Urban and regional change and conflict in post-socialist societies.* Ed. Gregory Andrusz, Michael Harloe, and Ivan Szelenyi, 70–99. Oxford: Blackwell.

Solinger, Dorothy. 1993. *China's transition from socialism: Statist legacies and market reforms 1980–1990.* Armonk, NY: M. E. Sharpe.

———. 1995. The floating population in the cities' chances for assimilation? In *Urban spaces in contemporary China.* Ed. Deborah Davis, Richard Kraus, Barry Naughton, and Elizabeth J. Perry, 113–139.New York: Woodrow Wilson Center Press.

———. 1999. *Contesting citizenship in urban China: Peasant migrants, the state, and the logic of the market.* Berkeley: University of California Press.

———. [2004] 2006. The creation of a new underclass in China and its implications. *Environment and Urbanization* 18 (1): 177–193.

Song, Jessook. 2006a. Family breakdown and invisible homeless women: Neoliberal goverance during the Asian debt crisis in South Korea, 1997–2001. *Positions: East Asia Cultures Critique* 14 (1): 37–65.

———. 2006b. Historicization of homeless spaces: The Seoul train station square and the house of freedom. *Anthropological Quarterly* 79 (2): 193–223.

Stacey, Judith. 1983. *Patriarchy and socialist revolution in China.* Berkeley: University of California Press.

Stam, Erik, Jeroen P. J. deJong, and Gerard Marlet. 2008. Creative industries in the Netherlands: Structure, development, innovativeness and effects on urban growth. *Geografiska Annaler: Series B, Human Geography* 90 (2): 119–132.

Stivens, Maila. 1998. Sex, gender, and the making of the new Malay middle classes. In *Gender and power in affluent Asia.* Ed. Krishna Sen and Maila Stivens, 87–126. London: Routledge.

Strand, David. 1989. *Rickshaw Beijing: City people and politics in the 1920s.* Berkeley: University of California.

Su, Wenming, ed. 1985. *The open policy at work.* Beijing: Beijing Review Publications.

———. 1986. *The 14 coastal cities and Hainan Island.* Beijing: Beijing Review Publications.

Sum, Ngai-ling. 1999. Rethinking globalization: Re-articulating the spatial scale and temporal horizons of trans-border spaces. In *Globalisation and the Asia-Pacific.* Ed. Kris Olds, Peter Dicken, Philip F. Kelly, Lily Kong, and Henry Wai-chung Yeung, 129–146. London: Routledge.

Szelenyi, Ivan. 1996. Cities under socialism—and after. In *Cities after socialism: Urban and regional change and conflict in post-socialist societies.* Ed. Gregory Andrusz, Michael Harloe, and Ivan Szelenyi, 286–317. Oxford: Blackwell.

Tan, Songhua. 1994. A realistic approach to human resources development in China: Education, the system of labor, and human resources development. *Social Sciences in China* 15 (1): 33–45.

Tang, Wenfang, and William Parish. 2000. *Chinese urban life under reform: The changing social contract*. Cambridge: Cambridge University Press.

Tang, Wingshing. 2000. Chinese urban planning at fifty: An assessment of the planning theory literature. *Journal of Planning Literature* 14 (3): 347–366.

———. 2006. Planning Beijing strategically: "One world, one dream." *Town Planning Review* 77 (3): 257–282.

Tang, Zhihong, and Xiaohua Wang, eds. 1992. *Bangzhu ni jiuye* [Helping with your career]. Dalian: Dalian University of Technology.

Thompson, Michael W. J. 2006. Dalian: China's Bangalore. *Global Dateline* (Winter): 21–23.

Tomba, Luigi. 2004. Creating an urban middle class: Social engineering in Beijing. *China Journal* 51:1–26.

Tu, Wei-ming, ed. 1994. *China in transformation*. Cambridge, MA: Harvard University Press.

UN (United Nations). 1999. The China human development report. United Nations Development Programme (UNDP), China. New York: Oxford University Press.

Unger, Jonathan. 1982. *Education under Mao: Class and competition in Canton schools, 1960–1980*. New York: Columbia University Press.

Verdery, Katherine. 1991. *National ideology under socialism: Identity and cultural politics in Ceausescu's Romania*. Berkeley: University of California Press.

Vorley, Tim, Oli Mould, and Helen Lawton Smith. 2008. Introduction to geographical economies of creativity, enterprise and the creative industries. *Geogafiska Annaler: Series B, Human Geography* 90 (2): 101–106.

Wakeman, Frederic. 1993. The civil society and public sphere debate: Western reflections on Chinese political culture. *Modern China* 19 (2): 108–138.

Walcott, Susan M. 2003. *Chinese science and technology industrial parks*. Burlington, VT: Ashgate.

Walder, Andrew G. 1995a. Career mobility and the Communist political order. *American Sociological Review* 60:309–328.

———, ed. 1995b. *The waning of the communist state: Economic origins of political decline in China and Hungary*. Berkeley: University of California Press.

Wang, Fei-ling. 1998. Floaters, moonlighters, and the underemployed: A national labor market with Chinese characteristics. *Journal of Contemporary China* 7 (9): 459–475.

Wang, Hui. 2004. The year 1989 and the historical roots of neoliberalism in China. *Positions: East Asia Cultural Critique* 12 (1): 7–69.

Wang, Jing. 1996. *High culture fever: Politics, aesthetics, and ideology in Deng's China*. Berkeley: University of California Press.

Wang, Wei. 2003. Building "Greater Dalian": Considering a new strategy for urban development in the twenty-first century [Jian she "Da Dalian": Tan xin 21 shi ji cheng shi fa zhan de xin si lu]. *Journal of Dalian University of Technology (Social Sciences Edition)* 24 (2): 79–82.

Wang, Xiufang. 2003. *Education in China since 1976*. Jefferson, NC: McFarland.

Wang, Yi. 2007. Dalian: The shining pearl of the north. *China Daily*, September 6, 2007. Available at www.chinadaily.com.cn/china/2007-09/06/content_6085189.htm.

Wang, Yonghe, and Fengping Zhao. 2004. Strengthening the city with science and education when building "Greater Dalian" [Jian she "Da Dalian" bi xu shi shi ke jian qiang shi zhan lue]. *Journal of Dalian Education University* 20 (2): 1–4.

Warner, Malcolm, and Grace O. M. Lee. 2007. Setting the scene: Unemployment in China. In *Unemployment in China: Economy, human resources and labour markets.* Ed. Grace O. M. Lee and Malcolm Warner, 3–16. London: Routledge.

Webber, Michael, and Zhu Ying. 2007. Primitive accumulation, transition and unemployment in China. In *Unemployment in China: Economy, human resources and labour markets.* Ed. Grace-.O. M. Lee and Malcolm Warner, 17–35. London: Routledge.

Wen, Fuxiang 1996. Enhancing students' overall quality and promoting society's all-around development. In *East-West dialogue in knowledge and higher education.* Ed. Ruth Hayhoe and Julia Pan, 266–279. Armonk, NY: M. E. Sharpe.

White, Gordon. 1987. The politics of economic reform in Chinese industry: The introduction of the labor contract system. *China Quarterly* 111:365–389.

White, Lynn T., III. 1978. *Careers in Shanghai: The social guidance of personal energies in a developing Chinese city, 1949–1966.* Berkeley: University of California Press.

Whyte, Martin K. 1992. Urban China: A civil society in the making? In *State and society in China: The consequences of reform.* Ed. Arthur Lewis Rosenbaum, 77–102. Boulder, CO: Westview Press.

———. 1993. Deng Xiaoping: The social reformer. *China Quarterly* 135:515–535.

———. 2004. The victory of materialism: Aspirations to join China's urban moneyed classes and the commercialization of education. *China Journal* 51:27–51.

———. 2005. Continuity and change in urban Chinese family life. *China Journal* 53: 9–33.

Whyte, Martin K., and William L. Parish. 1984. *Urban life in contemporary China.* Chicago: University of Chicago Press.

Williams, Raymond. 1983. *Keywords: A vocabulary of culture and society.* Rev. ed. New York: Oxford University Press.

Wolf, Margery. 1985. *Revolution postponed: Women in contemporary China.* Stanford, CA: University Press.

Wong, John. 2001. The economics of *nanxun.* In *The nanxun legacy and China's development in the post-Deng era.* Ed. John Wong and Zheng Yongnian, 35–50. Singapore: Singapore University Press.

Wong, John, and Yongnian Zheng. 2001. The political economy of China's post-*nanxun* development. In *The nanxun legacy and China's development in the post-Deng era.* Ed. John Wong and Zheng Yongnian, 3–17. Singapore: Singapore University Press.

Wong, Kwan-Yiu. 1987. China's special economic zone experiment: An appraisal. *Geografiska Annaler Series B, Human Geography* 69 (1): 27–40.

Woo, Margaret Y. K. 1994. Chinese women workers: The delicate balance between protection and equality. In *Engendering China: Women, culture, and the state.* Ed. Christina Gilmartin, Gail Hershatter, Lisa Rofel, and Tyrene White, 279–298. Cambridge, MA: Harvard University Press.

World Bank. 1997. *China: Higher education reform: World Bank country study.* Washington, DC: World Bank.

Woronov, Terry. 2002. Transforming the future: "Quality" children for the Chinese nation. Ph.D. diss., University of Chicago.

Wu, Fulong. 2003. The (post-)socialist entrepreneurial city as a state project: Shanghai's reglobalisation in question. *Urban Studies* 40 (9): 1673–1698.

———. 2006. Globalization and China's new urbanism. In *Globalization and the Chinese city*. Ed. Fulong Wu, 1–18. New York: Routledge.

Xiao, Guirong. 2007. *Urban tourism: Global-local relationships in Dalian, China*. Ph.D. diss., University of Waterloo.

Xiao, Jin, and Mun C. Tsang. 1999. Human capital development in an emerging economy: The experience of Shenzhen, China. *China Quarterly* 157:72–114.

Xin, Gu. 2001. Employment service and unemployment insurance. In *The nanxun legacy and China's development in the post-Deng era*. Ed. John Wong and Zheng Yongnian, 143–169. Singapore: Singapore University Press.

Xu, Feng. 2008. Gated communities and migrant enclaves: The conundrum for building "harmonious community/shequ." *Journal of Contemporary China* 17 (57): 633–651.

Xu, Luo. 2004. Farewell to idealism: Mapping China's university students of the 1990s. *Journal of Contemporary China* 13 (41): 779–799.

Yahuda, Michael B. 1994. North China and Russia. In *China deconstructs: Politics, trade, and regionalism*. Ed. David. S. G. Goodman and Gerald Segal, 253–270. London: Routledge.

Yan, Hairong. 2002. Self-development of migrant women: Production of suzhi (quality) as surplus value and displacement of class in China's post-Socialist development. Paper presented at the Association for Asian Studies Annual Meeting, April 4–7, in Washington, D.C.

———. 2003a. Neoliberal governmentality and neohumanism: Organizing suzhi/value flow through labor recruitment networks. *Cultural Anthropology* 18 (4): 493–523.

———. 2003b. Spectralization of the rural: Reinterpreting the labor mobility of rural young women in post-Mao China. *American Ethnologist* 30 (4): 578–596.

Yan, Xiaowen. 2006. Implementing urbanization and the construction of "Greater Dalian" [Cheng shi hua dong yin yu jian she "Da Dalian"]. *Journal of Neijiang Teachers College* 3 (21): 157–159.

Yan, Yunxiang. 2002. Managed globalization: State power and cultural transition in China. In *Many globalizations: Cultural diversity in the contemporary world*. Ed. P. L. Berger and S. P. Huntington, 19–47. Oxford: Oxford University Press.

Yanagisako, Sylvia, and Carol Delaney. 1995. Naturalizing power. In *Naturalizing power: Essays in feminist cultural analysis*. Ed. Sylvia Yanagisako and Carol Delaney, 1–22. New York: Routledge.

Yang, Mayfair. 1988. The modernity of power in the Chinese socialist order. *Cultural Anthropology* 3 (4): 408–427.

———. 1989a. Between state and society: The construction of corporateness in a Chinese socialist factory. *Australian Journal of Chinese Affairs* 22:31–60.

———. 1989b. The gift economy and state power in China. *Comparative Studies in Society and History* 31 (1): 25–54.

———. 1994. *Gifts, favors, and banquets: The art of social relationships in China.* Ithaca, NY: Cornell University Press.

———, ed. 1999. *Spaces of their own: Women's public sphere in transnational China.* Minneapolis: University of Minnesota Press.

Yang, Xiaowen. 2006. *Cheng shi hua dong yin yu jian she da Dalian* [Urbanization results and construction of greater Dalian]. *Neijiang Teacher's College Journal* 3 (21): 157–159.

Yardley, Jim. 2008. China seeks to calm fears amid scandal. *New York Times,* September 21, Section A.

Yeung, Yue-man. 2000. *Globalization and networked societies: Urban-regional change in Pacific Asia.* Honolulu: University of Hawaii Press.

Yeung, Yue-man, and Xu-wei Hu, eds. 1992. *China's coastal cities: Catalysts for modernization.* Honolulu: University of Hawaii Press.

Yin, Qiping, and Gordon White. 1994. The "marketisation" of Chinese higher education: A critical assessment. *Comparative Education* 30 (3): 217–237.

Young, Louise. 1998. *Japan's total empire: Manchuria and the culture of wartime imperialism.* Berkeley: University of California Press.

Young, Marilyn. 1989. Chicken Little in China: Some reflections on women. In *Marxism and the Chinese experience: Issues in contemporary Chinese socialism.* Ed. Arif Dirlik and Maurice Meisner, 253–268. Armonk, NY: M. E. Sharpe.

Yu, Kaicheng, Wang Wenbo, and Wang Xiaoyun, eds. 1994. *Xiandai renli ziyuan guanli* [Contemporary human resources management]. Beijing: Beijing University Press.

Yu, Ruizhou, ed. 1999. *Xin jiuye shidai* [New employment era]. Beijing: Reform Press.

Yusuf, Shahid, and Kaoru Nabeshima. 2006. *Postindustrial East Asian cities: Innovation for growth.* Washington, DC: World Bank Publications.

Zaloom, Caitlin. 2004. The productive life of risk. *Cultural Anthropology* 19 (3): 365–391.

Zhan, Mei. 2005. Civet cats, fried grasshoppers, and David Beckham's pajamas: Unruly bodies after SARS. *American Anthropologist* 107 (1): 31–42.

Zhang, Kevin. 2004. The evolution of China's urban transformation: 1949–2000. In *Urban transformation in China.* Ed. Amin Chen, Gordon G. Liu, Kevin H. Zhang, 25–39. Hampshire, UK: Ashgate.

Zhang, Li. 2001. *Strangers in the city: Reconfigurations of space, power and social networks within China's floating population.* Stanford, CA: Stanford University Press.

———. 2008. Private homes, distinct lifestyles: Performing a new middle class. In *Privatizing China, socialism from afar.* Ed. Li Zhang and Aihwa Ong, 23–40. Ithaca: Cornell University Press.

Zhang, Li, and Aihwa Ong, eds. 2008. Introduction: Privatizing China: Powers of the self, socialism from afar. In *Privatizing China, socialism from afar.* 1–19. Ithaca: Cornell University Press.

Zhang, Minxuan. 1998. Changing conceptions of equity and student financial support policies. In *Higher education in post-Mao China.* Ed. Michael Agelasto and Bob Adamson, 237–258. Hong Kong: Hong Kong University Press.

Zhang, Wei-Wei. 1996. *Ideology and economic reform under Deng Xiaoping 1978–1993.* London: Kegan Paul International.

Zhang, Wei-Yuan. 1998. *Young people and careers: School careers guidance in Shanghai, Edinburgh and Hong Kong*. Hong Kong: Comparative Education Research Centre, University of Hong Kong.

Zhang, Wei-Yuan, and Bo Qu. 1988. *School and vocational guidance*. Shanghai: Tongji University Press.

Zhang, Xia. 2008. Ziyou [freedom], occupational choice, and labor: Bangbang in Chongqing, People's Republic of China. *International Labor and Working-Class History* 73: 65–84.

Zhang, Xin. 1997. Daxuesheng: Ni yuan he yan xue. *Jingshen Wenming Jianshe* 6:36.

Zhao, Dingxiang. 2002. An angle on nationalism in China today: Attitudes among Beijing students after Belgrade 1999. *China Quarterly* 172:885–905.

Zhao, Shukai. 2007. The accountability system of township governments. *Chinese Sociology and Anthropology* 39 (2): 64–73.

Zhao, Shuming. 2005. Changing structure of Chinese enterprises and human resource management practices in China. In *China's business reforms: Institutional challenges in a globalized economy*. Ed. Russell Smyth, On Kit Tam, Malcolm Warner, and Cherrie Jiuhua Zhu, 106–123. London, UK: Routledge.

Zhao, Suisheng. 1997. Chinese intellectuals' quest for national greatness and nationalistic writing in the 1990s. *China Quarterly* 151:725–745.

———. 2004. *A nation-state by construction: Dynamics of modern Chinese nationalism*. Stanford: Stanford University Press.

Zhao, Ziyang. 1985. On China's open-door policy: Excerpts from Premier Zhao Ziyang's report on the work of the government delivered at the fourth session of the fifth National People's Congress. In *The open policy at work*. Ed. Su Wenming, 7–11. China Today 10, Beijing Review Special Feature Series, Beijing Review Publications.

Zheng, Tiantian. 2007. Performing media-constructed images for first-class citizenship: Political struggles of rural migrant hostesses in Dalian. *Critical Asian Studies* 39 (1): 89–120.

———. 2009. *Red lights: The lives of sex workers in postsocialist China*. University of Minnesota Press: Minneapolis.

Zhou, Daping. 1998. User pays Beijing. In *Streetlife China*. Ed. Michael Dutton, 100–103. Cambridge: Cambridge University Press.

Zhou, Daxin, ed. 2003. *Da Dalian: Xin shiji tou 20 nian de zhanlue jueze* [Greater Dalian: Strategic choices the first 20 years of the new century]. Dalian: Dalian Publishing.

Zhou, Kate Xiao. 1996. *How the farmers changed China: Power of the people*. Boulder, CO: Westview Press.

Zhou, Li. 2006. *Higher education in China*. Australia: Thompson Learning.

Zhou, Xueguang, Nancy Brandon Tuma, and Phyllis Moen. 1996. Stratification dynamics under state socialism: The case of urban China, 1949–1993. *Social Forces* 74 (3): 759–96.

———. 1997. Institutional change and job-shift patterns in urban China, 1949–1994. *American Sociological Review* 62:339–365.

Zhu, Jieming. 2000. The changing mode of housing provision in transitional China. *Urban Affairs Review* 35 (4): 502–519.

Zhu, Mingren, and Zhendai Li, eds. 1988. *Dangdai Dalian chengshi jianshe, shang, xia* [Contemporary urban construction in Dalian, vols. 1 and 2]. Dalian: *Dongbei caijing daxue chubanshi* [Northeast Economic and Finance University Publishers].

Zhu, Yu. 1999. *New paths to urbanization in China: Seeking more balanced patterns.* Commack, NY: Nova Science Publishers.

Zimmerman, Jeffrey. 2008. From brew town to cool town: Neoliberalism and the creative city development strategy in Milwaukee. *Cities* 25 (4):230–242.

Zukin, Sharon. 1991. *Landscapes of power: From Detroit to Disney World.* Berkeley: University of California Press.

Index